FAMILY THERAPY IN CHANGING TIMES

BASIC TEXTS IN COUNSELLING AND PSYCHOTHERAPY

Series Editor: Stephen Frosh

This series introduces readers to the theory and practice of counselling and psychotherapy across a wide range of topic areas. The books appeal to anyone wishing to use counselling and psychotherapeutic skills and are particularly relevant to workers in health, education, social work and related settings. The books are unusual in being rooted in psychodynamic and systemic ideas, yet being written at an accessible, readable and introductory level. Each text offers theoretical background and guidance for practice, with creative use of clinical examples.

Published

Jenny Altschuler
WORKING WITH CHRONIC ILLNESS

Bill Barnes, Sheila Ernst and Keith Hyde
AN INTRODUCTION TO GROUPWORK

Stephen Brigger
WORKING WITH ADOLESCENTS

Alex Coren
SHORT-TERM PSYCHOTHERAPY

Emilia Dowling and Gill Gorell Barnes
WORKING WITH CHILDREN AND PARENTS THROUGH SEPARATION AND DIVORCE

Loretha Franklin
AN INTRODUCTION TO WORKPLACE COUNSELLING

Gill Gorell Barnes
FAMILY THERAPY IN CHANGING TIMES (2nd edn)

Sally Hodges
COUNSELLING ADULTS WITH LEARNING DISABILITIES

Ravi Rana
COUNSELLING STUDENTS

Paul Terry
WORKING WITH THE ELDERLY AND THEIR CARERS

Jan Wiener and Mannie Sher
COUNSELLING AND PSYCHOTHERAPY IN PRIMARY HEALTH CARE

Shula Wilson
DISABILITY, COUNSELLING AND PSYCHOTHERAPY

Invitation to authors

The Series Editor welcomes proposals for new books within the Basic Texts in Counselling and Psychotherapy series. These should be sent to Stephen Frosh at the School of Psychology, Birkbeck College, Malet Street, London, WC1E 7HX (e-mail s.frosh@bbk.ac.uk)

**Basic Texts in Counselling and Psychotherapy
Series Standing Order ISBN 0–333–69330–2**
(outside North America only)

You can receive future titles in this series as they are published by placing a standing order. Please contact your bookseller or, in the case of difficulty, write to us at the address below with your name and address, the title of the series and the ISBN quoted above.

Customer Services Department, Macmillan Distribution Ltd
Houndmills, Basingstoke, Hampshire RG21 6XS, England

FAMILY THERAPY IN CHANGING TIMES

SECOND EDITION

GILL GORELL BARNES

palgrave
macmillan

First edition 1998
Second edition 2004

Published by
PALGRAVE MACMILLAN
Houndmills, Basingstoke, Hampshire RG21 6XS and
175 Fifth Avenue, New York, N.Y. 10010
Companies and representatives throughout the world

PALGRAVE MACMILLAN is the global academic imprint of the Palgrave
Macmillan division of St. Martin's Press, LLC and of Palgrave Macmillan Ltd.
Macmillan® is a registered trademark in the United States, United Kingdom
and other countries. Palgrave is a registered trademark in the European
Union and other countries.

ISBN 1–4039–0472–3

This book is printed on paper suitable for recycling and made from fully
managed and sustained forest sources.

A catalogue record for this book is available from the British Library.

A catalog record for this book is available from the Library of Congress.

10   9   8   7   6   5   4   3   2   1
13 12 11 10 09 08 07 06 05 04

Printed and bound in Great Britain by
J. W. Arrowsmith Ltd., Bristol

CONTENTS

Acknowledgements

I would like to thank all colleagues on whose research and ideas I have drawn in the second edition of this book; and in particular those with whom I shared clinical work, research and writing over the last five years: Charlotte Burk, Gwyn Daniel, Emilia Dowling, Gwynneth Down, Salvador Minuchin, Damian McCann. Renos Papadopoulos, Gerrilyn Smith, Jeremy Woodcock and the family team at the Medical Foundation; Lee Wai Yung and the family teams in Hong Kong and Beijing. I would especially like to thank my colleague and husband Alan Cooklin in the clinical work and teaching we continue to share and for encouraging me to link systemic practice and work in the family justice system. Thank you Liz Kyria Kides for your patient typing over the years and for helping to produce this text.

GILL GORELL BARNES

1

WHAT IS FAMILY THERAPY? PATTERNS OF LIVING, PATTERNS OF MIND AND PATTERNS OF THERAPY

When we approach a new model of therapy what do we want to know about it? The questions that students most frequently ask about how family therapy differs from other counselling or therapy models point to three areas that loosely distinguish a systemic approach from other approaches. First of all, family therapy looks at current context, what is going on in people's lives *now*, as well as what has gone on before: the voices that continue to shout down the telephone or speak in a derogatory manner at Sunday lunch, as well as those voices from the past that are carried in a person's head. Secondly, it listens to the ways in which current relationships, as well as former relationships, come to form patterns and conversations in people's minds, and therefore influence their beliefs and daily practices. Thirdly, the way in which these inner and outer conversations are arranged, the importance the individual accords to each of them and the way some are privileged over others are seen as related to how individuals behave in their families, in their circles of intimate relationship and in wider social contexts. Identity is therefore primarily considered as a self negotiated in relation to others from our infancy onwards. While developmental processes play a key part in how we experience and perceive interpersonal processes, the idea of a 'core inner self' is always seen as contextualised by the mutual influence of family and other intimate relationships.

The term 'family therapy' itself encompasses a number of different activities in relation to these ideas of mind and relational context: (1) a philosophy of how to observe, describe, and frame relational events; (2) methods of description that explicitly make interactive connections between people and their wider social context specifically noting mutual influence, feedback, and circularity; (3) a relational and contextual *approach* to treating dilemmas and problems in families; and (4) a number of therapeutic modalities addressing these relational contexts, with particular skills devolving from each approach. As a therapeutic approach, family therapy as a whole considers problems in the context both of people's intimate relationships and of their wider social network, as well as the social and political structures of which the family and the therapist are each an evolving part. Thus the focus of a family therapist is the relationship of the individuals, their beliefs and behaviour to the various collective practices and beliefs in which their lives evolve, and to the ways these collective, social, religious, and political practices offer continuity and coherence or discontinuity and a disjunctive sense of self over time.

Family therapy focuses on the ways that patterns of behaviour – those that are problematic and those that promote well-being – operate at different levels within the lives of individuals. Identified problems may be described within the context of a number of overlapping social systems, the family household, the extended family, and institutions with whom household members have daily contact such as schools, or doctors, health services and other professional services that may be concerned about or stigmatise the family. In recognition of the attention paid to the multilevel social systems intersecting with family life, reference is often made not to 'family therapy' but to systemic therapy or the 'systemic approach'. The descriptions of family life generated within these different levels of social system may all be operational in different ways in the family's descriptions of themselves. They may therefore also appropriately enter the texts and the language of therapy. Personal views of the 'self', and the connections between such subjectively held views and pathologized definitions created by the accounts of others, are an integral part of what emerges in discourses created within the therapeutic context.

The systemic approach

The principles of the systemic approach underlie all models of therapy used within the broad heading of family therapy. They can be summarised as follows:

- People in families are intimately connected, and focusing on those connections and the beliefs different members hold about them can be a more valid way of understanding and promoting change in problem-related behaviour than focusing on the perspective of any one individual.
- People living in close proximity over time set up patterns of interaction made up of relatively stable sequences of speech and behaviour.
- The patterns of interaction, beliefs and behaviour that therapists observe and engage with can be understood as the 'context' of the problem and be considered as both 'cause' and 'effect', acting as feedback loops that create the 'fit' between problem and family. These are often referred to as 'circular patterns of interaction', in contrast with the cause and effect 'linear' thinking of the psychology from which early systems thinkers were trying to break free. Such patterns involve mutual influence and mutually regulated learning.
- Problems within patterns of family life are often related to dilemmas in adapting to some environmental influence or change. Such changes may already have happened or are about to happen. For example a young person leaving home, a family migrating or an impending divorce all involve the development of new patterns and the loss of old ones. The minute details of the ways in which families describe such changes – the language within which constructions of problems, both past and anticipated, are generated – are of key importance in understanding the nuances of family thinking; the 'discourses' or discussions about family life and its problems and solutions. These take place both within individuals and between them. All the adults who form part of the family may carry different discourses in their minds, which while often unspoken in the room nevertheless carry powerful imperatives for action or restraint in their thinking about themselves and the processes they are engaged in.

Change in systemic therapy is therefore usually conceptualised as possible at a number of levels: in relation to the presenting problem, to the relationship pattern to which it is connected and to wider social factors that are currently affecting the family. Historical patterns, both those created in former generations and in earlier contexts of a family's life, and the relationship of these to current beliefs will also be areas of interest to many therapists (see Chapter 2). Many of the differences between the systemic approaches themselves derive from which level of the social system a therapist makes their primary focus of attention; systematised patterns of thinking about the self manifest in language about the self, the intimate unit of the immediate family, the wider family and kinship groupings and the social context of the life of the family in a broader political sense.

Families in transition

There are many situations in which the organisation of family life is in transition. In such situations systemic work with *individuals* – exploring beliefs and feelings in relation to the changing contexts of which she or he is a part – is likely to be useful (for example, when a child's parent has died, when a parent has lost their partner in circumstances they do not wish to describe to the children, when parents are getting divorced, or when a child is moving between one family and another). In these as in many other circumstances people may feel that to speak in front of one another without first exploring their own views further would be harmful. As more parents are separating and new partnerships are formed, I have found it helpful to work with the many subsystems involved in the changing family and to respect the differing views that are held at the time of family break-up and new family formation (see Chapters 5 and 6). Recent research (Dunn, 2002) has also drawn attention to the importance of attending to children's views about the biological family and their more intimate connections within that framework, including the extended family, and respecting the distinctions between biological and step-parents.

The systemic approach is constantly in change in response to family and social change, and the early pioneers' insistence on 'seeing all the family' in the room has been replaced by recognition of the importance for the therapist to 'hold all the family' in mind and to enquire how members not present are held in the minds of those who are. This takes into account the many people in an intimate social network who at different times have contributed to 'voices in the mind', inner conversations, or components of self. These voices come from many differing contexts, some of which may compete with one another. Any individual may have to negotiate a pathway through relational contexts representing conflicts of interest. Gender, class, ethnicity, religion and culture, which may include the expectations of extended families in this or other countries, may each bring different perspectives to bear on current individual and family discourses. People originally categorise the world the way they do because they have shared social and cultural practices, including ways of thinking about and talking about their lives. The term 'discourse' encompasses this notion of shared meanings of events within relationships, relationship patterns over time and the development of shared meaning at many different levels. However, these shared notions may change through necessity or choice as people in transition through change of partner, change of country (or both) negotiate new meanings to make sense of their lives. New meanings and old meanings can give rise to great tension within and between generations, and the negotiation of *shared* meaning is not always possible. Thus, for many adults and children where the context has changed dramatically, it is important to respect the notion of 'parallel lives'.

Social discourses, the common descriptions of ourselves by others that also make up aspects of our own identity, such as 'single parent', 'black person', 'adoptive mother' or 'underclass', are also voices that may be essential to deconstruct in therapy. By considering wider social discourses and their specific effects on individuals and their thoughts about themselves, a family can gain a clearer understanding of what is contributing to their own perceptions and daily exchanges.

Stressful life events and family life: patterns of stress and patterns of affirmation

In the last decade much of the research into family life and the onset of different forms of psychological illness has explored the impact of stressful life events within the family such as sudden death, the loss of a parent through acrimonious divorce, serious illness or accidents, as well as larger external events such as civil war, enforced migration, and other unexpected disaster in terms of the meanings that these events are given by individuals and families, and the potential impact of such meanings developed in one context on subsequent choices. Other research has considered patterns of early childhood deprivation and the way that, as a result of childhood experience, negative meanings may be attributed by any of us to subsequent life events. Anticipating that bad things are bound to happen may itself contribute to subsequent experiences developing a negative way. However, studies have also looked at how patterns of deprivation can coexist with alternative patterns of affirmation; patterns in which a positive self-image is fostered that promotes the resilience that enables people to get by. The effects of former patterns of deprivation can also be changed by subsequent intimate relationships. Research studies therefore give us broader evidence to back up our clinical and subjective knowledge that people's former life experience is intimately connected to how they manage the present, to the choices they consider they are able to make, and to their ability to respond in the face of further life stress (see Chapters 3 and 4). In the process of therapy, affirmative stories that the family may have deleted from their narrative about themselves may be brought back into their way of thinking about and describing strengths or assets. This can help to shift the habitual pattern of looking at the problem-focused story about themselves, to developing more varied and richer descriptions. Some therapists focus on bringing out these patterns of affirmation (often subjugated by the greater pressures created by stress) and make competence, what people have done well, the primary focus of therapy. Others believe that to affirm in the absence of empathetic enquiry into the negative effects of stress will be perceived by clients as facile, and therefore choose a 'both/and' approach to acknowledging what the family has endured.

As migration from around the globe has changed the living patterns of our cities, much family work takes place with cultures and ethnicities that are different from the therapist's own. While the need to understand differences created through ethnicity has long been a part of family therapy thinking in the United States, the many acute and subtle differences in the understanding of life experience that this requires from a therapist only began to be addressed in the UK in the mid-1980s. There are different beliefs about why there has been reluctance to document patterns of breakdown, and patterns of resilience for different ethnic groups. One school of thought has argued that to make such distinctions based on ethnicity could be construed as persecutory or prejudicial, by those who were subject to such distinction, and that it might also contribute to the creation of unitary, stereotypical categories of 'peoples' that are unhelpful to individuals. Another viewpoint might be that failure to distinguish between diverse peoples is a further instance of 'fuzzy thinking' derived from former traditions of global colonisation. Following these legacies, the need to respect difference and be curious about it failed to enter the minds of therapists, born into a predominantly white society, in ways they could utilise positively. In the latter years of the 1980s, black professionals in the UK began to voice the need for white professionals to face up to differences, and to the implications for new constructions of theory and practice that this would involve. White professionals were challenged to take a pluralist view of society that acknowledges there are many equally valid perspectives of reality, and to recognise that these may be *in conflict*. The attempt to construct a homogeneous view of reality between black client and white therapist in therapy may disqualify the experience of black families, especially when inequalities of structure and power built into mental health treatment systems are taken into account (Hardy and Laszloffy, 1994, Fernando, 1991). Thomas, a black psychotherapist, has pointed out that it is in the areas of racism and sexism that 'psychotherapists are at their weakest and not in a position to help their clients who might not only turn to them for solace but to understand how their inner structures have responded to or accommodated the external realities of racism and sexism' (Thomas, 1995, p. 172). The growth in the number of black professionals in the UK has also led to greater diversity in what is thought about and written about in international work.

Patterns and problems over time: changing constraints and developing new solutions

From a systemic therapist's viewpoint, then, social patterns and attitudes are seen as interweaving with and likely to affect family patterns and self-descriptions. The longer-term effects of family patterns of the past on the present, the present on the future, and whether such effects carry forward in positive or negative ways, are obviously questions of great importance. If current intervention is also potentially related to future prevention, our work has relevance not only for what is going on now, but also for future generations within a family. There is considerable evidence from research of different kinds to show that the influences that come from the establishment of negative ways of interacting with other people – negative patterns of feeling, thinking and behaving – are hard to change. Much depends on whether alternative positive frameworks for problem-solving are available to growing children, so that they can learn affirmative possibilities, and the skill of developing solutions. Children learn patterns or principles of relating, rather than just 'behaviours', and these affect both the way they see themselves and their role in family life, and the development of ongoing ways of relating to others. Children whose families are very closed to influences from the outside world have particular difficulty in developing other models of relating. In particular, unhelpful patterns develop in relation to aggression, quarrelling and the inability to set up models of problem-solving within the family.

Family therapists look not only at what has brought about behaviour that is considered a problem, the history and the circumstances of the problem, but the contexts in which over time the problem has been shown to the world, the different ways people have responded, and whether these differences offer *new* ideas in the current context. They enquire about and elicit stories that may be less prominent; stories of former solutions and resources that may emerge from members of the family who are not the 'frontliners', and whose voices are usually given less time or attention. These marginalised voices may come from a different gender or generation, or from extended kin. Family therapists also try to develop some specificity about the context of the problem – *where* it is shown, to whom, and by whom the problem is considered a problem. Why now? Why has the problem arisen at this time? In relation to what other events in the lives of the family members is the problem located?

Historical and current dimensions

Each problem or dilemma is likely to have a historical as well as a current dimension in terms of the family's perception of life events and the difficulties that go alongside these, and different ways of responding to or dealing with them are likely to have developed at different times. The patterns that people use to cope with changing life circumstances may be based on old models rather than ones that suit the current circumstances. Assessment therefore involves joint appraisal by family and therapist of how these areas have been handled in the past, and why former solutions have been forgotten or do not work in the current context. The therapist will try to elicit what new dimensions of family thinking, feeling or behaviours the current problem is challenging, and where the family members see that their own resources, as they currently define them, cannot meet the changes required. What shifts in gender arrangements may new solutions involve? Whose voice may need to have more executive power? This provides a rough map of what may be possible from the family's point of view, as well as highlighting constraints on thinking or action. Co-constructing knowledge of what can and cannot be handled from within a family's own resource pool will help the therapist to formulate a realistic plan of their own outsider input. By input, the therapist may have in mind the provocation of new ideas and curiosity by asking previously unasked questions that will lead to the family considering the problem in a new way. Alternatively, he/she may make an active contribution by advocating the healing of emotional or relational connections that have been lost, either within people's minds or between members of the family. The therapist may also address the patterns of behaviour she or he can see taking place in the room, and start creating new pathways of communication, listening, talking, and observing (see Chapter 2).

Family systems, transitions and non-biologically connected families: implications for a family therapist

Early family therapy training was based on a theory of the family as a stable two-parent social system that remained together over time. However, we will rethink continuously throughout this book how constructions of family life have changed in the last two decades, and consider a number of influences which have contributed to new thinking. Firstly, the structures for bringing up children in the UK have diversified. Patterns of cohabitation, childbearing, marriage, and divorce are all different from a generation ago. Up to one-third of all live births precede marriage. While marriage follows birth in many instances, there remains a larger number of cohabiting couples than ever before. Lone parent households now form 23 per cent of all households with dependent children in the UK, composed of the two groups of never-married parents, and divorced and separated mothers, with a smaller, but substantial group, of fathers heading up families (Haskey, 1998). About one million children live in step-families (two-fifths the number of those who live in lone-parent headed households). Movement in and out of these different structures for family living means that transitional experience characterises the lives of many adults and children, and is often insufficiently enquired about by therapists. In addition many families undergo major life transitions as a result of economic pressure, particularly drastic changes in employment patterns at the local and global levels. Huge shifts and dislocations in lifestyle also follow the migration of a large number of families following civil wars and religious persecution.

Thinking about what therapeutic work with families is now likely to involve has therefore also undergone change. While a systemic approach based on introducing variety into rigid family structures is still likely to be of use to family therapists, they will equally require an ability to look for and help the family think about the effect of different transitions, of different pathways into family life, of losses and subsequent adaptations to their lives. Therapists may also need to help families to value coherence or core characteristics of family life. It may be important for parents to hold on to these in their minds, both as part of their own internal equilibrium and on behalf of their children. To know what they are looking for in what keeps life viable for a particular family unit, therapists need flexible mental maps of family possibility to equip them to explore diversity. In addition to knowledge about how transitions have an impact on human behaviour and the way life changes of different kinds may undermine people's ability to maintain a sense of effectiveness, counsellors, mental health professionals and therapists need to develop an understanding of the many different ways in which families are created, constructed and maintained, and the potential effects of these differences on subsequent relational dilemmas.

Diversity also includes non-biologically created family forms. The families we see as well as the families we are part of may be created by adoption, by fostering and adoption, by artificial insemination, by surrogacy. Couples may be heterosexual, gay, or lesbian. While each family will have its own unique properties, there will also be commonalties created by the different pathways into family life. Research is one of many voices now contributing to a wider acceptance of lesbian parenting, although we still know little about the issues faced by gay fathers (see pp. 64–8).

All couples are vulnerable to change. Just as heterosexual couples split up, so do gay and lesbian couples. The couples with whom children begin their lives may not be those with whom they spend their middle childhood or adolescence. How will therapists bear in mind the balance between acknowledging losses and the need for parents to negotiate a coherent identity for the developing child? Children may have the complex task of developing their own sense of self and family out of shapes that do not compare easily with those of others in their neighbourhood or in the children's books they read at school. Imaginative ways of talking and connecting may need to be found by therapists as well as parents to help them construct their own story out of more than one parental meaning system (for example, a divorced heterosexual mother and their now openly gay father), and to negotiate the mystery of 'hidden meanings' in relation to parents they have never met and may never meet (for example, donor sperm fathers, or biological parents in an adoptive family). Therapists as well as families are often sailing in uncharted waters, and they need to be open to their own lack of knowledge in relation to these new constructions of family life and family relationships. None of us know what questions children will have in the future about the connections between constructions of family and self, and the most important thing therapists can do is to help parents to be open to questions and to be ready to try to think about them when a young child becomes a young person.

Rethinking family bonds: diversity, intimacy and identity

The diversity of race and culture within UK society has slowly led to greater curiosity about similarities and differences in structures, loyalties, and beliefs about family life. In Western societies, theorising about the family has traditionally privileged the significance of the husband – wife bond, taking as desirable norms equality between partners, empathy with each other's experiences and a willingness to collaborate around both meaning and action (Rampage, 1994, 2002; Gorell Barnes, 1994a). The importance of connectedness in other relationships – mother/son, father/brother, sister/brother, mother/child – that give meaning to the idea of 'family' have been marginalised in western theorising about family, and therefore also in theories informing family therapy. Similarly, there has been a lack of knowledge about relationships that through their inbuilt structures of power can be disqualifying or pathologising. Two that I have become more familiar with in clinical work include firstly the formal relationship of daughter-in-law to mother-in-law in some Indian and Chinese families: where the new wife is in effect subjugated to the will of her husband's mother, and secondly the extent to which the extended family on either side can actively exacerbate marital distress by their insistence on their own 'share' of their family entitlements. Such kinship groups continue to carry active power in the adult life of the next generation, both as physical presences, but also in the mind (Ma, 2000). In spite of the wide knowledge available through sociology, anthropology, or writings from cultures other than those that are Northern-European-based, that draw attention to the significance of intimacies within larger kinship groups for secure family identity as well as for secure gendered identity, the psychotherapies have been slow to recognise these. From these kin come beliefs qualifying the limits of intimate relationships of different kinds, and the effect of these beliefs on different behaviours in families – what is permitted in the way of open talk within different sections of a family and what is forbidden, distorted or concealed. Therapists therefore need to develop both curiosity, and sensitivity in enquiring what may or may not be openly talked about and with whom.

Family therapy teaching and research, therefore, has moved towards considering the diversity of processes in family life and away from ideas of family 'normality and pathology'. Assumptions based on the stability of family life and the internal coherence of systems patterned over time (which developed in the 1960s) have to be reconsidered in the light of the transitions and disruptions experienced by many families seen in clinical settings in the new millennium. The theoretical focus on patterns and rules that were seen as maintaining symptoms over time, which it was the therapist's job to 'discover', has changed to a more humble professional curiosity in which therapist and family together consider the changing field of life relationships and intimate experiences.

How do cultural values underpin family life?

For all of us, ways of life are both constituted by and express culture. Values exist at some deep and often unexamined level, and are held not only within but between people connected by kinship, by family of choice, by culture at macro and micro levels. The degree to which families believe and experience themselves as connected to 'cultural communities' varies widely, and many families express themselves as suffering as a result of disconnection from that wider community because of mobility, migration, exile or loss of faith. The degree to which the values of a culture are embodied within a family is likely to vary from member to member, so that the use of 'culture' as an external reference point may well be a matter of ongoing controversy in the family (particularly between generations, but also, often less openly expressed, between genders, brother and sister, or a husband and wife). The absence of a wider community and its appropriate representatives in this country may be felt as a loss by many of those who would have had recourse to elders in their countries of origin. However, ingenious ways of reconstructing such groups are being created by different communities.

Culture is part of the make-up of each of us. All too often we make crude assumptions about a person's culture based on their country of origin, ethnicity or religion. Culture is more intangible than any one of these things and makes up the self in many subtle ways, affecting the meanings which we attribute to our experience. In this sense, culture is constitutive of the self (see Gorell Barnes, 2002a).

By participating in our culture we also contribute to it. Each individual's and family's interpretation of culture is unique to them, even though it also expresses the larger collectivity. For a therapist, then, understanding something of the larger collectivity illuminates potential aspects of what is being expressed by the family, but is not equivalent to 'understanding' the family.

Culture, gender and development

For young children, home and culture are synonymous. At a very early age, therefore, certain concepts of human behaviour, with overarching principles relating to the learning of gendered behaviour (what belongs to 'men in the home' and what belongs to 'women in the home') will begin to form images of living that carry powerful impressions. It has been argued that gender concepts in particular are formed when young and are extremely resistant to change (Maccoby, 1980, 1986). Such impressions derive both from what is observed in the behaviour of others (witnessed behaviour) and what is experienced and fantasised by the self (lived experience). The two together in the daily proximity of family life create legacies of beliefs about behaviour that re-enter the working contexts constructed by the boundaries of therapy or counselling. Family therapists not only work with families as a living presence in the room, but also with the families in people's minds. Both in systemic work with individuals and in family sessions, the therapist may experience a tension between the adults present in the room and a version of themselves to which they seem to refer, but which is not apparent to the therapist. This version of another self may continue to hold dominant meanings, influencing aspects of family life in the present.

What is the job of the family therapist?

The special job of a family therapist is to understand the 'meaning making' particular to each family; the therapist has to be able to attend to each individual as well as retaining a sense of the overall family (Reimers, 1999). In addition he/she has to be aware of how the larger culture, with its many layered meanings, is also a part of this family, as well as the variations in meaning held by the individuals who make up the family. Understanding also involves the distinctions of generation and gender. Cultures are not always benign to the individuals within them, and this may need bringing into the open. Culture can be used to hide behind, as in recourse to a man's 'rights' over a woman, which may be seen by another person from a different culture as the right to abuse or terrorise her. Deconstruction of the particular use made of a *culture* to justify a position of power by an *individual*, (in relation to gender, age or status), is one of the many discourses that accompany a central therapeutic purpose. Gender and its accompanying uses of power, developed over centuries, is often one of the vital discourses that affect the mental health and emotional well-being of certain individuals in the family. Therapists require a number of positions, so that they can keep in mind questions that relate to potential discourses outside the room. In this way cultural practices that appear abusive to the therapist can be openly questioned in the context of therapy as 'larger social issues', relating for example to men and women, and to the 'use of power', while their validation through other levels of historical or cultural meaning can also be acknowledged. In relation to such questions, other holders of knowledge – religious leaders, family elders or people of the same community of beliefs with the authority to dispute the subject – may usefully be involved as the appropriate people to ask questions that the therapist or the family may feel the therapist is not empowered to ask.

A function of therapy as I practice it is to bring hidden meanings into the public domain – 'public domain' meaning that a person (the therapist) other than the family is involved. Such 'bringing forth' involves new negotiations of these meanings. The very act of bringing out meanings that may have been deeply coded into the life of a family at levels that may even have been non-verbal, involves new, often slow and painful, often angry and acrimonious negotiations of meaning. Shared procedures of 'interpretation', understanding who understands what meaning is attached to which behaviours, arriving at a joint negotiated position about those meanings, or agreeing that agreement may never be reached, require the therapist to retain a clear head and not to become confused, enmeshed or inappropriately confrontative. Recognition that certain meanings, in relation to practices involving dominance and submission, are areas of fundamental disagreement between generations or genders in a household can be of vital importance to members 'locked into' an abusive situation.

Listening to families and to the family in individual stories: internal and external discourses

This book is about listening to families, to couples, to parents and children, to adults and their own parents, to the way they talk about intimate relationships and the things that are going wrong with these relationships, and the ways in which they relate these 'wrong things' to the past, the present and forces external to themselves, as well as blaming themselves for what is happening. A goal would be the negotiation of viable selves that they can live with, and that he/she/they can stand by when challenged. When listening we pay attention to the recurrence of themes, phrases and ideas or powerful 'internal discourses' that suggest in what arenas tangled thoughts and emotions may be keeping people in positions that are not currently useful to them. We also consider what *external* discourses in their earlier lives, as well as those current in our society today, may be responsible for people maintaining a lowered sense of self-esteem, disempowering them and their ability to act effectively (for example, discourses of oppression, of enforced migration, of poverty, interrupted education, and unemployment) (see Chapter 4). For each of the families you will meet in this book, *family* life has different meanings that are made up from components such as intimacy, loyalty, mutual support, trust, commitment and dependability. The family is a place within which one ideally could be taken for granted for better or worse, relate and converse according to old habits and principles, and take up comfortable, expected familiar roles. However, these very familiarities, as noted above, may be the breeding ground of misunderstanding, misperception and attributions that do not fit easily with the individual in receipt of them. 'Home' therefore also involves conflicts of interest, oppressive experience, discord, aggression, violence and abuse. 'Home' is also embodied at more abstract levels in emblematic stories that family members tell about their families that illustrate plights, tragedies and their outcomes, symbolic and amusing resolutions; and less pleasantly, stories of horror and pain, misunderstanding without resolution; of deprivation, madness, cruelty and death. The effort of wiping these from the mind or distorting them to rewrite a better story can lead to confusion in later generations, who sometimes need to return to the original sources or texts in order to reinterpret a new generational understanding.

When listening to an account of an individual's life experience or a family's description of how they manage their daily lives, we are continuously involved as therapists in identifying key moments or key transactions that give subjective meaning to the lives being described. We listen on more than one level: to factors contributing to stress, which may amplify previous experiences of stress, and to factors that contribute to, or demonstrate strength and resilience in the face of difficult life situations. We also try to note what values are placed on these. Within the themes that emerge we begin to identify recurrent patterns that work for and against different family members, or different relationship constellations in the group that is with us, and between them and the family beyond the walls of the room; patterns of stress and coping in the way accounts are given – both as they show now and have shown in former times.

The way in which an individual may develop a sense of identity, effectiveness and continuous sense of self over time, and how this emerges from the stories that are told, can be linked to, and validated by, various areas of research. Research conducted from a psychoanalytic perspective on coherence in narrative has links with earlier research on childhood resilience (Fonagy *et al.*, 1993; Rutter, 1987). Each set of studies points independently to the importance of the capacity to appraise, the ability in any of us to sit back and look reflectively at ourselves and the way we are living our lives from a position where we can make choices. This is more easily described in research studies than done in real life, where any coherent stories about ourselves have continuously to be carved out, negotiated, protected or manipulated through the hazards of life events and their sequelae. Nonetheless counselling and therapy do offer (as do many other life events away from the therapy room) the opportunity for a second chance or a second look – what in systemic therapy has been called 'a meta-perspective' (or getting an overall view) of what is going on. The opportunity to sit in a neutral but friendly space defined by time and geography for the purpose of reflection, is a declaration that meaning may be found in what as yet seem incoherent or out-of-control events. As systemic therapists we remain concerned with the experience of the individual even when the key structure of our work is with the family. We are always curious and respectful about what has helped an individual to do well or maintain a sense of self despite multiple setbacks, and why some people feel so vulnerable that in spite of good life circumstances they are unable to believe in their ability to manage their lives, their relationships or their children.

The family as the template for intimate relations: three ways of looking at what goes on

As the family both constructs intimate relationships in which individuals grow, and becomes a construction that individuals subsequently hold in their minds, three different ways of reflecting on family processes and asking myself 'what is going on here?' are described below.

Intimacy and confusion

The emotional dimensions of family life contain many physical components. I always think about the ways that people in families affirm one another: for example in preverbal experience of a very primitive kind, such as skin care, hair care and certain kinds of touching or massaging; and in certain kinds of soothing and tonalities, as well as reliable expectations of having needs met through food, warmth and closeness. I often talk about these experiences with families. The 'taking one another for granted' in meeting primitive needs that much of family life involves, encompasses many facets of intimacy, power and control, since an act as simple as making someone a cup of tea can be an act of loving or an oppressive experience, depending on the way the request is contextualised. Partly because the continuity of patterns and habits in family life hold the possibility of a continuity of self over time, and partly because those continuities are so often tied up with intimate processes such as eating, sleeping, habits of health and hygiene, sex or its absence, talking, laughing and crying, the time-frames available to any of us *within* the context of a family situation are often confused, however much autonomy we achieve away from the family. Like Dr Who's Tardis, within an instant we can be carted backwards to an earlier time by a moment of strong emotion, shared hilarity or deep grief, or by rituals of birthdays or religious festivities. But the time-frame to which we are returned may no longer be available to us as a resource in the present. Indeed those around us may have no knowledge of that earlier family life and its representations that we refer to inside ourselves. Such moments of loss can create acute confusion in adults and often lead to the search for outside help. For many therapists, as well as for many of the people we see as clients, the relational systems within which currently held meanings were originally constructed have either dramatically changed or are no longer available. This absence can be an enormously powerful disqualifying factor in feeling able to cope in the present, even when past experience is reported as negative.

Power and blame

In intimate human systems, connected and developed over time, systemic therapists formerly took the view that there are no 'protagonists' or 'victims', but that each member enters into the interactions in the ways that are complementary to the overall balance of the family as a whole. Systemic theory was initially constructed by white middle-class men in the 1960s and 1970s, and these views have subsequently been widely disputed. Researchers and women therapists from differing perspectives began to change theorising in the 1980s by drawing attention to the imbalances of power in the structure of families as systems with developing and dependent members. A debate was created in which a wider discussion of power and coercion in social systems enforced the need for more distinctions in systemic thinking as it related to therapy with families and intimate human relationship groups. The way in which people become drawn into habitual patterns that may not be to their individual liking, for reasons of economic survival for protection of their young and their elderly dependents, requires a different lens for examining theory, as does the creation of abusive patterns through structures of race, class and caste. In any interactions people may not be equal in the degree to which they choose to be bound by a particular set of beliefs imposed by one or more members. Choice will also be dependent on relative power related to age. While to some extent most adult participants may be said to 'choose' to continue to participate in their life in a family, the cost of trying to give up that participation may be dramatically different for different family members. Children obviously cannot easily leave home; this is frequently also true of abused women and the elderly.

Systemic therapy has therefore adopted a number of different lenses through which to consider the relevance of interconnection through choice and interconnection through circumstance. These distinctions affect people's freedoms within families and households. Recent writing indicates the variety of applications of systemic thinking to interdependence in families among therapists of different ethnicities and cultures. Feminist perspectives on the issues of power and abuse reflect the tension between attempting to hold a 'non-blaming' systemic position at the level of 'family' and the anger deriving from the recognition of how such imbalances are built in and reinforced at wider and more powerfully institutionalised levels in society.

Family pattern and individual habit

Bateson, arguably the most influential early theorist affecting the practice of systemic family therapy, described 'habit' as a 'major economy of conscious thought' (Bateson, 1973a, p. 115), the sinking of knowledge to less conscious levels. 'The unconscious contains not only the painful matters which consciousness prefers not to inspect, but also many matters which are so familiar that we do not need to inspect them' (ibid., p. 114). Much of what systemic family therapists do, therefore, is to help families reflect about their own 'habits' which incorporates dimensions of family living discussed in this chapter. Different techniques that stem from the therapists' different belief systems and methods of utilising themselves are oriented to restoring the capacity to think and reflect in situations where this capacity is lost. Family therapists look for 'habit' or ways in which families behave, which are not necessarily just responses to the current situation, but are ways of behaving laid down at levels not immediately accessible to awareness. Some of these behaviours may be redundant, that is, they no longer have a relevant meaning, and may actively impede the development of behaviours that would be more functional for the family in their current context.

Summary

Family therapy addresses itself to changes in patterns of relationships, to those which are lived and witnessed on a daily basis, and to those which are carried in people's minds (Reiss, 1989). The fact that members of a family not only live an habitual pattern but also witness it around them, allows the development of different degrees of reflective capacity within different families and between different members of different families. Families are often interested to talk about what they do in detailed and passionate ways. Much of what may be shared as an area of interest between a psychodynamic approach and a systemic approach relates to this question of how the reflective capacity of different members develops, how it is protected or destroyed through individual developmental processes and how the capacity to reflect on experience affects children when they grow up and become parents (Fonagy *et al.*, 1993). The way a reflective capacity can be monitored and supported within therapeutic intervention of any kind is of key concern to all professionals working with children or adults, as well as their wider families.

One way of describing the job of the therapist, then, is that he or she explores the different power accorded to the voices that contribute to descriptions in the family and give these descriptions and definitions emotional and moral power at the expense of alternative descriptions. When appropriate, therapists reintroduce marginalised voices or silenced voices. Where voices are contributing to ongoing negative images of self for any individual, alternative descriptions will be sought within the family, or the family's wider milieu. If more positive or benign descriptions become part of the language spoken about the person, then the person's inner images, the voices with which she or he speaks to her- or himself will also change. In therapeutic conversations, whether with an individual or with the family as a whole, the inner 'negative' monologues or self-descriptions may be invited into conversation and challenged by or tested out against other more positive views of the self. If alternative descriptions can be heard and accepted they may be incorporated into the language and interactional pattern of the family and subsequently into the self (Penn and Frankfurt, 1994). However, this is unlikely to come about easily; it is likely that it will need to be repeated and reaffirmed on numerous occasions and may require the therapist to encourage the discovery of appropriate allies to back up these new definitions. Much family therapy theorising has tended to neglect the hard work that change involves if it is to last. Emphasis has been given to the exhilarating effects of initial therapeutic intervention. While such shifts may well create new trajectories that can amplify in positive ways, life experience teaches us how difficult the maintenance of such patterns can be and therefore the importance of allies (team mates in daily life and in the mind) to help see changes in pattern through to a secure new position.

2

Changes in Families: Theories in Change

In this chapter I will also discuss some common themes that characterise the systemic therapies, and provide some brief examples of work with families that illustrate aspects of the theoretical and clinical influences of the last twenty years, without giving detailed accounts of the different approaches alluded to. The way in which I work as a therapist will be related to a number of different family therapy approaches.

Systems thinking, family pattern, family coherence, and dominant discourses

In early family therapy theory, systems thinking used to centre around concepts of mutual causality or mutual influence, the interrelationship of events within a given living system, such as a family; the importance of a 'required balance', or 'homeostasis' between the subsystems, and around the familiar, but abstract, notion that the whole is greater than the sum of its parts. To distinguish a systemic approach from a more individually oriented psychodynamic approach, family therapists were encouraged to look at the individual in the context of the intimate connections of which he or she was *currently* a part, rather than focusing on current distress as a product of former developmental experience. The isolation of the individual from the context in which she or he lived was described as delimiting 'the arcs of the circuit' (Bateson, 1973b, p. 420) with the attendant danger of making too simplistic an assessment. Therapists attempting to describe 'family systems' struggled to define what Lynn Hoffman famously described as 'the thing in the bushes', the elusive but essential tension between interdependent and coordinated aspects of actions, behaviours, and beliefs mutually influencing one another over time. Therapists also tried to recognise the way in which an individual often carries representations or elements of that larger whole.

Attachment theory and subsequent developments of attachment ideas in family-focused research have lent new validity to these ideas of individual 'patterning' in relation to family patterns , by making explicit connections to the relationship between behaviour, beliefs and intergenerational pattern (Main *et al.*, 1985). The original experimental observations of exploratory behaviour on which subsequent classifications of secure and insecure attachment were based, recognised the tensions between parents protecting their children and letting them go. What was observed was a kind of dance in which the behaviour of one had to be understood in the context of the behaviour of the other. Secure infants looked for and found parents when they felt uneasy, protested if they did not like the separation, and were comforted when reunited. Parents were both attentive and responsive. Insecure infants showed a number of different patterns mirroring the behaviours of their parents, disconnection, inability to be comforted and ambivalence about reconnecting. The researchers related behaviours to theories of how each category of child and parent 'held each other in mind' when separated from each other. This work lent confirmation to Bowlby's earlier theories about the way in which outer 'constellations of relationships' become embedded in the child's internal world and persist over time. Bowlby referred to these as 'inner working models' (1969, 1973,1980). The construction is valuable in relation to many different research studies both in systemic practice and child and adult development over the life span (Clulow, 2001; Parkes *et al.*, 1991).

The notion of a 'reciprocal arrangement' of influence in family life, a family's own declared and undeclared system of checks and balances, is often referred to in different modalities of family research as the 'coherence' of the family. Family coherence also contains the idea of 'core family characteristics', or features that distinguish *that* family from other families, and that the family themselves would recognise as being an aspect of 'this particular family'. Such characteristics are held in balance in relation to one another (Dunn, 1988); and may be taken in by children developing within them as whole patterns – mental representations of relationships. These may be carried forward into subsequent social contexts. At the everyday level of family behaviour, Bateson called these core characteristics 'habits', and defined them as those aspects of living together as human beings that have sunk to a level where we no longer consciously have to attend to them, although they continue to influence the way we subsequently behave (Bateson, 1973b, p. 115). Working with habits and the beliefs that may or may not be associated with them is one key to a family approach, and the one that I have found most central and adaptable over the years. Attachment theorising and the links made in subsequent research into adult narratives of childhood (Fonagy *et al.*, 1993) are also valuable in understanding family stories. Byng-Hall (2001) has consistently theorised family therapy in relation to attachment principles and has focused on creating more coherent narratives within families in treatment. He has recently summarised the position of attachment theory in a world of postmodernist philosophies and theories.

> Over the last decade the field of family therapy has placed much emphasis on post modern philosophy which suggest there is no one truth, but many stories to be told about the same situation. This has been helpful in that family therapists are more likely to listen to their clients and less likely to impose their own model of what happens in families. However...clients wisely do not want any old story, but the most useful available story. Research can indicate what are the most probable stories. Attachments have been shown to be clinically relevant as insecure attachments are more likely than secure attachments to be associated with the development of problems. In my experience attachment directed interventions are more likely to lead to fundamental changes. The story about attachments is also readily understood by clients and therapists (2001, p. 32).

In a world of separations, transitions and new beginnings, I have used attachment principles as one pathway to understanding conflicts of belief and conflicts of interest. It is important to be aware that not all members of a family are likely to describe and understand family arrangements, however habitual, in the same way. Critics of the systemic approach, from the perspective of both gender and ethnicity, have highlighted how the illusion of' 'coherence' as a goal in a family's presentation to a therapist could conceal oppression, as it was likely to favour some family members more than others in order for the 'harmony' of the family to be preserved. Many therapists now prefer to consider the 'hierarchy of discourses' in a family, and reflect on which of these discourses are privileged over others, as well as the way in which some discourses and stories about family life and family functioning predominate. Exploring ideas about 'dominant discourses' in the family, and noting which voices become silenced or marginalised in relation to any particular discourse that has the dominant place, has for me become a regular therapeutic approach, particularly when exploring practices in family life that have become oppressive or constraining. I prefer the concept of 'discourse' to that of narrative in working with more than one person as the concept of therapy as discourse takes into account the interactional components of thought and exchange of ideas, beliefs, and attachments that shape 'narrative' within people's minds. In the family discussed below we will explore ideas of coherence, dissonance and the hierarchy of discourse by deconstructing a piece of passionate interaction in one family session and linking this to two influential theoretical approaches, structural family therapy, and the Milan approach. This family is a first-marriage, biologically intact family of mixed cultures. (Subsequent chapters will represent different structures of both family and ethnicity.)

The Xavier family

The Xavier family came to therapy, as many families do, because of fighting within the home. The father, Jorge, of Argentinean – English descent, fought with his middle son, Sal, who fought with his younger sister, Carlotta. The mother, Eva, a Scandinavian woman, and the older brother, Jamie, held a silent but truculent peace. The father had to travel the globe a lot in his job, and when he was at home he wanted a harmonious and united family life, which he felt desperate about failing to achieve.

I have edited extracts from the second session with the family to indicate connections between two levels of pattern – what was going on in the room, and intergenerational legacies affecting the current pattern (relationship beliefs about these, and emotions surging from the experiences of a previous generation). These created a dominant discourse around dilemmas of masculinity, power, closeness and exclusion. Other potential discourses, to do with women, sexuality and father–daughter relationships, were marginalised in this session, as they were in the life of the family. The parents were both clear that while the problems now being highlighted had always existed, they had intensified since the boys were in their early teens. In using an approach that takes personal family history into account, a phrase of Whittaker's allows for the acceptance of intergenerational and life cycle ideas while rejecting an over-determined approach to the inevitability of patterns repeating themselves over time: 'families are too complicated to simplify with a theory of life cycle development. The strongest determinants for continuity and change are the patterns that emanate from past families, and the patterns that look for something to attach to, shadowy fabricated patterns' (Keith and Whittaker, 1988, p. 447).

Intergenerational patterns, while often unvoiced in the early part of therapy, usually become a part of the family work that I do. The exploration of earlier contexts in which each parent has acquired beliefs about gender and role, about identity at different developmental stages, about attachment closeness, and distance in family life, can offer important clues to their current beliefs and dilemmas. (Byng-Hall 1982, 1986, 1991). They may spontaneously emerge in the course of the family's own exchange; or I may introduce questions relating what is going on to other experiences either parent may have had, when what is taking place in the room appears to carry an emotional loading that is disproportionate to the events being discussed. Elsewhere in the book I will describe how shadows of this kind may come not from an earlier generation, but from another phase in the life of the family; as for example when a family migrates but still live their lives according to patterns that belong to their homeland; or when part of a family moves on to form a second family either through re-cohabitation or marriage, or through a child being fostered or adopted in later childhood. A guiding principle of my own thinking is that 'constraints' carried within any individual adult may no longer have acknowledged or known sources, in the same way that, at the time they sit down with a therapist or counsellor no one in the current family may know where the habits and apparently deeply held beliefs in the family originated. Such constraints may emerge when some aspect of current family life provokes them and they can no longer be avoided. At that time they may need to be 'deconstructed', or taken apart and looked at afresh to assess their current relevance. In many families, certain patterns of living together may be consciously promoted by fathers or mothers on the basis of awareness of what they themselves missed in their own childhood. Determination that the children will have what a parent did not have can be as strong a constraint on family life as determination that something negative experienced by a parent will not be part of their own child's life. By being non-explicit as principles, neither is open to scrutiny, so that the power of the original message or guiding principle cannot be looked at afresh for its current relevance. We can see this happening in the Xavier family below.

In this, the second session, the family are talking about the fact that they are in less trouble now than they were the previous month, and we discuss where the 'hot' moments now show themselves. In spite of the fact that things are going better, the father remains dissatisfied, 'Yes, it hasn't been trouble free but compared to the past it's a lot better' and the 'neutral' older brother, Jamie, gives his opinion reservedly: 'Better, but not much'. The focus of argument between father and sons has now moved from Sal to Jamie, because he would rather be in his room doing his homework than join in the family activities that the father would like him to be part of. This upsets the father greatly, and Sal adds that it is unpleasant all round: 'If Jamie annoys my dad then that makes him angry and he gets annoyed with everyone in the family'. I invite the children to describe their understanding of their parents' view of family life: 'Okay, do you three children know what your mum and dad's idea of a proper family is? Do you share the same idea? Is it a family that does certain things together or everything together?' After a general factual description from Sal, Jamie replies with great feeling: 'If you spent all your life with the family, if you eat with them, play with family, go out with family, work with family, if you do everything – that's family'.

GGB: How old are you now?
Jamie: Fourteen.
GGB: So do you have the same ideas as your dad about closeness in family life, or are your ideas different?
Jamie: I don't particularly care about the family.
GGB: Is that a view that has any listeners in the family? Any sympathetic listeners?
Sal: Sympathetic but not really.
GGB: Is your mum's view the same as your dad's?
Jamie: [Looking at mum] Don't know, think so, expect so, yeah.

I explore whether the mother (Eva) and father (Jorge) have the same ideals of family life and it emerges that the father's current wish to be together is stronger than the mother's, because she has habitually spent much more time with the children in their growing years. Jamie's campaign – 'Nobody's entitled to their own right even to do their homework' – finds subdued echoes in Eva's contributions to the discussion. I ask the father why he took this unusual attitude towards homework: 'Many fathers would be delighted their sons were working so hard, so how come your philosophy is so different?'

Jorge reiterates his wish for more shared family activities: 'I do see Jamie on his own now and again; we go and play football together every weekend now, that pleases me but I have given up trying to do things as a family because it is always such hard work, and that is my heart's wish'. I ask Jorge to explain to the younger child, Carlotta aged six, who is busy turning somersaults, what he means by family activities.

Jorge: I like doing things. Can you listen to me? It would be nice if you did, easier to talk to you when you are listening to me. You know that I like to do things as a family: have long meals together, go for walks sometimes, sometimes to play games and to share things in the house as well...so everybody is part of doing something for the family and for the house and each other. Yeah? You know that don't you?' [Carlotta still says nothing, and continues her play.]

Jorge expands his speech on the difficulties he experiences with each of his sons and becomes more emotional.

Jorge: Just a couple of things, the thing that I find most difficult about Sal, that makes me pull away, is where he just goes on trying to get me to hear his point of view and goes on and on so that I listen...And the thing that I find difficult about Jamie is when he withdraws...

Eva brings the discussion back into focus by pointing out a change.

Eva: I'd like to come back to this idea of the family that we were talking about right at the beginning. Because I feel that what has been difficult is the fundamental shift in the family that has happened. And the pattern used to be that we weren't operating as a family all that much, because Jorge was working so much and away so much, and for all sorts of other reasons when there might have been time, we didn't use it in that way and now Jorge has changed a lot and has redefined his way of wanting to be with the family and it coincides with the age, where, of course, Jamie is becoming more and more independent.

The family have brought along a genogram, or family tree, mapping the family relationships over time, which it was agreed they would construct together, and after a few minutes of looking at this Jorge makes a connection to his own experience at Jamie's age.

Jorge: Why am I so upset when you don't want to do things as a family?...I am acutely aware of the misery that I had when I was eleven, you know, I was sent home to England to live with my grandparents and it was as if I had no father. He never did anything with me, never! And I just don't want you to have that. I want to be a good father to you. I want to be a good father to all three of you.

The children all want to shout and comment and Sal takes the floor:

Sal: There's two things. One thing from just now and one thing from further back which is on the same subject. The thing that was further back was: when you said to me about Jamie working after school..., like my dad is away working and is not with the family as much as he would like to be and he didn't use to be either. I think Jamie is trying to take on board that he is not supposed to be with the family as much, which would be like Dad.

GGB: Well, I think that's very interesting. Do you think they have understood what you have just said?

Sal: Yeah but...

GGB: [remembering this is similar to something Eva had said earlier] Do you think your mum understood? Why don't you ask her?

Sal: [nervously] You ask her.

GGB: What do you think about what Sal just said?

Eva: I think it is a perception that I have had.

GGB: So you agree with him?

Eva: Yes, I agree with him.

GGB: Why would it be just now, do you think? How do you account for Jorge coming back in and wanting his family at this time, just as Jamie is getting the idea that men stay out?

Eva: I think it was a realisation for Jorge how much he had missed out on family life.

GGB: Right, and what led to that?

Eva: Dramatic recognition of family values...hoping that he'd have more regular time at home, and I think it coincides with Jorge identifying with that age when he sort of was aware that he didn't have a father to look after him in Argentina.

Jorge: I am intensely aware of my family and the impact of being sent away. I saw very little of my father after that, and for me this is a dark void. He is still alive and I still long to be close to him... Of course it has just occurred to me is that the crisis that changed me and reoriented me, happened when Jamie was eleven. Which is exactly when I was sent away. That was a moment of tremendous crisis for me.

GGB: Is this something that you have ever shared with the kids, or...

Jorge: I am just intensely aware of how much I missed out on, how much I missed out on as a father, and as a son in never having had a father myself, how much I missed out on eleven years of our own family life. I know that we can't bring that time back; I grieve for that time; I would so like to have more time with you kids, in order to be able, not to have time with you in a sense, so that we could have time together and then be perfectly comfortable about not being together, but being in the same house.

Sal: It does seem now like you are forcing us together.

Jorge: How can I do it differently, tell me? How can I be different, how can we be different?

Sal: Everybody should just be themselves without pressurising them to be with the family... If you don't pressurise people so much then I expect they would feel more comfortable to spend time with the family knowing that they aren't under pressure to do certain things with the family. For me I expect this would make quite a lot of difference.

GGB: Do you think your dad, I mean, I think it is like he can hear the words but he can't quite understand the message.

Jorge: I understand the message loud and clear. What I panic about, I suppose, is that if I don't try and actually help the family come together and god knows I'm around so little anyway, that you'll leave home in three years' time, four years' time and it won't have happened. We won't have been together and then it is too late. We can be together later as grown-ups occasionally.

It can be seen how this period of the boys' lives was a sensitive period for the father in terms of reliving the 'shadowy patterns' of his own experience. Using a genogram or family tree had highlighted for him specific reasons why this was so (in terms of it being a period in his own life when his already tenuous relationship with his father was finally disconnected when he was sent to the UK to live with his aunt and finish his schooling). However, looking at the family tree had also provided a period in which the understandings of the young adolescents could be brought into the open talking of the family, providing the father with different glimpses of what it was possible to expect from them.

The therapist's thinking

In my clinical work I focus on small pieces of family interaction – sequences of behaviour that in families are always laden with emotion and meaning developed over one or more generations. In this I was particularly influenced by a structural approach to family therapy, which pays close attention to the way members of families speak to each other and behave towards each other, in both their verbal and non-verbal behaviours. It offers ways in which family members of all ages can examine meanings that lie within their own behaviour by thinking about small events in everyday life. Subsequently, an analysis of my work through the discipline of 'discourse analysis' (Cederborg, 1994) reinforced my attention to patterns of speech and their arrangement within sessions, and helped me further relate to the text in a number of ways looking at allocation of space, turn taking, and interruption, each of which allows a different examination of power and influence in the pattern of the family.

In the sequences related above and in other brief extracts that follow, I see five main influences on my work. The first two are the direct use of understanding derived from psychodynamic thinking and attachment theory. These provide a way of looking at how our current behaviour may be influenced by the emotional legacies of earlier experiences in our lives. This relates to both individual developmental experience, and to the patterning of attachment and 'mental representations of relationship' (the patterning of family experience within the mind of the growing individual). The framework provides principles for understanding, rather than models for how to *practise*. Emotional force charging current events may shape our current life experience in powerful ways that stem from an earlier point in our own development, and carry with it the emotional rawness of that time (Gorell Barnes, 1994b).

The third influence derives from structural principles. Structural family therapy offers both a model of theorising family life, and a model for practice advocating close participation in the detail of what is taking place between the family members in the room, and including direct provocation of the family's own curiosity, comment and discussion. As the majority of families I work with include children, and teenagers, under sixteen years of age, I try within this model to make the medium of the discussion the smallest inter-actional sequences of behaviour that all the family members can rec-ognise and relate to from their different ages and perspectives. The sequences they can talk about together provide the basis for exploring the different constructions of meaning attributed to behaviour by the different family members. These in turn are contextualised by their age, generation, and gender. The fourth influence (to be discussed later in the chapter) is the Milan approach with its major emphasis on the development of curiosity and reflective mental function in the family as the resource for change. The fifth influence is my lifelong interest in language, which in therapy has developed through ideas about discourse analysis, narrative work, and the use of imagination.

Influences from structural family therapy in the Xavier family session

Everyone except Carlotta talked a lot, often over each other, and I spent time bringing in Carlotta's non-verbal behaviour and the ways the other family members related to or ignored this. One sequence of behaviour (a repeated 'redundancy') was that Sal would often be told off by his father following a series of events that had in fact been started by Carlotta, his younger sister. Catching this in action, and discussing it at the same moment changed one of the key problem-atized ways in which Sal was seen: rather than being 'overactive and a troublemaker', he was trying to maintain one of the family rules – 'keep the peace' – so that his father could have a more uninter-rupted hearing. After one such sequence, in which Carlotta had been turning somersaults and Sal had stopped her and then been yelled at, Eva described how she, as a woman who believed she should be a calming influence, held back from disciplining the children: 'So I hold back and then somebody picks it up and then usually it does blow up'.

GGB: Is it part of the family style that you have developed this, not to express annoyance in order to keep things peaceful?

Eva: Oh yes, very much, very much indeed.

GGB: Have you ever thought that it could be the other way around? That if you express more forcibly what you felt was not being said, the others might need to say less at times?

Eva: I have been thinking that... yes, but quite often in the past I feared that once I start expressing things they then escalate more. It was that if I lost *my* temper with the children, then Jorge would pick it up... and would get even madder... and things would blow.

GGB: [indicating Carlotta] If we just stick with this one example of this young woman here, who has gone head over heels about eight or nine times, the fact that neither of you parents expressed *anything* led to Sal stepping in. What then happened was that Jorge blamed Sal for a piece of behaviour he hadn't initiated at all. I think Sal was trying to stop something else happening so he could listen to his father. I wonder how much of that goes on in the family.

Sal: It does happen a lot, being blamed for things that...

GGB: ...that have started somewhere else but it just gets picked up at a certain point...

Sal: Being blamed for something that isn't actually your doing. That does happen a lot.

In the next session Sal and Jorge both described how having this small event openly noted and discussed had affected each of them and brought them closer together in thinking about it.

Perhaps the most valuable principle I have found from this insider (structural) approach to working with a family's own style, and ways of meaning making, has been the emphasis on working with the repetitive habitual sequences that carry the details of other everyday transactions in families (Colapinto, 1991). Such small repeated sequences carry the 'coding' for more abstract family rules, meta rules that govern larger classes of behaviour. Many of the things that happen between people in a room, such as Sal stopping Carlotta turning somersaults while Eva chose not to step in, are likely to be working to the same meta rule: 'keep the peace at all costs'. However such 'hidden rules' or organising principles of family life and the patterns that derive from them can often become out of date as the family grows, develops and changes. One episode such as a child endlessly doing somersaults while others talk, and the way it is contextualised within the family's responses, is therefore not an isolated event because it reverberates and has relevance in relation to other transactions within the family system (Gorell Barnes, 1981b).

With the Xavier family different lenses might have been used by the therapist to contextualise this behaviour within different frames of meaning. For example, was Carlotta drawing attention to the more subdued female voice in this session, or to the needs of children to express themselves other than through lengthy verbal exchanges? Was she perhaps challenging the view that 'peace should be maintained'? Structural family therapy is of particular value when working with small children because it allows their own behaviours to be part of the medium of therapeutic action. It moves discussion from taking place above the heads of children, to involving them in the process of thinking, and of potential change.

The Riordan family

In this female headed family unit Clara talks *about* Pat, her five-year-old son, and the terrible nightmares he has experienced after his father (Clara's ex-husband) broke down the door of their flat and fought with her about contact with his son. She talks as though Pat is not part of the conversation. She uses a low monotonous voice and refers to Pat with a nod of her head, as if by talking this way she will protect him from the content of her story. On one level Clara is reporting that she has taken charge of safety in the home, but her manner is not conveying to Pat a direct sense of her ability to stop the frightening intrusions of his father. She is also giving him the message that she is anxious about speaking to him directly. During the discussion Pat bangs file drawers and pulls his hat down over his eyes, making funny faces while he does so. The therapist's goal is to encourage Clara to convince Pat that she can now take charge of frightening events.

GGB: Tell me Clara, do you think you've found a way to stop these fights happening?

Clara: Yeah, by him not coming to the house.

GGB: Can you tell *Pat* rather than me how you have thought of a way of it not happening.

Clara: [nervous, giggling] Daddy is not coming to the house any more so there won't be any more fighting.

GGB: Do you know if he can hear you under that hat?

Pat: [to Clara] I knew that.

Clara: [pulling him closer and tipping his hat up so she can see his eyes] He's not coming any more cos I've put a stop to it... You can still *see* him whenever you want to, well, Sundays... you can *ring* him any time and *see* him on Sundays.

Pat settles down, and being offered paper and pens, draws a big fight between mum and dad. In the drawing he shows himself as a helpless little person, waiting to run away. He wonders aloud if *he* should have done something to stop the fight and I begin to explore whether he thinks, as children often do, that it is partly his fault that his parents broke up. He says he does worry about that and that he wants me to speak to Clara about it – 'You ask mum' – so I ask her 'If he says "Mum, was it my fault?", what do you say to him?'

Clara: I tell him that it is not his fault, it was just that Mummy and Daddy could not get on.
GGB: Can you say that to him now and I'll see if he seems to be to be hearing you and taking your meaning...
Clara: It's not your fault, it's never your fault, it is just that mummy and daddy could not get on together. Do you understand?
Pat: Yeah.
GGB: Do you think he believes you? Do you really? [to Pat] Might she need to say it very often, many times?
Pat: I do believe her... but sometimes in the night I don't.
GGB: ...you still sometimes secretly think it might be something you have done or didn't do.
Pat: Yeah.
Clara: [now speaking directly to him with conviction] No, never you darlin', you're too little to cause any trouble, it's Daddy with his drinking coming in and causing trouble.
Pat: [looking at her intently] I know that now.

The value of a structural approach is that it aims at directness of communication between family members in the session. The therapist uses him- or herself to create focused episodes where this can be achieved. In the 1980s the approach came under heavy criticism as it was seen as upholding 'normative' standards for family life, placing one set of family arrangements – that is, the father as head of the family, the woman as his 'more tender' helper and the two of them joined in authority over the children – as the ideal way for families to be (Minuchin and Minuchin, 1974). This led to many interventions based on a supposed view of 'healthy' family functioning in which women were disqualified in order to correct the 'balance' in the couple or family. Many of the families that I have worked with, past and present, have either had no father or had two or three male figures in intermittent partnering roles, since at different times the mother had relationships with men, and children by each of them. In households headed by women the arrangements for men, women and children are likely to be diverse, and since I believe it important to respect these differences, both as a woman and as a therapist, it has led me away from techniques that are oriented towards destabilising existing family arrangements in the service of constructing more 'functional' ones, as perceived and determined by the therapist. Techniques such as 'intensifying' existing tensions and 'unbalancing' supposedly dysfunctional power arrangements were based on changing existing relationship patterns within the family (Minuchin and Fishman, 1981). While intended to empower 'weaker' members in an alliance that is seen as 'dysfunctional', the realities of social existence outside the therapy room often led to the failure of such rearrangements. However, enactment, the creation of family patterns in the room remains a key tool for providing a shared framework for exploration of new solutions, 'how it can happen'. New solutions can be tried in the session and reviewed and critiqued by all: the success of these will depend on parents feeling sufficiently empowered to maintain them once they get home. Much depends on the skill of the therapist in pacing and handling these techniques, rather than the technique itself. Community support may also be needed to keep the new patterns going. Asen (2001, p. 34) using combined structural and group work has commented 'I prefer to work on an empowerment principle focusing on strengths and taking things more slowly as seems necessary, using multiple reinforcements of similar empowering principles'.

One of the qualities in family life that structural work has relied on, while not explicitly articulated within the theory, is the innate resilience or 'bounce-back' quality intrinsic to a theory of biologically intact families that have lived together over time. Cooklin has called this quality 'elasticity' (personal communication). My work with non-nuclear families, step-families and post-divorce reconstructions of family life in various forms, as well as my own lived experience, have led me to believe that many constructions of family do not contain this 'bounce-back' or 'elastic' quality, but have a fragility in the maintenance of relationship arrangements that require both respect and more attention to therapeutic holding, with more shared talking about 'how things have come to be as they are'. It is often the case that families who have undergone many transitions need time to process these and to catch up with and reflect on changes already undergone, rather than emphasis being placed on creating change.

Nonetheless, the strength I derived from experiencing the positive effects of more interventive work has remained central to my work with many couples and families, particularly when working with young children, and with families managing three generations. In recent work with Indian couples trying to manage the integration of their own parents whilst dealing with the demands of full-time careers and small children, a focus on talking directly to each other about key issues of annoyance and discord during the session has been specifically welcomed. 'When we try and move away from a hot spot or talk about three annoying things at once, you keep us focused. If we talk at home and disagree one of us will move away and refuse to continue. A third party is essential'. Ways of keeping focused on troubling subjects (such as how much time at weekends should be devoted to husbands' parents, how much time to wives' parents) might include the observation of the lengths of speech devoted by each party to each side of the family (did it allow for the interjection of the thoughts and feelings of the other or did it become a righteous and uninterruptable monologue; did a question posed allow for an answer to be given; did a response amplify the areas of possible agreement or narrow the possibilities of a solution?). I attempt in my use of questions to link action to both feeling and future conse-quence: 'In what ways could you show commitment to your wife's parents that would allow her to find more room in her heart for your own?', and use comments that emphasise mutual influence and reciprocity, 'If you want to change the way he responds to you, you will have to change the way you say "I need your help"'. In a three generational family situation where the parents of either parent are also heavily involved in child care, roles can become genuinely con-fused. For example, paternal grandmother can become involved in real everyday competition with her daughter-in-law about the young male child in the family: who does he 'belong to' first? Conflicts of interests develop. Does the husband act primarily as son to his mother, or as husband to his wife? If he acts as son to his mother does this place him in a position which renders his wife less empowered and forced always to function first as a grateful daughter-in-law, rather than an adult woman with her own mind? Minuchin (2001), interviewing a Chinese couple in Beijing confronted such a situation in a Chinese family with great simplicity: 'Talk to him as though he is your husband, not as the son of his mother'. Bringing these hidden rivalries into the open can lead to a temporary increase in tension, but can also lead to a greater relief and recognition of what needs to change in the longer term. Inviting new ways of talking that specifically allow the recognition of the sexual relationship as a powerful potential force for good, can also create new pathways for a different distribution of power within the larger construction of three-generational family life. Ma (2000) talking of work with Chinese families in Hong Kong reports that structured help in analysing and thinking about the problem, focusing and planning, providing alternatives and new ways of coping were cited as especially welcome. In addition, the creation of a context in which family members listened and talked among themselves in a social culture where drive and bustle were the organising principles, was seen as giving rise to new behaviours, observation, reflection and the development of play with children.

The Milan approach

A fourth major influence on how theory and clinical work have woven together for me stemmed from the Milan approach, originally developed by four Italian psychoanalysts who came together to develop systemic work as a team in the 1970s. The approach offered a framework within which a psychodynamic and intergenerational understanding could be incorporated into a systemic approach to work with families. In particular the Milan approach offered useful ways of addressing the complex and often conflicting systems of meanings people attribute to their own actions. It attended to the power of belief systems in which both individuals and families may either be trapped or flourish over time (Campbell *et al.*, 1991; Tomm, 1984). The approach offered a method of linking the understanding of unconscious intergenerational processes that control family relationships over time with a systemic approach to changing the hidden rules in families' current interactional patterns of communication (Cecchin, 1987). Whereas questions were originally a way of extracting information that could be used by the therapist and the team, noting the impact of the questions on the family as they learnt about themselves through the responses of the other members, rapidly became an intrinsic part of the therapeutic process, and the curiosity invoked by listening to the therapist's questions about relationships in the family and the answers other members gave became the main vehicle for inducing changes in thinking and belief (Tomm, 1987, 1988). Questioning was seen as 'circular' in that the interviewer attempts to follow feedback closely so that the answer to a previous question, (and the wording of the answer) plays a part in shaping the subsequent question. The interviewer also pays attention to distinction, to definitions, and to difference, and follows the pattern of thought in response to prior responses (see Jones, 1993, and Jones and Asen, 2000, pp. 22–31, for clear elucidation of this model). Cecchin (2001, p. 35) has said of questioning that 'we are interested in eliciting differences that move a system along, and we are interested in family members' opinions regarding various sorts of differences'.

The formal method the Milan approach offered to professionals for teamwork with colleagues and for systematic thinking about clinical dilemmas – the consistent use of a hypothesis to guide therapist's questioning, the recognition of circularity and mutual influence in the therapeutic process as well as in the family process, and the idea of neutrality in relation to the therapist's stance towards family members – have all been further developed throughout the field of family therapy (Jones, 1993). Milan work, originally rooted in three-generational Italian family life, addressed the way family identity becomes organised around meanings that are handed down, often without examination, and also brought back therapists' attention to family myths as a powerful force in the inner lives of families. The Milan approach freed the thinking of many therapists who, like myself, had previously felt they were not being effective enough as 'structural intervenors'. The emphasis on contextualisation as the essential factor in defining the meanings embedded in family relationship patterns, the use of direct and indirect questions to elucidate meaning and provoke family members' own curiosity about what is going on, the emphasis on circularity (actions as responses, and also as triggers) took into account processes of mutual influence also emerging clearly from the separate field of infant development (Hinde and Stevenson-Hinde, 1988), and offered therapists a way of intruding into complex family patterns without arousing personal feelings of misuse of therapist power and self.

The pleasure and interest of working in teams has also been a formative influence on the development of this model as an aid to working with families. In my own view, teamwork is at its most valuable when working with families that are too closely 'cross-joined' to be offered a difference by a single therapist. However, the freedom the model created by encouraging therapists to always consider taking a number of different positions in the mind in relation to clinical dilemmas (Reimers, 2000) has been one of the particular contributions to helping therapists do something useful, independent of whether they have access to a team.

Returning to the Xavier family, the use of indirect questions was a useful way of getting the less speculative members of the family to think more about the powerful ideas other members were carrying in their heads. We have seen how Jorge (the father) was more preoccupied with the context of the message, his relationship with his sons in the intergenerational *context* of his own unmet fathering needs, than with the *content* of either of his sons' answers. This preoccupation dominated the exchange, at the expense of any content in the messages they sent him. Thus whatever meaning was attributed to an action by either son was read by him primarily as a signal to come closer or go further away, interpreted either way as a conflict-laden message ('the thing that I find most difficult about Sal, that makes me pull away, is where he just goes on trying to get me to hear his point of view and goes on and on so that I listen ... And the thing that I find difficult about Jamie is when he withdraws'.)

Very simple questions invited family members to think about the differences between how they as individuals may see things, and the way the other family members may see things. The constant comparison between self and other in the course of a session directed at one person, but heard by all, opens up what may previously have been rigid positions and encourages people who are intimately connected but engaged in defending their rights or their position to become anxious about one another in new ways, and from this, new negotiations can develop. Here are some individual examples:

GGB: So Jamie, what do you think your dad's idea of being a proper family is?

Jamie: If you spent all your life with the family, if you eat with them, play with family, go out with family, work with family, if you do everything – that's family.

GGB: How old are you now?

Jamie: Fourteen.

GGB: So do you think you have the same ideas as your dad about closeness in family life, or are your ideas different?

Jamie: I don't particularly care about the family.

GGB: So when you're doing your homework do you think your dad sees this as just the need to do your homework, or does he see it as opting out of the family?

Jamie: Oh, I think he sees it partly as both, but probably more opting out of the family.

Another indirect question, this time to Eva:

GGB: When Sal stops Carlotta from interrupting what his dad is saying, how do you think Jorge frames this behaviour to himself?

Working on my own with families, which is the case with about three-quarters of my work (the rest being with different co-therapists in the room), I often use the multi-positional approach that post-Milan thinking encouraged therapists to develop. This allows me to formulate questions that address aspects of what is going on in a family that I think are being ignored. Thus I might ask Eva, 'as a woman, why do you think that your daughter, the only other female in the family, somersaults while her father is talking...what do you think she might be trying to tell him?' Or to Jorge, 'if you had two daughters and a son rather than two sons and a daughter, how do you think the family might be different for each of you two parents?' Sometimes I use other members of the family who are not present as aids to the discussion: 'if Jorge's father – who disappeared from his life when he was eleven – was here now, what advice do you think he would give him about how to be close to his sons?'. Sometimes the invocation of others is less specific: 'who in all your family would be of most use to you in thinking about this dilemma now?'. Once the absent persons are named, I go on to involve them in thinking in terms of what they might say if they were present. This can also lead to additional family members joining in the work with the family in a later session if they live within reasonable reach. Much of my work combines an exploration of the influence of other people (who may not be in the household or in the country) on the thinking of the people in the room, with the subsequent bringing in of those people if they live reasonably near by or are visiting the family.

Moving forward with theory

Like many other family therapists in the UK whose practice developed under the umbrella of the NHS and within a welfare state offering some collective ideals, I was suspicious of new waves of theory that claimed to be a total approach. I am more interested in 'adding on' factors to my basic repertoire, in line with the changing climate of family life and also of the changing nature of the work I do. My basic repertoire, grounded in the reality of social inequalities of gender, class and ethnicity, has always consisted of verbal exploration with individuals, couples and families, connecting their internal and external experiences as they see these intersecting and interacting over time. My interest in text, what people say, and how they say it pre-dated my training as a therapist, and has remained at the centre of how I think with clients about their own narrative and discourse. Listening, exploration, and the expansion of text is combined with a number of ways of engaging families in change. Talking and writing, the use of life-story material in the session (both verbal and visual), photos, drawings, reflections and stories about these, are combined with interactive tasks between sessions. My own input has always included highlighting resilience, picking up positive story lines around distress, positively connoting behaviours and attention to clients' unique creativities within the ordinary nature of living. This has meant that certain 'waves' of theorising or practice speciality have passed by me without my practice being centrally changed by them. Certain ongoing 'lenses'(Hoffman, 1990) from other aspects of living, as well as from within the systemic field, have been key to connecting theory and practice more closely for me over the last fifteen years.

Feminist theorising

Feminist theorising offered a way of starting a different quality of examination to any approach that was currently claiming 'totality' within the field. It offered an emotional and intellectual lens through which to explore the balance of my own practice, as well as my own life. I found much to re-describe my own experience which did not previously have a theoretical attribution. During the 1970s, women therapists began to develop a more collective voice, which they identified as having features distinct from the preoccupations of the men working alongside them. In the USA many of these centred around unacknowledged inequalities in the field, both in what was addressed in theory and what was ignored in practice. Walters (1990) summarised the early feminist approach as including four major components, and these appealed to me as action points: (1) the conscious inclusion of the different experience of women in their professional, social and family roles in a culture largely organised by male experience; (2) a critique of therapy practices that devalued women and their roles; (3) the integration of feminist theory and women's studies into family therapy thinking; and (4) the use of female modes and models in practice and teaching.

Many women re-framed techniques that had formerly been described within a male domain in new ways that emphasised the positive intention in behaviours formerly ascribed to pathology. Peggy Papp and Olga Silverstein took ideas from the Mental Research Institute (MRI) 'the problem theorised as the solution to another problem' and worked as a team in ways that had similarities to the Milan team (who had also trained at the MRI). They specialised in delivering a 'both and' message to the family at the end of the session in which 'the pros and cons of symptomatic 'behaviour were described, the positive intention of the patient was ascribed and a potential let out clause was provided: the patient's belief in the essential nature of their job may have been mistaken/no longer necessary'. No one was 'to blame' (Papp, 2001). Joan Laird rewrote myth into family therapy as a universal cultural process with positive healing aspects, rather than myth being described as something with primarily negative binding powers as had previously characterised its theorising within the field (Laird, 2001). The feminist approach in the 1980s also included a much wider re-framing; important debates about the need for altered consciousness among therapists about the realities of power and control in families, especially those aspects of physical and economic control that oppressed and isolated women and children (MacKinnon and Miller, 1987; Perelberg and Miller, 1990). The development of 'women's talking' as part of what was discussed in the domain of therapy, the making of space between women for experience that had not previously been voiced, as well as sharing the common elements derived from being a human female intersected the systemic field (Gorell Barnes and Henesy, 1994; Burck and Speed, 1994). Working with colleagues of different ethnicities and the entering of these additional diverse voices, further moved the field away from the objectification of people, categories and knowledge in the unitary principles which often obscured and disqualified the significance of differences (Phoenix, 1999). Burck and Daniel (1995) also challenged therapists not to resort to gender stereotyping with regard to differences between men and women themselves, but to recognise the contextualisation of gender:

What is femaleness and maleness? The question implies that somewhere, somehow we could really find out what womanhood and manhood is. We take the view that these categories have been created through language which in turn has real effects on how we live, think, feel. This is not to deny that there are actual biological differences, but that these are so profoundly mediated through culture that it is impossible to find a gendered essence: we can only discover the ways in which we 'perform' these differences. (Burck and Daniel, 1995, p. 11).

Harding (1987, p. 6) also put it thus: 'Once it is realised that there is no universal "man" but only culturally different men and women, then man's eternal companion "woman" also disappeared ... that is women come only in different classes races and cultures, there is no "woman" and no "woman's experience".' Gendered experience may vary not only across cultural categories, but within the individual experience of any one of us as we move between different social contexts, some of which may be in conflict. If brought into conversation with one another in a therapeutic context, however, these points of conflict can offer richer possibilities for thinking about what change involves. A further feminist point of inquiry, which 'joins other underclass approaches in insisting on the importance of studying ourselves and "studying up" instead of "studying down"' (Harding, 1987, p. 8), became more acceptable in practice after a period in which professional training had moved practice away from using the personal self of the therapist as an important component in therapy.

Post-modernism and social constructionism

The assumption of a 'post-modern era' in family therapy theory, as in other theories, relies on an earlier assumption that once there were grand collective beliefs characterising a 'modernist era'. Diversity undoubtedly existed then as now. However, certain 'truths' were certainly privileged above others for long periods of time, and held more influence within the public discourses of family therapy theory than others. For example, one story characterising the family seen in family therapy, as taught in the 1970s would read like this. Family structures were hierarchically arranged, the family was considered as an 'objective entity' independent of the prejudices, biases and preferences of the observer and describer, most families studied were white and middle class from which generalisations applying to all families would be drawn, and the therapist, usually white, male and middle class, had an expert position. Research was based on similar assumptions about 'the family'. While certain key influences in that period, for example the Philadelphia Child Guidance Clinic, specifically worked with poor 'underorganised' families and employed black therapists, the differences offered by class and ethnicity that they emphasised in their early work had little impact on wider teaching and publication in the journals of the time. 'Normative' family development, including recommended gender arrangements were held as a hallmark of healthy growth and functioning. This description may be believed or dismissed by current readers, but the strength of determining statements that used to be made about family life and the roles of men and women is now hard to grasp.

Discovery of the body of theory that was developing under the general heading of 'social constructionism' was important for me because it provided a way of theorising more clearly my background in sociology and my ongoing interest in social research within the different arenas of family life. In post-modern or social constructionist thinking, the self, like the gendered self, is not conceived as a single entity, but as continually in evolution; not a text inscribed in early childhood on 'tablets of stone' or intrapsychically inscribed with one narrative to be interpreted within a particular framework, but as many potential selves evolving in different ways that are 'elicited' or 'brought forth' by different contexts. Many of the narrative therapies derive from this principle of language as constitutive: that as we speak we not only recount our lives, but through conversation make up the possibility of new futures. In my own construction of what therapy involves, it remains important that such ideas about the fluid self do not gain more prominence than alternative discourses that acknowledge the power of social realities such as poverty, sexism, nationalism and racism. Belief in the powers such realities hold and the way we bring these into the work we do with families may determine whether any of us see ourselves as constructivist or social constructionist therapists. The constructivist paradigm itself, at its most free floating, has been widely criticised, primarily for failing to take account of the structural imbalances of power in society, which controls how such problems are thought about and discussed at both the visible and the invisible levels (Speed, 1991). In my experience, holding socially constructed realities in mind alongside the exploration of possibilities for any newly emerging family reality or self in therapy prevents the therapist from engaging in false optimism in constructing realities that are dissonant with the worldview of the client (Reimers, 2001).

Social constructionism includes a recognition that people categorise the world the way they do because they have participated in social practices, institutions and other forms of symbolic action (that is, language) that give shared meanings to events within relationships and relationship patterns established over time. The many discourses and conversations developing around the patterning of ethnicities and cultures within the UK contribute constantly to evolving philosophies of family life, theory of family, and dilemmas of change (Gorell Barnes, Down, and McCann, 2000). Social constructionist ideas give the therapist more flexibility in creating options deriving from the family's account. The therapist focuses with different members of the family on how the story is constructed, how it came to be constructed that way, and why it is being told in this way in this setting now. Therapist and family may share areas of 'communal' or socially constructed beliefs about how the world works, which they are *all* party to as men, women, mothers, fathers, children, sisters or brothers, and *differences* between them. Problems can be explored through a personal focus – 'myself as a woman' – and then move into the socially constructed and shared domain – 'myself as an unmarried, educated Greek Cypriot woman still living in an Orthodox community in Camden Town in 2002' – and back into the personal domain elaborated with new meanings. The emphasis is thus not only on the individual mind and individual responsibility, but on the meanings collectively generated by the individual, couple or family within larger communities. The therapist will also look for differences in 'voicing': which descriptions have the most power, who has most voice in the family in relation to which area of discussion, and who loses out as a result.

Two key ideas from influential social constructionist theorists are highlighted here. The first derives from the work of Harlene Anderson and Harry Goolishian (1988), two American systemic therapists. In their view social constructionist concepts emphasise meaning as an intersubjective phenomenon created and experienced by individuals in conversations and actions with others and with themselves. This assumes that human action is given meaning through the way that we tell our stories and have them responded to by others; and that language is a powerful shaper of human experience. If problems are created and told in language, they can also be changed in language. The second idea derives from Tom Andersen, a Norwegian family therapist, who argues that by expressing oneself one is simultaneously reforming oneself. 'The process of talking is both informative and formative' (Andersen, 1992a, p. 89). Andersen also asks a question that is key to the maintenance of any attempt to change: 'Who is the reference group who will affirm that which the person is trying to become?' and this is addressed further in later chapters.

The use of research

Research has always influenced my work, particularly research that looks at the effects of social adversity, stressful life events and what develops resilience in families and children (Gorell Barnes, 1985, 1990, 1994c, 1999). Early in my development as a systemic therapist I found the use of research studies relating to different aspects of interactional relationships in couple and family life, a valuable adjunct to less grounded theory. Research can indicate stories that are not in the therapist's knowledge base, and act as an adjunct to appropriate curiosity. In the last twenty years I have been particularly interested in the areas of family life covered in the following chapters of this book and the research that relates to these areas; as well as conducting research with colleagues based on life story interviews, and subsequently in clinical work. I try to use research reflexively, that is, to inform my own living as well as my work. This is not because I believe in 'objective' truths, but to offer another perspective or 'voice' in interpersonal debates. Supervision of the research of others has led to ongoing interest in the relationship between what is observed and described within the research domain as well as the clinical domain. Similar questions of privilege and marginalisation exist in both. As a therapist and researcher I see myself as influenced by social constructionist ideas in relation to the way I look at how people give accounts of their lives. I am interested in the external realities that contextualise family life as well as the medium, the discursive or narrative form, that families choose to describe their experience and try out new ways of thinking about relational issues.

3

CULTURE, DIVERSITY AND DEVELOPMENTS (1): RETHINKING CONTEXTS FOR GROWTH AND CHANGE

The family and life cycle ideas: a pluralistic approach

When you hear the term 'family life cycle' what image of a family comes to your mind? How many adults live in the household; in what ways are they connected; are they of the same gender or different genders? How many generations are there? What are the arrangements for child-care? How does the family allocate the daily tasks of family life? What rituals does it have for transitions from one state to another (birth, birthdays, rituals of joining and separation, rituals of parting and death).

The processes of change required for therapists to develop a pluralistic approach to families, one that can take account not only of lone-parent families, as well as post-divorce diversity, gay and lesbian families, as well as the variations of family form contextualised by world migration, ethnicity and culture, have been slow in coming about in UK professional thinking and teaching. In practice, the former theoretical model of nuclear family life – a heterosexual, biologically intact family headed by a couple where the man brings in the money and the woman keeps the home – is increasingly rare in the UK. The definition of a 'normal mother' as one in a stable, hetero-sexual partnership rules out one-third of UK mothers of infants today. Although many women marry after the birth of their first child, there are still 23 per cent of UK families with dependent children living in lone female-headed households, with 80 per cent of never-married mothers dependent on State income support, and

60 per cent of who have been previously married. It is clear therefore that one normality in a lone-parent headed household is to require additional financial support (Burghes, 1994). The differences in the way mothers and children lead their lives do not need to be 'problematized'. The current suggestions from research are that about one-third of these children will be disadvantaged in terms of education outcomes (Dunn, 2001; Kiernan and Hobcraft, 1997), and point to the need for additional supportive structures to their progress through school. (Dowling and Osbourne, 1994). Children from these families are also more likely to have to contend with depression in their parents, as well as transitions in and out of cohabitation-based households, which will have their own hazards for relationship ties (Dunn, 2002). However, the recent ongoing Avon Longitudinal Study of Pregnancy and Childbirth (ALSPAC – 14 000 families) from which these figures are drawn has also highlighted the importance of variables within broad generalisations of family categorisation:

- the significance of parents' life course experience (teenage pregnancy, number of relationship transitions, and fathers' number of relationship transitions, and the amplifying cross-parenting effects of earlier negative experience for some families).
- the significance of biological relationships for children
- the significance of within-family variation (59 per cent of variance within families in relation to the adjustment of children) (Dunn *et al.*, 2000; Golding, 1996).

With reference to clinical work, children drew researchers' attention to the importance of grandparents (usually maternal, rather than paternal), the importance of friends, particularly in step-mother headed families, and the dangers of distance from their own fathers. Children under eight, who place their fathers as 'not close' on a simple family map, were three times more likely to show behaviour difficulties, than children who place their fathers in the central circle (Dunn, 2001, op. cit.). Other researchers working on the material generated by this longitudinal survey have pointed to the value of a second parent of either gender in the family (Golombok, *et al.*, 2002). Single mothers reported more negative relationships with their children, than did mothers with partners, and the children of single mothers showed a higher incidence of psychological problems. These findings suggest that it is the presence of two parents, rather than the presence of a parent of either gender, that is associated with more positive outcomes for the children's psychological wellbeing. Moving more specifically into the vulnerabilities of lone-parenthood, Moffit (2002) found that young mothers as a whole, for example, those who had their children under nineteen, had more socio-economic deprivation, less resilience, and more mental health difficulties. Where they had live-in partners they also tended to have partners who were less reliable and supportive, both economically and emotionally. The partners tended to be more anti-social and abusive. However, 90 per cent of births occurred outside marriage. Young mothers, therefore, often cannot rely on a partner for support. As Moffit points out, state support for families with children has decreased since the early 1980s, and there is no state supported childcare. Children at age five were rated as having more emotional and behavioural problems, were at increased risk of maltreatment, or harm, and showed higher rates of illnesses, accidents, and injuries.

To the complexities of family structure, and potential risk, we also need to add ethnicity and culture as mediating variables: the shared history, practices, beliefs and values of particular groups of people, 'operating dynamically and permeating the way people live their lives' (D'Ardenne and Mahtani, 1999). This may involve particular connotations in terms of relationship to three-generational family patterns: respect for an older generation, as well as expected support from grandmothers to grandchildren. Although active involvement of, and respect for, the older generation can also contribute to tension in a married couple attempting to balance loyalties to family of origin, against loyalties to each other and to their children, it can in other contexts provide secure support for parenting without a husband. While there is substantial evidence that young mothers, rather than single mothers, are a group requiring professional concern – the UK having the highest rate of teenage childbearing in Europe, twice that of Germany, three times that of France and six times that of the Netherlands (Moffitt, 2002, p. 727) – there is as yet insufficient research of this within cultural differences, and the mediating effects of these on successful child-rearing as a young mother. Family therapy in the UK is now well-rooted in its recognition that models of family development are culture-specific, and clinical work can be ahead of research in bringing this differential thinking to bear.

Multiculturalism and diversity

A multicultural approach offers a focus for attending to differences in hazards to family life and in resilience. Using a multicultural perspective, each of us can look at how our own culture has been a significant variable and how it has powerfully shaped our own realities and development as people and therapists. One of the most important developments in family therapy theorising in recent years has been the recognition of plurality: of family form, of gendered choice in relationships, of cultures within a multicultural society, coupled with an approach to people's life stories that takes into account ideas about hierarchies in discourse. In attending to the stories people tell, and to the way they carry a number of alternative descriptions of their own circumstances in their heads; the way these discourses about themselves become arranged within hierarchies of importance within their own minds, provides us with clues that guide our own listening and help us to attend to the particular beliefs that are shaping behaviour. Attention to how story and context interact keeps a therapist attuned to the impact of their own influence and how this in itself can shape emphases for empowerment or disqualification. The idea of a unitary dominant truth that people are finding unhelpful in relation to the life issues that confront them can be challenged.

Listening carefully also allows us to define with a particular family what is a transitional life-cycle crisis for them. What are their expectations, norms and hopes in relation to roles the children will perform, the men will perform, the women will perform? In what ways are family members such as brother, sister, aunt, uncle and grandparent expected to provide or be provided for; and in what ways are the family concerned that this is not happening 'normally'? What are they prepared to share with an 'outsider' to the family? Burman, in analysing her own interviews as a psychologist with children (1994, pp. 145–7), shows how a child's use of language is shaped by beliefs about what is legitimised in social exchanges between people of different generations and different cultures, within the family and outside it, an important point that should be borne in mind by family therapists working with adults as well as children (Gorell Barnes, 1996b). Variations on 'normality' are likely to be infinite, and only by enquiring about a crisis within the context defined by the family (and the community of which it sees itself as part); the defined 'hierarchies of importance' within the mind of the teller; will the idea of violated 'norms' with the attendant sense of 'failures and disappointments' become clearer.

Gay and lesbian families: diversity and homophobia

R. J. Green, a gay family therapist who has forced the academic collective of family therapy in the United States to question some of its own homophobic practices, listed five overlapping areas as important for preparing students in a multicultural society to work within a given cultural group. (The term 'culture' includes the changing micropractices that come to characterise different groupings of people choosing to live their lives in defined ways.)

- Didactic training: helping students acquire information through lectures and readings that are woven throughout the entire programme.
- Sensitisation: helping students to develop a comfortable awareness of 'not knowing everything', and an enthusiasm for learning about and forming multiple identifications with different cultural groups.
- Personal contact: helping students reduce their phobic and prejudicial responses through cooperative interactions with members of different cultural groups.
- Supervised clinical experience: helping students acquire intervention skills that are culturally attuned under the guidance of supervisors and cultural consultants with expertise on specific groups.
- Modelling by means of organisational structure: helping students become accustomed to seeking routine case consultation, personal guidance and instruction from minority group professionals holding positions of senior leadership (Green, 1996).

Many of these recommendations are similar to those advocated by Laszloffy and Hardy (2000) in creating contexts for therapists to examine non-racist practice. They add a number of issues of self-examination relating to developing racial awareness and differences of perception in relation to skin colour, arguing that individuals who understand and are resolved about their racial identity are more comfortable about discussing race and racism because they are less fearful of discovering or exposing parts of themselves which they or others would find objectionable. Gorell Barnes, Down and McCann (2000), Gorell Barnes (2002a), and Burns and Kemps (2002) have further examined issues involved in working professionally across gay lesbian and diverse ethnic cultures in UK contexts.

Culture and changing micropractices: keeping up with change

'Culture' itself is always in the process of change. Expectations, sometimes rooted in old traditions underpinned by religious beliefs, are constantly on the move as women and children – living in new countries and contexts and finding voices that formerly they may not have been allowed to express – publicly offer new critiques of what were previously privileged (male) traditional assumptions and structures, and move into them as they go. Men, particularly young men, also move into positions in the family occupied in former generations by women. Newer structures such as gay and lesbian families may not yet have developed a 'culture' of family traditions, and are constantly inventing them in response to a perceived or felt need. Lone parents, divorced parents and step-families, often orient themselves towards former assumptions about daily family living and may not take into account their own discreet differences as family forms. Ignoring difference can impede the development of thinking about the ways in which transitions in their own and their children's lives may affect the social, emotional, behavioural, or educational aspects of children's development.

Biological development can offer a basic framework upon which to build thinking about how parent figures and children are relating, and the need for secure attachments as a prerequisite for healthy emotional development. Recent research has emphasised the importance of attending to biology and to attachment (Dunn, 2001, 2002, op. cit.). Secure attachments are characterised by interactions where people are accessible and responsive to each other, offer a protective 'safe haven' and a secure base from which to learn and grow. Secure attachment is related to a capacity for intimacy and trust, to resilience levels and to the ability to adjust to stress as well as to meta communicate about relationships (Main et al., 1985; Byng-Hall, 2001). It provides an additional focus for family assessment and many aspects of thinking about family functioning, that is, an alternative axis to the socio-cultural dimensions (Minuchin, 1988). A systemically oriented curiosity about why a family's dilemma is as it is, which includes cultural and socially constructed perspectives, can be placed alongside a series of questions that may help to reveal whether the family is constructing itself in a way that does in fact promote the well-being and development of children, and indicate more clearly where new thinking, behaviours, or supports may need to be developed. Identification of the needs of any children in a family will also need to include the family's ability to access information and resources in an age in which access to resources has become increasingly complex. Minuchin and Minuchin (1974) conceptualised the natural family as developing through a number of stages that require it to restructure its organisation, while at the same time maintaining continuity on behalf of its members. They defined family structures as 'the invisible set of functional demands that organises the ways in which family members interact' (ibid., p. 51). While such continuities have often been fragmented in the lives of families in the UK today, especially in families presenting to therapists, it is important to note the value children continue to place on secure attachment to their primary parent figures even though the shape of the family structure has changed (Dunn, 2001).

Families, however constructed, are contextualised by two broad areas of concern. The first of these can be described as universal concerns since all families have to wrestle with them: nurture, the organisation of authoritative parenting and power, distribution between family members and interdependence versus autonomy. The second set of constraints relates to the ways in which these universals are housed within any particular family: the structure, organisation and daily behaviour within which they are negotiated. The Minuchins' particular contribution to the development of life cycle ideas as a way of thinking about family stress, has been the emphasis on the normality of stress, and the inevitability of developmental transitional crises for all families. The normative range of crises most families have to deal with include changes such as a marriage, a new baby or the lack of one, a second child or a miscarriage, a serious illness or death in the family, or the onset of Alzheimer's in a loved old person. Such changes force the 'pattern as it was' to evolve into a new pattern. A new balance has to be established within the range the family can manage. Families now, both of the therapists themselves and of the clients who form part of their working lives, have often had severe disruptions and multiple transitions to accommodate and in many cases traumatic assaults on their own developmental histories and bio-psychosocial rhythms as well as to their attachment systems. Many people may also find themselves rearing children in very different circumstances from those in which they themselves were reared. Ideas derived from normative life-cycle theorising require balancing alongside alternative frameworks for thinking about development and a focus on transitions and their effects. Families from widely differing cultures deal with the universalities of human development, but therapists are often not trained in the nuances of these cultural differences. This places a requirement on them to have a developed curiosity about differences in child-rearing and expectations of development as well as understanding about the effects of loss and change. Particular difficulties for individual families in relation to their current life experience will need exploring, as will the idiosyncratic variants of why any developmental dilemma is hard to think about. This may include attention to a 'higher organising principle', the weight of expectation, attitudes and taboos from the past. It may include attention to trauma and disruptive experience. Equally powerful may be the effect of *inadequate* past experience on the current situation; for example girls who have spent all their lives in care, as young mothers may struggle to find a family form that they themselves have never experienced (Quinton and Rutter, 1984), or men who are trying to parent their children alone following divorce may have never looked after children before (Gorell Barnes, 2002b). Carter and McGoldrick (1980) usefully defined two axes of stress as the horizontal and the vertical stressors. The horizontal stressors include predictable developmental stresses and unpredictable events, the hazards that life deals families – disability, long-term illness, mental ill-health, untimely death – as well as socially constructed and environmental stressors outside the family over which the family has no control. Vertical stressors include the experience of previous generations, as incorporated and transmitted by the parents in the family. To these two axes should be added experience *within the same generation* that has led to changes of context for child-rearing, or that has created traumatic disruption of attachment and anticipated patterns of child-rearing; divorce, re-partnering, enforced migration. The family will be most vulnerable at the point where a current crisis triggers or amplifies previous anxiety that has left the parents less able to cope in relation to a particular dimension of living. Whereas an intact family progressing through the life cycle would be likely to go through transitional stages that can be defined in predictable ways by developmental psychologists, many children and parents have been through a number of losses, transitions and regroupings, which inevitably create differences in developmental pathways (ALSPAC study; Dunn, 2001; Moffitt, 2002), as also those whose parents have been forced to flee from their own communities and countries (Woodcock, 2001a,b; Papadopoulos, 2002).

Ethnicity, culture, migration and family change

Ethnicity can be defined in terms of the orientation it provides to individuals by delineating norms, values, interactional modalities, rituals, meanings and collective events and the way these permeate and give meaning to people's lives. Sluzki (1979) once framed this sense of 'being in the world' as 'dialectically supported by regularities of the environment that generate the experience of consonance' (p. 382). Each individual subscribes to some degree to a certain organisation of reality and hence is able to make constant micro predictions of how things are going to be and how people are going to act and react. In life cycle theorising, as therapists we need to ask ourselves about the effects of unpredicted variations on a person's sense of self, created not only by former experience but by current context, the structural inequalities of the world in which we live as well as by nationalist and racist attitudes.

As a family experience, migration may be presented to a therapist as containing both loss and hope for the future. Identifying with a family the ways in which they have coped with migration can be an important aspect of identifying the way they see their own strengths, resilience and vulnerabilities. Two common features of early family adaptation to living in a new country take families in different directions. One adaptation may be to increase their assimilation into the new environment at the expense of reducing a collective affiliation or a historical perspective. For other groups, cultural and religious allegiances forbid these adaptations and the group retains a strong reference to itself, before all other reference groups. In this self-defined, relatively closed situation it may be wise to include as consultant an important senior person or religious leader from the community rather than try to impose an alien way of thinking (Lau, 1994). Migration ranges from the individual who is sent on his own to work or study on behalf of a family who has stayed 'back home', to complete families, where a large part of the meaningful network and frame of reference migrates collectively, reducing the sense of personal difference that an individual has to experience. An important question highlighting the way a family frames its own experience is the story a family tells as part of its collective belief system: did the family migrate in order to make a better living, or to escape from a bad living situation? How does this effect their attitudes to the old country and the new? Who initiated the move, and who were the gainers and losers of the move? (In terms of gendered constructions these questions can take on significant new meanings for the way the family reorganises itself.) An important issue in this regard stems from the frequent assumption that if the move had a positive motivation or has exceeded expectations of what would be achieved, mourning what has been left behind may be unacceptable; sadness or mourning may be labelled as pathological or an act of ill will in the face of family good fortune. The opposite situation can also cause a family to seek help: a family that has fled from persecution while others remain, may feel stuck in a state of ongoing mindfulness of and involvement with the dreadful political and social circumstances from which they and not the others in the family have escaped.

Refugees and family work

Papadopoulos (in Papadopoulos and Byng-Hall, 1977) describes competing discourses in refugee communities, in their search for home arguing on the one hand for letting go of old habits of attachment and declaring that, 'now we are safely here, let's get on with it', and on the other the importance of not forgetting where one has come from and its traditions. A paradox for many refugees is that although they are physically safe from persecution, they are not secure in other ways (Papadopoulos and Byng-Hall, 1997). Thomas (1995) has continually pointed out that for a black refugee in a racist climate, to be temporarily physically safe is not necessarily ever to be secure. Safety and security are important but not synonymous aspects of the settling-in process that therapists may encounter.

In a second or subsequent immigrant generation, from which many in our profession are drawn, there may be pressures to develop either way, to honour tradition or to let it go. For example the father of an Orthodox Jewish family in a London Lubavitch community was clear that there are quite specific societal expectations of what his children will do when they grow up, in particular getting married and having a family, and that these expectations will be met. Such expectations relate to the wider community not just to the nuclear or extended family: 'it's partly because my parents came out of the holocaust and...I suppose this is rebuilding the family, rebuilding the Jewish family.' For a young man from the Middle East however, having settled in school and anglicised his name at 16, the reality of his country's dictatorship and the agonising experiences his parents had suffered meant that he could make no sense of their loyalty to their country of birth. His eagerness to be assimilated into his peer group at school led to constant, ongoing fights with his mother, who contrasted his current freedom with her own sacrifices at his age for the cause of freedom, and with the bad conditions in which his cousins remained. His lack of regard for the underlying causes of her outrage and the comparative pleasures of life outside his household in Britain, in contrast with the miseries expressed within it, indicated that for him assimilation would indeed be the way he would choose to define his life, in distinction from his parents.

The tension between holding things the same, which is likely to be done within the larger body of the family, and the need to adapt rapidly, which is being done by individuals, can lead to family conflict, in particular when the younger generation is changing more quickly than the older one. However, culture clashes between family members may also be between genders, the men and the women taking opposing positions on the degree to which the family should be moving towards assimilation, as well as between the generations, with children keen to make the most of the opportunities that school offers them and the parents fearing that they will leave the old value systems behind. More painfully, the divisions may accentuate losses already felt by the adults, so that a daughter, moving ahead with opportunities that her mother has never experienced, may find herself blamed for failure and neglect in relation to household duties and her mother's emotional needs; or the healthy growth of a son is feared by a mother who was imprisoned and raped by 'large' young men of the age her son is now reaching. Such fears can result in unbearable tensions and outbursts in families that are already struggling to cope with the privations of a life of endurance and relative inactivity compared with the political and social activity they had engaged in when protesting against conditions in their own country (Woodcock, 1994).

Creating conditions of safety

In the years since the first edition of this book, policy in relation to refugees and asylum seekers has veered wildly from apparently humanitarian intention to dislocated practices. The dispersal policy and the devolvement of responsibility on to local authority asylum teams led to widely differing ideas about what support should be provided to both primary health care and social service teams. Workers found themselves profoundly at odds with management about what they believed they should be doing for their clients. The Immigration and Asylum Act of 1999 removed the right of asylum seekers to access mainstream welfare benefits, public housing and services to meet needs arising out of destitution. The National Asylum Support System (NASS) was created but there was little analysis of the impact dispersal would have on services or on clients themselves who were often subjected to local ignorance and racist attacks. For the very people for whom the possibility of new community was important, the constant threat of dispersal intensified former anxieties. The current introduction of asylum centres in a society where we have spent the last thirty years deinstitutionalising both childcare and mental health provision will pose new issues for us all to address. In situations of such contextual insecurity therapeutic attention must first of all be towards creating some containment for any refugee family before attention to within-family differences are addressed.

What can a family therapist do that is useful? In my experience families in transition require a safe and welcoming space in which they can be listened to carefully; where in the absence of their own wider kin the decisions they are taking are validated as going in the right direction; where information can be obtained about resources that they may not know exist; where they can be put in touch (sometimes) with networks from their own country; and where they can be helped to sort out the areas of their own experience they feel they are not coping with (Sveass and Reichelt, 2000). As therapists in the context of families in transition, we are working with situations of maximum destabilisation, often involving the loss of all personal identity as it was formerly defined: loss of home, loss of relationships with the wider family, loss of possessions and loss of country. In addition, one of the paradoxes of being a political refugee is that fellow countrymen and women living in this country may not be seen as safe. Many of the features that characterised living in opposition to a particular political regime – adaptive survival features such as secrecy, cliques and a lack of open debate – may have travelled with the groups fleeing to this country. Women may not wish to mix with other women who they see as malicious or gossips, and men may be suspicious of affiliations that could prove dangerous. This can further isolate a family that is already coping with painful or traumatic memories, since the family members may initially believe they have only each other to rely on. In addition, aspects of family patterns developing in the home may carry larger aspects of political or gendered fear from a previously oppressive situation. A therapist therefore needs to be aware when dysfunctional patterns are setting in that can be halted by helping the family identify what is different in the situation in this country, and to draw out resources they have already exhibited. It may also be important to remember that because of the tension of existing in an alien culture, the therapy room may be the one place where the family feels free to 'let go', without it being assumed that this is characteristic of their usual interactions.

One characteristic of those who have had to leave their family in another part of the globe through enforced severance, is that they may find it hard to put together the self that existed in the country from which they came and the self who is in this country now. Dislocation from family and place of origin, the loss of a working life and of social role (CVS Consultants, 1999) contribute to potential fragmentation of self which can often be compounded by practical difficulties in the UK, as well as suspicion and mistrust within their own communities in exile (Harris and Maxwell, 2001; Woodcock, 2001a,b). Former experiences such as atrocities committed in their neighbourhood, the rape or murder of relatives or the torture of loved ones or themselves further damage identity. Sometimes atrocity is not the reason, but deprivation and humiliation, both in the country they have left and in this country, in which they have arrived in search of asylum but where they have not been welcomed. Much of what we can do involves listening – bearing witness, as Smith from the tradition of the black church has put it, which allows people to assimilate their story in the repeated process of telling it. The therapeutic purpose of listening is usually to allow the development of coherence of narrative in the teller, so that past and present may fit together in some way that allows the teller to think about a viable future. However, work with people who have themselves been subjected to persistently discrepant stories over time, 'oppositional voices' each making a claim for their loyalty, suggests that aiming at coherence may be an inappropriate framework, and that highlighting unbearable discrepancies may be of greater value to the person trying to make sense of things that may be irreconcilable. Avigad and Pooley (2002) in a moving account of therapeutic work with a young man define how the experience of rapid and violent change can also result in the creation of several identities, that which was present before the trauma and those co-constructed with others at different points in surviving and fleeing from danger. The conversations in therapy move backwards and forwards between earlier identities and current emergent identities. They describe a process in which talking to a new emerging identity involves talking to different voices at different times in quick succession. Woodcock (2001b) has emphasised this 'to and fro' aspect of working with narratives of extreme events, 'allow [the narrative] to come forth by working in the here and now of their relationships, with each other, their histories, their futures, their relationships with you' (p. 25).

Changing gender roles for men and women

Meanings are also constantly changing for men and for women as the different contexts in which they mix challenge former arrangements within families and communities. As women increasingly work outside the home in mixed cultural settings, they meet one another and have the opportunity to compare their images of family life, energising and learning from one another. This is probably one of the greatest subversive forces in the face of the conservatism of those family lives that were formerly organised into more patriarchal structures. Such changes can create complexities. In a number of families of mixed ethnicity seen recently, the women have challenged the men's value systems by (1) refusing to uphold the traditional values expected by the husband, (2) refusing to accept a value system that contains elements such as physical discipline of both wife and children, (3) making a bid for individual meaning to be worked out within the family, rather than subscribing to the ascribed 'role' upheld by the community, and (4) holding out for challenging 'elders' in a family where the insistence on superior knowledge or 'right to respect' has interfered with meeting the needs of the children. New cultural conditions also lead to new possibilities for women, for example divorce, which may have been forbidden by the community at home. Although women may have been seen as the strong members of the family in their country of origin, it requires a move to a different community of voiced belief before this strength can be expressed and their decision to divorce validated: 'we had this strength inside us but we had to learn how to express it more by seeing other strong women getting what they want'.

Many families have also described shifts in the gender roles within their families – in ways valued by both men and women – to meet a temporary need in a family that is geographically separated from extended kin. Changes in childcare practices can develop in new and unexpected ways in the absence of female relatives in the household, as in an Indian Sikh family from the Punjab where the husband, to his wife's amazement, 'took two weeks off and did all the housework chores and the child care... helped with bathing, feeding, putting to bed, all for the first time'. Women from religious backgrounds as different as Greek Orthodox and Hindu, have begun to speak of contraception with their daughters when the norms of their mothers and grandmothers had previously precluded the explicit discussion of sexual issues in general. In a household with no sons, a daughter may take on roles that are traditionally assigned to men following the father's death. How will this in turn impact on the role she is prepared to take when she is married? Where men have traditionally been accorded more respect because of religious tradition, how does this change in terms of how men and women are subsequently respected – is there a real change or a temporary convenience arrangement? Will it change in the terms of a reinterpretation of the original text from which the rules of gendered behaviour were derived? In exploring these issues with families, it can be valuable to investigate whether such shifts in arrangement are temporary or in which ways families still believe gender characteristics are immutable. What are the messages about the strengths and weakness of either gender that they would like their children to absorb from these new arrangements? How are shifts in one generation (say, woman as wife) counterbalanced by restraining moves within another generation or from different positions within the wider family (for example, husband's mother, brothers or husbands sisters).

My own curiosity is always provoked by the reflexivities of social change. For example, an attitude voiced by a young woman who had recently arrived from Jamaica – 'I haven't yet met a man who I think is going to be a good enough father for my child' – echoes the voices of many young women in the UK who now choose to rear their babies in female-headed households. The idea of an emotional, nurturing relationship with a man 'as a bit of a bonus' is echoed at a number of levels by British-born white women who do not have the strong matrilinear culture of their Jamaican sisters. To what degree is our society moving in this direction, bearing in mind that one-third of all first live births occur outside marriage and that this forms a much higher percentage among younger women?

Recent research into normative family arrangements across a range of ethnicities and cultures has highlighted the importance of attention to dyads that a UK-trained therapist might not normally recognise. Part of a Jamaican family's central strengths must be the mother-daughter dyad in a family that is now scattered across the world. In one such family the daughter had received serious advice from a senior woman relative: 'have your own daughter to replace your mother when she is gone'. In an Indian family the importance of a wife's relationship with her mother-in-law is another dyad that may have important implications for the children's development. Within the logic of a system where a woman has to move to her husband's household upon marriage, her own home being a temporary base from which she may come and go in relation to pregnancies and births, the wife chosen has to be a woman whom the mother-in-law will get on with: 'my elder brother says he wants my mum to choose him a wife, because he wants all the women in the household to like each other, so he'll ask her to choose the best one'. Where girls are temporary members of their own family and join their husband's family upon marriage, there can be overwhelming sadness at the loss of their own family as well as difficulties in adapting to life as subordinate women in their husband's household. There can also be rage, and where there is economic independence refusal to submit and requirements put to the husband about changing his position. The effort of maintaining traditional household and hospitality roles in a family where the wife is also sustaining a 'modernised' working life can create rifts of a different kind, and husbands may be reluctant to join their wives in trying to work out more equitable systems of household management. A refusal to move to a different position can also be backed up by the frame of 'disloyalty to husband's mother' or allowing less time to attend to the affairs of younger brothers.

In the context of families spread around the globe, it is essential for the therapist to bear in mind the extended family and how they might appropriately be included in family decision-making. While families are not always 'on the spot', they can be included in innovative ways, including the use of telecommunication systems conferencing and consultation. Sometimes 'appointed' elders in this country can be invited to stand in for families in cases of marital dispute (Nwoye, 2000). As in all matters, it is important to establish the gender of those to be consulted; in some families it will be affective relationships through the female line and couples may delegate decisions to collectives of elders thousands of miles away.

Racism in daily life, and in the therapeutic context

The question of how a family is empowered to develop a positive family and individual identity in the context of a racist society poses a particular challenge to any therapist. Different perspectives might include their own ethnicity, the nuances of how this is constructed for the way they think and how these nuances are brought into play in the context of the differing ethnicities of clients, the lives their clients lead and the different meanings embedded in their cultural practices (Hardy and Laszloffy, 1994; Laszloffy and Hardy, 2000). Pride in colour, and strong connections with a peer group of the same ethnicity are important elements in developing a positive black identity. Barbara Tizard and Ann Phoenix, in their book *Black, White and Mixed Race* (1994), address this question in terms of what protects children from the effects of stigma: 'if the majority stigmatize one's colour then to be proud of it is likely to be a protective factor'. In their study, young people of mixed parentage speak of racism at their primary school as the most painful thing to manage: 'When you get called names when you're younger, that can affect you for quite a long time, because you keep thinking about it and you get hurt easier then'. The most protective thing is having parents who discuss race and racism, but 'do not go on about it' and provide positive active models of dealing with it. Like many other aspects of stressful experience, such as aggressiveness or mental illness, children learn the experience by living it and by witnessing it happening to others, including friends and parents. Children describe 'dealing' with it at the level of both heart and head. Strategies that parents have offered but not practised are not admired as much as those which parents practise themselves and are seen to work. In many families (from one-half to two-thirds of the samples), racism is discussed and strategies suggested. Two that have worked are: telling the children to be proud of their mixed parentage (but this could also have a negative effect if a child lacks confidence or is highly anxious) and telling them about famous black people as role models. However, for half of the adolescents questioned, there has been little discussion either at home or at school. Those who are able to discuss racist experiences with their parents seem more confident of their ability to deal with racism, but this may be related to their generally closer and more positive relationship with their parents.

Hardy and Laszloffy (1994) assert that therapists must begin with the ethical imperative that change begins with 'self' not 'other', pointing out that it is often assumed that it is 'other' rather than 'self' who must change. They assert the principle, also held by many women thinkers and researchers, that we can only change 'self' not 'other' and have to begin with a 'looking within process'. Boyd Franklin (2002) emphasises how the 'looking within process' requires therapists to explore their backgrounds, racial identities and beliefs, cultural expectations, internalised racism and ideas of what constitutes health and pathology and to challenge the ways in which their role as therapist is affected by these. A number of ways in which colour blindness leads to other kinds of insensitivity and 'therapist generated micro aggressions' in relation to a number of areas of marginalised human experiences have been listed including ageism, sexism, homophobia, classism, offences of religious belief or custom (Hardy and

Laszloffy, 1994). They also list a number of ways in which theory has been maintained from a white male perspective, placing a high premium on patriarchal Eurocentric principles such as individualism, competition, autonomy, mastery of and control over the environment and dualistic thinking (while also acknowledging the feminist critique). In contrast many non-white, non-European groups emphasise group identity, cooperation, harmony with the environment, reciprocal obligation and holistic thinking (Lau, 1994; Tamura and Lau, 1992) as aspects of family to be cautiously and individually deconstructed by therapists. Furthermore, African–American culture is structured around the principles of group unity, cooperation and mutual responsibility. These principles are rooted in an African philosophical heritage, as well as present-day, racially based oppression. These differences in outlook relate to the way concepts widely accepted in family therapy are to be scrutinised (Patel *et al.*, 2000). In relation to clinical practice between clients and therapists of different ethnicity, Hardy and Laszloffy point out that clients rarely directly communicate the significance that race holds for them, but do so through the use of racial metaphors that therapists, because of lack of attunement to the subject, may fail to spot or know how to respond to: 'when therapists do not validate the ways in which clients communicate racially, they tend to lose points, thereby undermining the establishment of trust in the therapeutic relationship' (Hardy and Laszloffy, 1994, p. 15). Failure to be attuned to race as a key component of identity may also lead to a lack of understanding about its appropriate connection to the presenting problem and an inability to explore this. Miller and Thomas, writing from the positive perspective of valuing differences created by race and ethnicity, remind us of the importance of finding the strengths in families, the beauty in families and families' capacity to find their best modus vivendi; of the value of empowerment through allowing the emergence of subdued narratives, and of the intricacies of change that this can bring about in therapists (Miller and Thomas, 1994).

Gay and lesbian families: similarities and differences in life cycle issues

Various surveys indicate that most family therapists work with a substantial number of gay and lesbian clients. However, very little has been written about the cross-cultural issues for straight therapists working with lesbian and gay couples and families (for an exception, see Siegel and Walker, 1996). Teaching that marginalises homosexual lifestyles uses heterosexuality to define what is 'normal' and 'healthy' in family life; and might generalise findings derived from heterosexual populations to gay, lesbian or bisexual people and their lifestyles. In therapeutic work there are a number of ways in which bias can be shown, including outright prejudice or discrimination, sometimes under the guise of 'pathologising' a gay or lesbian life-style; ignorance of the special issues of lifestyles; and stereotypical assumptions. Discriminatory practices may need to be handled at a number of levels, between clients in partnership, between therapist and client, or between therapist, clients and a supervisory team. There may also be issues within the wider context of the work-place or training context that are not addressed. For example, does the training material or reading list contain gay and lesbian families, family-related research and relevant clinical material? Does a couple's reading list contain references to same-sex couples? Under stereo-typical assumptions, what popular concepts are privileged in ways that may pathologise aspects of psychological development? A recent survey of gay and lesbian couples showed certain things that they would like a therapist to know about being gay or lesbian. Responses included the following: the invisibility of their relationship to the majority of persons with whom they come into contact every day; knowledge about the 'coming out' process, including dealing with family and friends, and 'coming out issues in the work environment'; knowledge of the history of the gay rights movement; awareness of the major social battles facing gays and lesbians and an awareness of the effects of homophobic actions including the fear of being harmed or killed because of sexual orientation (Long et al., 1996). There is now a wide US literature on these issues (see Laird and Green, 1996) and important UK research and clinical writing has brought lesbian families into the family therapy domain (Tasker and Golombok, 1997; Malley and Tasker, 1999; Tasker and McCann, 1999; Golombok et al., 2002).

Since stereotypical thoughts in the absence of broader knowledge hinder therapists' ability to be effective, some of these stereotypes are listed below. A stereotype is seen as dangerous because it is based on normative assumptions derived from heterosexual relationships rather than from research or personally derived awareness of what relational aspects may distinguish heterosexual and homosexual life-styles. The mind of the therapist may therefore not be open to the particular nuances of concern in a gay or lesbian couple or family. First, therapists may believe that homosexual relationships are less permanent than heterosexual relationships and therefore pose more dangers to stability in child-rearing. Research indicates that up to 80 per cent of lesbians and 45 per cent of gay men are involved in steady relationships and many establish lifelong partnerships (Peplau and Cochran, 1990). Secondly, while therapists may believe that gay and lesbian relationships are less satisfactory than homosexual relationships, research indicates that when compared with hetero-sexual couples, few if any differences emerge (Kurdek and Schmidt, 1987). Thirdly, lesbians and gays are considered not to be effective parents, yet various studies have noted that being gay is compatible with effective parenting while lesbian mothers have been found to be more child-centred in their responses than heterosexual mothers (Golombok *et al.*, 2002). Other studies have not only found no differences between lesbian and heterosexual mothers in terms of maternal interests, current lifestyles and childbearing practices, but have found that as step-parents, they have been rated higher by stepchildren than stepfathers (Tasker and Golombok, 1997). Fourthly, the psychological theorising that suggests children raised by gay or lesbian parents will be psychologically damaged in some way (poor social adjustment, confusion about sexual identity) has been disproved in a number of studies of lesbian parents, but has not yet been adequately researched in relation to gay men.

Life cycle rituals: new constructions

Malley and Tasker (1999) have drawn attention to the work of others in attempting to delineate a lesbian family life cycle (Slater, 1995) and a gay male couple cycle (McWhirter and Mattison, 1984). However useful these are in highlighting issues of development and defining relationship patterns in same gender relationships, there are many variations within the range of homosexual and lesbian families as there are in heterosexual families. These include, for example, diffi-culties created by prior marriages in one or both parties, children from one or both former relationships and the managements of hostilities from former partners who remain current parents.

Many gay couples have raised the question of how ceremonies signifying commitment could be constructed that would have a coherent, integral meaning to themselves as gay men, rather than meaning derived from a heterosexual ritual such as marriage. As with many heterosexual couples, events of declared union are likely to follow a period of committed living together, and ques-tions of public commitment may focus on the sharing of property in some legally documented way. Coming into mainstream family discourse from minority family discourses are many issues relating to the public and social signifying of new constructions of family, of which property and clarified ownership are important components.

A second way that such commitment is publicly made is through the decision to have or to share a child. 'The only thing I do regret about being gay is I'd loved to have had a kid' (personal interview 1997) is a separation between two kinds of relationship that many gay men in the USA and a few in the UK have moved beyond. Some of the personal and emotional difficulties involved in the everyday process of carrying this idea through has been movingly documented, as have the joys, pleasures and differences of gay and lesbian family life with children in this country (Frommer, 1996). For a family therapist, key issues may present around a couple's differential longing to have a child, with one man or one woman wanting it more than their partner; as well as issues to do with ownership, parental authority in relation to the child and questions of proximity and satisfaction in relation to the child, especially for lesbian couples where the donor father is sharing a parenting relationship with them as the couple who bore and are rearing the child. The 'magic' of assisted fertilisation and surrogacy in childbearing has created the possibility of children being born into all family constructions, but the tensions of couples, threesomes or foursomes in relation to negotiating questions of shared parenting with regard to future or present children, require therapists to attune their ears to the particular differences that these new constructions of family involve. While many of the issues are similar to those that arise in second families where children have been born to a former partner, in my experience, the gendered issues amongst gay and lesbian couples carry a particular power and weight that involve heightened therapeutic sensitivity to gay concerns. Recent research (Golombok *et al.*, 2002) indicates that the greater proportion of children growing up in lesbian parent families have been born into heterosexual partnerships and have therefore experienced both heterosexual and lesbian couple parenting. As with all second families the therapist will therefore have to consider that the adults with parenting responsibilities do not all live under the same roof, may have very different views on family life and that these differences will be looped through the children participating in both households.

Tasker and McCann (1999) have written a comprehensive review of therapeutic issues around a young persons decision to 'come out' in the context of family responses. They emphasise the work required with the parental generation and the extended family. They also emphasise the importance of therapists' comfort with issues of homosexuality. Gorell Barnes, Down and McCann (2000) have explored this further in relation to training and supervision. Writing that focuses both on the coming out process (LaSala, 2000; Armesto and Weisman, 2001) and on the formation of successful gay male identity (Elizur and Ziv, 2001) emphasise the importance of the adjustment of family members for self acceptance. Whereas the notion of 'families of choice' has emphasised the importance of social support provided by the gay/lesbian friendship network, families of origin themselves also have a significant effect on well-being. A number of studies testify to the negative effects of hostile and critical atmospheres. LaSala in particular provides useful elaborated case examples of longer work with families.

Another issue raised in the context of therapy concerns 'openness' about donor insemination: the question of discussing this with the child in the future and how a model of family that fits the child's understanding will be developed in the family.

This further relates to the building in of 'reliable others' as part of the child's ongoing family world. Who will be built in as 'extended family', how open will they be, and what kind of prejudices might anyone who is built in now, contribute in the future? While careful planning can never rule out future hazards, it does allow the construction of multi-positional and reflective conversation, in which couples themselves face up to areas of doubt and taboo in their own thinking. Former sperm donors who have since had their own children within an ongoing relationship have also found themselves preoccupied by the lives of their unknown children. The question of whether these 'shadows', or absent children, should be brought into the light of ongoing conversation with present children will become a more frequent therapeutic issue in the future as the laws change around the openness of information.

Poverty and stresses

Too many of the social and family factors that create a stressful context for children growing up are related not to family life itself but to poverty, and the discrimination of various kinds that this creates. The way in which life expectations can be adversely affected by economics, deprived urban surroundings, poor housing and disaffected peer groups is likely to be very familiar to all of us in therapeutic work. A number of authors (mostly women) have drawn attention to the feminisation of poverty, and have emphasised how this dimension of stress should not be ignored when attending to family life that is based on a single income (Haskey, 1998; MacLean and Eekelaar, 1997). An understanding of some of the effects of structural inequalities created by poverty therefore needs to form an important part of the therapeutic sensitivity of all who work with families. The survival skills that poverty requires may have prompted particular forms of adaptation and resilience in families as a response to this. In my opinion, recognising survival skills rather than focusing on 'failures in management' is vital in fighting the contaminating effects of such stigmatising categorisations as 'underclass'.

The way that environmental factors can seriously affect children's development has been demonstrated in a number of epidemiological research studies. The Newcastle Study of 1000 families demonstrated that the cumulative risk for developing children, changed in response to improvements in their social milieu (Kolvin et al., 1988a,b; Masten and Garmezy, 1994). When deprivation increased over time, so did social offending; when it decreased, so did the subsequent rate of antisocial acts. This research identified stressful social factors such as dependence on the state for subsistence, and overcrowding in the home, together with family factors that may have developed within the context of such structured inequality, as risk factors for children without distinguishing 'cause' and 'effect'. The family factors include marital instability, parental mental illness, poor physical care of the children and poor domestic care of the home. Rutter (1990) adds paternal criminality as a hazard for development, and makes a distinction between families with only one risk factor and families where risk factors amplify one another. Rutter found that a child with only one of these family risk factors fared almost as well as children with none, but the presence of two risk factors increased the probability of disorder fourfold. Among children with four or more risk factors, 21 per cent manifested psychiatric problems. While poverty does not actually create the interactional features of family life that are associated with particular risks for children, it is likely to exacerbate them. Such risk factors include repeated conflict between parent and child, and a family climate of conflict and discord, ranging from quarrels to hostile abusive acts and family violence. Another family feature that affects development is neglect: lack of parental supervision and the absence of discipline in the home, and lack of parental response to children's antisocial acts. A third group of dangers includes deviant family values such as drug or alcohol abuse and the modelling of antisocial behaviours by parents for their children (Gorell Barnes, 1996a).

Within the larger collectivity of families adversely affected by poverty lie a small group of families with multiple problems. Asen (2001) has described these families' presentation of themselves as united in relation to the world outside while failing to organise internal family affairs such as finance, household work, childcare, employment and day-to-day activity. Reactivity and violence are common features: violence between parents; parents and children; between children; and between parents, children and professionals. From the family point of view it is the 'system ' that is violent to them, wanting to take their children away. The Marlborough Family Service has developed several models for working with these families that take into account the interface between family and the world outside. These include multi-family groups, working within and outside the unit, as well as having a school that involves parents in working with their children's behaviour in the classroom. The approach aims at multilevel interventions: addressing the individual and how they see the problem–solution pattern, the relationship of these to their own childhood scripts; the parental level in terms of management of their own children; and the family level in which the interactive problematic sequences are both enacted and discussed. The family team use both structural techniques such as enactment, the 'showing' of problems that the family have, either directly between parent and child or role-played if they are not already happening, and reflective techniques; for example 'stop starting' the problem sequences and getting parents to reflect on what went wrong and how might it be done differently. This last problem-solving may take place with other parents contributing their own ideas and observations. This allows parents to consider and organise change at their own pace and therefore differs from those parenting programmes that offer more direct advice (Scott, 2001).

Factors that buffer individuals against stress

Certain positive dimensions in family life are shown to be of primary importance for mental health in Eurocentric family schemes. These include a good parenting bond for later self-esteem; the importance of an intimate peer relationship for women with young children; and the value of a good marital relationship in repairing the effects of earlier deprivation and contributing to good parenting. In addition certain qualities of family life contribute to the well-being of children:

communication that is relatively free from aggression, and the capacity to appraise stressful situations (Rutter 1987, 1990; Quinton and Rutter, 1984; Hawley and Dehaan, 1996). Some families lack many of these dimensions, and pose additional questions for therapeutic intervention in relation to length of intervention, the quality of proximity and nurturance that characterises the intervention, and intervention that incorporates both psycho-education and a committed therapeutic alliance in a way that is experienced positively by the family.

How might these contributions to individual or family resilience differ according to ethnicity and culture? What would other ethnicities or cultures show us we need to add to the dimensions of family life shown to correlate with individual resilience in white families in western society? Do any of the features looked for by researchers or therapists need to be changed and described in different ways, or is it primarily a matter of enlarging the lens and including aspects of family life and family arrangements that researchers have not yet examined? As Froma Walsh commented in a recent review of resilience, there is remarkable consistency in the findings across a number of studies that such interactional processes as cohesion, flexibility, open communication and problem-solving skills are essential to basic family functioning and the well-being of family members. 'It is not family form, but rather family processes and the quality of relationships that matter most for evolutionary hardiness' (Walsh, 1996, p. 277). However, the families studied were settled in communities, rather than being families in transition.

When considering family issues using a life cycle or developmental perspective, the complexity and inbuilt inequalities in the lives of many families means that therapists have to position themselves in relation to *each* family's particular life challenges and family resources (Wolin and Wolin, 1993). Processes that are effective in one family may not work for another, and therapists therefore need to understand how these operate uniquely within any one family. Very small practical differences such as the provision of a telephone for a young mother in a high-rise block, or an appropriate wheelchair or bath seat for a disabled person, can strengthen a family's ability to withstand crises or prolonged stresses, and may be more vital than talking about the effects of stress on family life. Defining with a family what they see as vital to contributing to a degree of autonomy that will make their lives meaningful is an important therapeutic skill. Many studies emphasise the variety and diversity of resilience of families suffering financial hardship, but nonetheless finding unique ways of getting by and getting on, but many are also non-specific in their analysis of resilience-promoting features (Rutter, 1999). However, once we consider resilience as context specific, and begin to consider the specific hazards affecting families and the specificities of their idiosyncratic resilience, we are more likely to place our interventions in appropriate, or 'fitting' ways.

Intimacy and resilience

In considering resilience I am particularly interested in the concept of intimacy in relationships as a protective factor that can moderate many kinds of social adversity. Intimacy in relationships between adult partners has been shown to be both crucial and difficult to define in studies of adult mental health (Brown *et al.*, 1986). Understanding intimacy means understanding diversity in family structures, as well as the effects of family reordering so that we have a clearer understanding of where intimacy is allowed and fostered (Gorell Barnes *et al.*, 1998). As briefly described in this chapter, people in families derive their strength from different family subsystems, depending on culture and custom. We need to understand more about shared relational resilience within cultures of different kinds as resources in different life situations. Dunn (2001), from a detailed current research perspective, advocates attention to children's own accounts of where they derive resilience in family relationships, looking to the importance of *one* good parental bond, to biological connections within reordered families, including relationships with out-of-house parents and with siblings, and to intergenerational connections with grandparents. The involvement of support networks, extended 'families of choice', and larger systems to foster community connections may be important aspects of thinking that a systemic therapist can add to a family's own thoughts and daily resource pool. Resilience is also gained through contact with other individuals or families going through similar life situations, facing similar challenges, and learning from one another. Group work can be a valuable adjunct to work with individual families.

What can we look out for in processes that foster relational resilience within the family, patterns which in turn will create more functional patterns in adverse times and in times of crisis? Research indicates much which is obvious common sense; for example, that systemic patterns featuring good communication and problem-solving capacities as well as good community links and affirming belief systems all enhance relational resilience. An approach to families that searches out the degree of resilience a family has tries to look beyond problem-solving and towards the prevention of future problems by expanding the parents' ability to look at and think about their lives and their children. In my experience this involves working at a family level of micro details, analysing what has and has not been effective in previous situations. It also involves assessing the quality of a child's attachment with at least one parent, and the quality of parenting offered to the child, and building on these features. Learning to anticipate future challenges by using past experience to plan more effective ways of handling things the next time is usually seen by parents as good sense. Whereas some families have the ability to do this, given sufficient time and space, others welcome a more structured approach. Within a context of normalising and contextualising the stresses that have been experienced by a family and by working out with them guidelines for future coping, many families feel more actively in charge of daily processes (Place *et al.*, 2002). They are consequently more likely to feel in charge of, rather than at the mercy of, emotional events in the future. Before ending work with a family, I therefore often pose questions that relate to how what has been learnt in the current context might be applied in the future situations. By 'learning' I include what I have learnt myself, and often thank families for what they have taught me.

Summary

The intimate relationships within which a young person develops and changes, themselves notionally develop and change in response to the different needs and requirements from adults that development elicits. Depending on how these sequential and mutually influencing relationships operate, they can amplify or compound things that went wrong early on, or they can operate as moderating factors that compensate for what went wrong. The contexts for development may also change through transitions of relationships and of country. Parents may need to be alerted to the effects of transitions, and to the expectations and attitudes that the larger culture will have for their children, and be helped to equip their children to handle these. In addition gender will create widely differing expectations in relation to roles within and outside the family, and potential dissonance between the two domains. Stress and coping need to be considered at all these levels – familial, social and ecostructural. Each level provides a different viewpoint and issues to be addressed. All are likely to be important.

4

CULTURE, DIVERSITY AND DEVELOPMENT (2): LOSS AND TRANSITIONS IN CHILDHOOD

The previous chapter discussed different transitional experiences in relation to life cycle expectations using the lenses of diversity: in particular, differences arising from ethnicity and gay and lesbian lifestyles. Discourses that may affect the constitution of these lifestyles, such as racism and homophobia, were discussed. Poverty as a socially structured dimension of society that may impact on any lifestyles, and in turn affect children's development and life cycle expectations, was also flagged up for therapists' attention. In this chapter the focus is on loss, the absence of intimate experience and some of the subsequent effects on people's lives as adults and parents.

Thinking about the effects of loss on family life requires family therapists to operate well in at least two ways. First, they have to find a genuine position within themselves from which they can recognise that the ongoing reorganisation of the family is being managed in a way that is 'the best they can do'. At the same time, as therapists, they need to be aware that the way society manages loss is mainly by denying its importance. It is therefore likely that the family will incorporate aspects of this social denial of loss in its own functioning facade. For therapists to challenge such denial as 'pathological' is unlikely to be useful. At the same time, as therapists they have to be attuned to what may be 'unsaid', to absences within the family's account of itself, to denials, and to decide how they as professionals who are supposed to function outside the 'social mode' and are allowed to operate as 'rule breakers' will respond to this. Where such intervention challenges a family taboo, for example by discussing death or desertion when to do so has been 'forbidden', this may be useful for children whose inability to voice their lack of understanding in a context where these events have taken place is shown in many studies to have future negative effects.

For children who lose a parent by death, the acute pain of loss of intimacy may be re-experienced at different points in their adult lives including in the context of their own development as parents (Brown, 1991; Harris and Bifulco, 1991). This was reported by a number of young parents in *Growing up in Step-Families* (Gorell Barnes *et al.*, 1998). Of the children who had lost a parent through death, few felt they had been helped to understand the reasons for the death. It is significant that in spite of close relationships among female relatives, a circle where intimate family matters are usually discussed, there was a taboo on the subject of death. Other research has shown that family meetings focusing on promoting shared grief and mourning within the family reduce the adverse effects on children (Black and Urbanowitz, 1987). Families however, often believe that it is more protective to focus on other things. In spite of wanting to ask about death, children felt they should respect both their parents' and their relatives' choice not to talk about it. In the step-family study, it was shown that sleeper effects from the death of a mother in particular might emerge with fresh pain when young adults become parents themselves. One mother believed that because her mother had died young, she would do likewise and was depressed for the whole year leading up to the significant birthday. 'I just kept thinking, "What are my kids gonna do, who's gonna look after them?" And I used to say to my husband, "If you meet somebody else, don't let them be nasty to my kids", you know, and it was all just the fear of what I'd gone through.' Susan, who had lost her mother when she was six years old, re-experienced the loneliness of not having a mother; and the difference between having a step-mother who had done her duty by her, and a mother with whom she had had a special intimacy. Speaking of her stepmother she said, 'I will do anything for her, and I do appreciate what she did for us when I was younger...if anything happened to her I would be upset because I do care about her, but I don't think I care about her like a mother, and I don't think I ever will.' When thinking about her own position as a young mother she contrasted herself with her friends at the antenatal clinic: 'All the others who had children at the same time said "Oh, I'll go to my mum's and she'll show me what to do" – whereas I didn't have anybody, and also I was lonely.' In therapy this absence of a loved parent has been expressed by both men and women as an absence of adult reassurance: 'I just want somebody to cuddle me, and tell me it will be all right.'

Many facets of the processes of mourning that allow the resolution of loss have been documented in classic studies (Parkes *et al.*, 1991). While the absence of these characterise families who attend clinics in search of help, more surprising is the way in which the absence of such resolution features in families who do not attend clinics. Walsh and McGoldrick (1988), who have written movingly about loss and family functioning in a number of publications, suggest that at least three family tasks can be specified as part of the resolution of loss. These may follow one another or may happen in a more random manner. They include shared acknowledgement of the reality of loss (death), which is helped by clear information and open communication about death and the reality of death, especially through funeral rites and visits to the grave; and shared experience of the pain of grief, which requires mutual understanding and acceptance of complicated and mixed feelings, including anger and guilt. These are notionally followed by a third stage: reorganisation of the family system.

Reorganisation, however, may be complicated for many reasons. Family members may try to hold on to old patterns that are no longer functional, or seek replacement attachments for people who have gone. Such replacements may be good or bad for the person concerned, but either way, they may not be valued by others, creating family conflict. The many ways that families find to hold on to the past may usefully be understood not only as 'memories' but also as wishes and fantasies about what 'might have been'. People of different ages and positions in the family will respond to death in very different ways. A father may accept the loss of a child which a mother cannot bear to accept, feeling that she will in some way be disloyal to her dead child if she lets the pain of strong grief diminish. A sibling may take on aspects of a dead brother or sister and develop these attributes in themselves 'on behalf of' the one who has gone. In a step-family the loss of a biological parent may be much more poignant for one subsystem in the family than another. Children will often have ideas about a death which adults cannot imagine.

Communication and loss

Many studies have indicated aspects of family communication that can help children adjust to loss. However, when helping parents or other relatives to consider these it is important to remember that they themselves are likely to be suffering from complicated and often ambivalent feelings about the experiences they have been through, which may render such 'open talking' difficult. They may wish to show the child their best 'coping' side and keep their grief private. In turn the child may believe that his or her mother or father 'does not care'. Some balance between coping, showing grief and allowing the children to grieve while they also get on with their daily lives seems to be the best 'mix' reported by various studies. Something all parents can be helped with is to give explanations to children that are adjusted to their ages, rather than making them too abstract to comprehend. In relation to death, it is wise not to explain death by the use of other life events such as 'going to sleep', 'going on a journey' or, as one parent put it, 'working away from home'. These can lead to heightened anxiety in the child's mind about daily experiences from which people do not return, rather than clarifying the mysterious and unexplainable thoughts about where a person has gone. A child will continue to ask 'why' and may have to accept that a parent doesn't know. However, even short conversations that allow the subject of death to be part of family life are valuable in helping the child gain cognitive mastery, as is looking at photographs and having conversations around these. Some families like to visit the grave; others prefer to visit places where they went with the dead person so that memories can be evoked and discussed. Each family has different rituals, but perhaps the most important thing a therapist can do is to ask questions that stimulate the family's own ideas about how these may be developed, with some ideas on hand to offer if the family, for reasons relating to their own fear or trauma, perhaps has no ideas. This may be particularly likely after an untimely death where the issue of 'why' has never been resolved. Reminders of the dead person that a child has chosen for her-or himself may also be helpful in overcoming the absence of the person.

Guilt about a death can further interfere with the resolution of a loss, as studies of suicide within families have shown (Dyregov, 2001). Where a parent or sibling has died in distressing ways, many stories about the death told to a child may contain deliberate distortions, and where a child tries to unravel a truth that may be closer to a memory they themselves have, adults can attribute 'confusion' to the child. A therapist therefore may need to help a family re-travel the journey around the death and piece together the differences in their stories. Dyregov (2001) emphasises that the therapist must spend time helping the family construct open ways of talking with each other. The therapist will have to model empathic listening, ways of asking questions, clarifying feelings (including anger) and showing that children must be allowed to have their say. Children's understanding of why something happened should be processed and responded to by other family members, rather than hushed up. Like Black (Black and Urbanowitz, 1987), he suggests that the effects of traumatic deaths can be mitigated by formulating a narrative soon afterwards; allowing the opportunity to describe what happened, understanding where possible what caused the event and describing related thoughts, feelings and sensory experiences and the reactions that ensued. In my own experience, families are more likely to organise willingly around a traumatic event such as a 'disaster', where blame can be attributed to factors outside themselves (Gorell Barnes, 1991b). Where personal guilt is involved, such 'unravelling' may be impossible because of the layers of different realities constructed within the family over time. A workable reality that frees children from blame and guilt may be a more therapeutic goal. Separate work may also need to take place with the parents or remaining adult. Dyregov (2001) summarises ways in which children can be excluded from knowledge: providing wrong information and withholding information; not explaining certain facts or relating new facts as these become available; not answering the actual questions children ask. In relation to feelings, he points out that parents often hide feelings or do not bother to explain them. Through their behaviours both verbal and non-verbal they also signal to children that they should not bring issues up in conversations. Parents may also prevent children from meeting people who could relay new facts to them and exclude children from rituals such as funerals, or visiting the grave. Dyregov also quotes Bowlby (1979) on 'knowing what you are not supposed to know and feeling what you are not supposed to feel', times when the child is told not to cry, not to show sadness or anger, and is under pressure to exclude feelings from consciousness.

Maintenance of the children's daily world, whether the loss they are grieving is death, desertion or a change in their lives through parental separation, is an important factor in stimulating their ability to cope. Continuity in peer group, whether in school, play group or 'playing out', and continuity of place and home milieu, even of meals, TV programmes and bedtime routines, have all been shown to be of value by young adults remembering loss. Less professionally discussed but clearly key to older boys was sport, particularly the camaraderie of the world of football. Avoiding further minor separations or losses that children might normally take in their stride helps maintain evenness in family life, even though their remaining parent may long to go out and to develop a new life for themselves. The value of good extended-family support or friends who will sit in is therefore an important dimension for a therapist to bear in mind when exploring a family network.

Where loss has remained an overriding preoccupying factor for a child, it can affect the capacity to look forward. This can be compounded by living with a parent who is also continually preoccupied by the loss. In the step-family study referred to earlier, one young woman had not been 'allowed' to recover from her father's death because of her mother's obsession with 'getting an answer'. One of the effects of being locked into her mother's embittered relationship with loss in her childhood was that she had decided, after a long cohabitation, that she could not marry anybody. 'I like me freedom, I do like me freedom and me own space and being able to do what I want'. The question that remains is whether it was the single event of her father's death that caused her ongoing restlessness, or her mother's continuing and overriding preoccupation with her father's death, even in the context of a second marriage: 'she's still like me, wants an answer. She still wants to know why. Yes, she went very very bitter... against life, against everybody in general... on the verge of a nervous breakdown.'

Death is not the only powerful loss experienced in childhood that creates painful legacies for adult life. Desertion by a parent was reported by many young adults as contributing to their lack of self-esteem, especially when the parent who had gone was seen as the parent to whom they had previously been closest. Many stories were recounted of the absence of intimacy in transitions following loss and family reordering. The long-term effects of remembered absences showed in different ways. Sometimes it was subsequently experienced in relation to the absence of closeness to partners, sometimes in relation to an inability as parents to be close to their own children. Such constraints ranged from the effects of traumatic episodes 'perpetually running' in people's heads well into adult life, affecting the well-being of life as a whole, to lesser interactional restraints on everyday behaviours within the family domain. Desertion by a mother, for example, had long-term traumatic effects and was still something that was very hard to think about: 'When you are seven you probably don't know how to take things like that. You don't believe people can go. People don't go, do they, when you're seven...you always wonder, will she turn up some day. I can't imagine it, but it's always there.' The possibility of moving this thought on to a new position through talking to the father about the mother and her 'desertion' was still felt to be taboo. Traumatic memories of a loss of this magnitude are likely to remain stuck when there is no opportunity to deconstruct them and see if there are fresh thoughts or feelings that can be brought into the memories of the person who has gone, by the person who remains and is still mourning. In many accounts of loss, this potent combination of trauma and taboo remains as a powerful constraint on the freedom to think or act in relation to some aspects of the experience of the person who remained.

Variations in childcare patterns and the loss of intimacy

Sociology and attachment theory can offer different and sometimes competing discourses when accounting for traditions and legacies that affect working women and provision for their children. These interact with both family expectations and society's capacity to provide for children of working mothers. These various discourses inevitably create changes in expected patterns of attachment within different families, as well as expected patterns of emotional development. An example of a long-term effect was given by a young woman in the step-family study about a mother/daughter intimacy that was wished for in childhood but not received. She related this to an inability to introduce such intimacy into her current everyday practice as a parent. In her family there was a three-generational family tradition where the younger women continued to work while the older generation raised the children. This was a tradition she was proud of and from which she had derived an identity that helped her find strength after the break-up of her marriage, just as she believed it had helped her mother a generation earlier. However, it was not her mother who had shown her affection as a child; it was her grandmother to whom she went for cuddles. Thus her childhood experience did not include a mother who cuddled, and now she was finding it hard to show affection to her daughter, although she longed to do so and was worried that her daughter in turn would not know how to 'cuddle'. 'I find that hard, to sit and cuddle...I just keep, I just keep telling her "I love you, you know" and then she'll shout "I love you Mum", as she's going upstairs. But she won't come downstairs and say, "I love you, Mum". It's always as she's going upstairs. I think she's the same as me, doesn't show all that affection.' Another woman, Dana, also talked about how difficult it was for her to show affection, even though she wished to do so. 'People put their arms round me now, it's the same with my husband ... affection is something I have great difficulty with, because, my grandmother always loved us and she'd put her arms around me now and again, you know ..., my mum could never do it, and very rarely did. My husband and I never did, I think I've grown, grew up never really knowing affection'. Speaking of her daughter she said, 'She'll sit on my knees, and I hope that she's not going to grow up like I am. I've tried to be affectionate, but I find it hard, and she ... she'll sit on my knees, "Give us a cuddle, Mum", and I can sit there for so long, and then I say, "Come on, off", you know. I hope she understands that I don't mean, I do love her, but I find it so hard.'

A study of Caribbean women whose mothers had left them with relatives 'back home' when they came to the UK to work in the 1960s, recognises similar complexities in the tensions created by being cared for first by extended family relatives such as 'granny' or 'auntie', and then rejoining a mother from whom they had been separated for many years. The tension arose less in the traditional provision of care by kin, and more from whether the child felt loved or cherished by them, and felt that the mother's leaving had meaning in terms of increased well-being for the family with whom the child remained. In addition, the question of whether the mother had been able to cuddle the child when they were reunited was important to how she later felt about bringing up her own children (Arnold, 1997, in Arnold and Adams, 2000).

It is therefore important for a therapist to enquire about *beliefs* about childcare, as well as expectations of children's development, as parents see these. It is also useful to see how mothers and fathers understand the different effects of the patterns of childcare they have set up in terms of the child's *own* experience. Rather than pathologise one form of care as 'inadequate care', we need to understand more about the pluses and minuses of shared care arrangements of different kinds. At the same time it is essential, in the interests of individual mental health, for family therapists to know something of the likely effect that the absence of emotional provision for children will have on their development and future well-being.

Loss and adaptation

When loss is expressed as a major theme relating to a problem presenting within a family, it is usually helpful to track the patterns of loss and the adaptations that families have made to losses over more than one generation. Charting major stress events as part of a family's own evaluation of their life experience forms a regular part of the way I work. This can either be done in conjunction with a genogram, or taken as a series of family stories characterising that particular family, the stresses and losses they have suffered and their resources and routines for adaptation and survival. In complex family situations of current crisis, I often see the 'parental couple', who may not be the biological parents, on their own for several sessions so that they can evaluate their stories of loss, survival and resilience with one another and look at how their stories affect their thinking about the current life situation, to think about or 'appraise' the subsequent effects they think events have had. For example, Marley and Yvonne were struggling to deal with Tammy, a fourteen-year-old who had been more interested in living with her boyfriend than staying at home since the accidental death of her father, from whom her mother had already been separated. I invited each of them to tell the other about what they had been doing with their lives at the same age. This produced a very reflective atmosphere, in contrast to the heated exchanges of former sessions when Tammy had been present. Yvonne described how *she* had left home at the same age as Tammy, following her own father's death and her mother setting up home with a man she did not like, a part of her life story that Marley had never heard and Yvonne herself had never reflected on. Having run away, Yvonne returned twice, but 'my mum being such a strict mum, I couldn't stand it, so she sent me away to my aunt and I worked in a supermarket, then I left her and went to Balham and just hung out for a while'. I asked Marley to express his thoughts about what he had heard:

GGB: In listening to Yvonne's story about that part of her life, what messages do you hear?

Marley: She missed her dad and she wanted to do what she wanted to do.

GGB: Do you see that as a positive message?

Marley: It depends on the individual.

GGB: In Yvonne's story though.

Marley: Yes, because in Yvonne's life I see her as strong...she does what she wants to achieve...even if she can't do it she will survive...but I can't answer it as a fourteen-year-old and whether that was right, whether she should have stayed and got to know that man.

GGB: What was going on for you at fourteen?

Marley: My step-dad at the time was OK, never troubled me, never tried to be my dad. By that time he would have had no chance anyway, and I was good at sport, had a really good sports teacher at school, I really valued school to get away each day.

Marley went on to describe an earlier part of his childhood when his mother had had a succession of cohabitees, and he had had a number of experiences of being fostered out himself. Unlike Yvonne's way of leaving home, which he felt showed her autonomy, his own experience was of being 'pushed around'. Tammy's current behaviour was again making him feel 'pushed around' and disqualified in the context of her wanting to live with another 'man' and echoes of his earlier life story. The way that earlier experiences of loss are brought in to the current telling of a story, not only in words but in the tone and mood of the teller, are important indicators of the power they continue to carry. Equally important, however, is what partners make of them and how they see these former stories as relevant in the context of their current life experience. I have found that partners often pick up details of stories in ways that are much more direct and confrontative than I as an outsider would feel it appropriate to do, and they can also offer more robust confirmation of the strong features they see in one another in ways a therapist might feel unable to do. 'She's bloody gorgeous, that woman, whatever her mum say' was a more powerful alternative voice to a disqualifying mother in the head than my own voice would have been; just as 'he's the most loving man when she [the speaker's daughter] don't provoke him to be crazy', was a good testimony emerging from a formerly oppositional partner. Very often, when recounting childhood experiences of loss in the context of the therapist's appropriately directed curiosity, the power of a dominant narrative created in the forum of *childhood* family life will be challenged in the process of telling. It can be useful to ask questions that allow the teller to elaborate or enrich a story that is too thin or rigid. It can also be useful to ask questions as though they were being asked by other members of the family who witnessed the child's life at that time. Who else could be a source of information? If they were to tell the story, how might it be different? When looking at current stresses, what might another person tell us about earlier experiences of loss that the current experience may be playing into or amplifying? What would this other 'witness' have to offer about how the child's family had coped at the time and what had gone well for the teller of the story (what are the life stresses that may have amplified early experiences of loss and what are the moderating factors in relationships that may have made a difference)?

I have encouraged sisters to write to older sisters and brothers to older brothers, women to write to their aunts and older cousins, and men and women to write to their parents in order to expand their knowledge of some aspects of their current lives that they see as having been affected by something that has gone before. In some families this has brought rich and complex replies, in others letters of outrage and protest at their 'peace' having been disturbed. Thus 'telling a story' is an ongoing, active changing process in which the writer engages with and challenges the 'family', in his head, sometimes by active discussion with living members of the family; and sometimes by bringing them in for a subsequent session. In ongoing family work, different adult members of the immediate family may want to bring in a person from their extended family to expand their own childhood story with the intention of throwing light on current stress or unhappiness. Sometimes a relative's story creates the possibility of different actions developing in the future. The way in which the interview process offers an opportunity to change positions in relation to a past self or to have a fresh look at how contexts, both past and present, relate to different aspects of self is exciting.

The importance of a safe place: former loss and current parenting

Exploring the current meaning of 'home' for adults who experienced significant loss and disruption as children, plays an important part in establishing the boundaries of a current family crisis, what is likely to be manageable by parents and what will not be tolerated. The sense of violation of 'home', the 'safe base', is often related to a 'crisis' in which anxiety is triggered beyond what can normally be tolerated. Franklyn, a young black British man, said of his home: 'The point about the home...the home is not just me and Jacintha and Stacy, it's more than that. Living in the city is living in a shithole; I hate the place most of the time...and you need a place you can go home and be alright...and that's what I'm frightened of in the future.' His fear and resulting rage related to panic in the face of his daughter getting caught up with the 'wrong' sort of man. Dope dealing, drug smuggling and prostitution were the worst fantasies he threw at her, while she answered back that as a street-wise four-teen-year-old, she knew her mates were just ordinary kids.

> I don't want that place to be a place where we can't go home and be all right, so I don't want you bringing trouble to our door...this must be a place where you can go home and this will be your bloody sanctuary...I'm not saying don't leave home and never come back...don't ever darken my doors again and such, but I'm saying keep this peace...I dread that my daughter goes after men simply to have a living, simply to be wanted, simply to have a roof over her head...these are the things I've been going on with since I was three years old.

In order to understand the particular terrors for Franklyn of 'trouble at his door', his own childhood experience was explored with both his partner and his sister. Franklyn was the third child and the first boy, and his two older sisters had been fathered by different men. Being a boy, he was both set up to be and felt himself to be special to his mother, who valued men as providers but did not value them for constancy in relationship. For a long period in his childhood he had been brutalised by one of his mother's partners, who had created a reign of real fear in the house. This was described by Franklyn and his sister, both of whom had been severely and regularly beaten: 'Do you remember anything about Franklyn getting hit?' 'No, because I used to get most of the beating...His routine was to lock us all in the room and he would badly beat us...I used to fight him and make him stop...I was so involved with that, that I don't remember what happened to Franklyn...he was around for at least five years.' Combined with fear was a sense of rage and impotence at not being able to take charge of the violent events as they were witnessed in relation to siblings, as well as anger with their mother for having allowed these things to happen. The way Franklyn was treated by his mother bore many similarities to the way the sexual partners in her life were treated. He was loved, but also despised and teased. 'How do you remember that, Soraya...what do you think the effects of that was on Franklyn and his ability to bear her inconstancy... there one minute, gone the next...how was that for you?'. Soraya answered thoughtfully about some of the effects, both on Franklyn and on the way she had brought up her own son:

> I never liked the way she was with men...I think it is different for a girl and it doesn't have the same effect, but having said that, it

did make an impression, because I am a lone parent and when I was bringing up my son, I was very careful not to show any relationships...they were either kept out of the house... I never wanted to live with anybody so I must have realised at the time that boys looking at their mothers don't like to see it... boys want to see their mothers as perfect and non-sexual... there must be a contradiction there for a son in his teenage years.

I commented, 'I had the feeling that much of this comes from way before the teenage years...that is why we wondered if there were things you could help him with...When he was about four or five and you were eight or nine, can you remember the comings and goings?'. As Soraya and Franklyn went through the process of 'remembering' together, the confusion of some of the early years was shared between the two of them, together with some of the 'horrible feelings'. As Franklyn said:

I certainly remember the outside looking in...I felt I was of no value...I don't remember the people, I remember the feelings... of being of no value and surplus to requirements...it's like you're in the next room and you can hear them laughing and fighting and horrible things, and you don't want to hear it... you don't want to...can just remember it. I remember going to sleep like this all the time, and can't wait to go to school.

In going through the story of their childhood lives together Soraya helped Franklyn think about whether the way he was worrying about his own daughter might connect to what had happened to their sister, who had left the family at fifteen to live with another man: 'A real power freak who will be violent to anything...she won't leave him, she depends on him, her dependence is total, nothing changed for her, she went from one life to the other at fifteen'. By reflecting on the differences in the life he was offering his daughter and the life his mother had offered his sister, Franklyn found the courage to confront his daughter with less panic and more humour. She responded with some small changes in her own street behaviour, as well as some small changes in what she did about the house. For Franklyn, tracking the original experience allowed him to see more of the differences in the current situation and to share with his partner Jacintha a more hopeful approach to their own daughter's future.

Transitions and second families

Many of the difficulties children in second families experience arise from the transitions that precede the family coming together. Second families may be formed as a result of separation and repartnering, by formal and informal fostering within and outside the extended family, or by adoption. For children who go through more than one parental break-up, it may not be possible to sustain the cumulative losses without some negative effects. For example in relation to divorce, in 1989 out of the total number of divorcing couples with children (150 872) there were 24 765 couples where one of the adults had been divorced before, and 12 455 couples where both adults had previously been divorced. For children in some families, therefore, transitions of home and relationship become part of their lives. Whether or not change itself makes it easier to accommodate subsequent change, and when further change becomes a factor for accumulated stress leading to disturbance, has not yet been sufficiently described and discussed from the perspective of children (Gorell Barnes *et al.*, 1998; Dunn, 2000, 2001). Family life after separation and divorce is discussed in the chapters that follow. In drawing attention to the losses experienced through transitions here, a family therapist can note that in addition to shifts in the patterns of parenting, children may change home, school and neighbourhood following a marriage break-up or a parental repartnering. Analyses of children in second families 'being looked after' by the state (Schlosser and De'Ath, 1995; Fitzgerald, 1992) have described family patterns marked by multiple transitions, and the effects of these on children that family therapists and counsellors need to be alert to. The analyses highlight a number of factors pointing to vulnerabilities in the lives of some step-families including poor accommodation, acute overcrowding and poverty. Many of the mothers studied were young and of mixed race. A problematic feature for children was returning to their parents from children's homes or foster homes to find that their mother was now living with a partner whom the child did not know. Parents' deprivation or ill health, as well as a history of abuse and neglect, were associated with the risk of their children being put into care.

Adoption

In the 1990s adoption has become both more open and more often seen as a 'partnership' between two families. In 2000 the government took a clear proactive stance towards adoption as an alternative to residential care. While adoption is therefore largely a more open and public procedure than in former times, many of those adopted in earlier times and their adoptive families have been provided with little or no information about the identity of their biological families, and the 'shadows' of these other families are likely to have increased as the adopted children matured and became more curious about the construction of their own identity (Forster, 1995). This is now more likely to be something for the therapist to bear in mind when a child is adopted overseas and brought to this country as a baby – currently around 30 000 babies and children are moved for adoption each year between different countries. Alongside the developmental pathways within the adoptive family, thoughts about the biological family are likely to be held at some level in the minds of the adoptive mother or father, as well as in the mind of the child. Awareness of the 'other mother' and perhaps the 'other father', whose existence may be denied or not discussed, creates other sets of relationships in the 'adoptive family mind' that may impact on everyday family experience, and therefore on the emotional development of the adoptive family. When working with an adoptive family it is therefore useful to bear in mind questions about the potential impact of one set of relationships at any point in time on the other.

Cederblad *et al.* (1999) have reviewed the development of a group of international adoptees in Sweden and found their mental health and self esteem to be as high as their non-adoptive peers. However, more difficulties occurred for those who most engaged with questions of identity and who felt disconnected from their countries of adoption. Both this and other studies emphasise the part that pre-adoption conditions play in a young persons sense of well-being. Haworth (2001) reporting from a British group of overseas-adopted children summarised their concerns as follows: knowing nothing for certain about core aspects of self – birth date, place of birth, given name, birth parents name and health history... lack of adoption awareness in schools... the desirability of buddying or mentoring (learning about culture and language through someone from the same country or origin)... the need for a central institution which holds information about their birth family... the need for support services when adopted people encountered racism or just wished to talk.

Adoption does not exist as a single life event and may not be the dominant event in connection with a problem being experienced by a family with adopted children. It holds power as one of a series of life events in a family that may be recontextualized by other stressful life events, or normal life hazards that subsequently occur. A therapist may need to position the adoption in relation to these other life events. Has the stress created by the adoption been amplified or lessened by other stressful events? If so, for which members of the family? In what way might other events have rekindled anxieties relating to the adoption, put them to rest or relegated them to a minor position?

Prynn (2000), a long-time worker in the adoption field, carried out a study of 50 adoptive parents in order to try and ascertain why some parents found adoption manageable and others did not. She created a richly patterned research design which took into account parents' own attachment histories and disruptions in their own childhoods, and that looked into their own internal models of parenting to see whether this included parenting biologically unrelated children. She included such questions as whether it was necessary for the adoptive parents to hold the birth parents in mind and whether previous knowledge of adoption made a difference. She found that most comfortable adopters saw themselves as members of a community which extended beyond the household; where only one parent worked outside the home, where parents took enormous pride and pleasure in any achievements of their adopted children. In addition, a difference was made where at least one parent had experienced major disruption in childhood which had been mitigated by extended family and community support that had helped them integrate their former loss. The families for whom life had been a struggle were characterised by a strained relationship with one or both of their own parents: they were older parents who had been married for some time before their children were placed there and there had been unhappy circumstances surrounding the arrival of children.

Archer (2000) has emphasised the importance of empowering adoptive parents in family work since they are likely to come with a heightened vulnerability to implied criticism of their parenting. From her long experience in Adoption UK she sees a primary issue for children in adoptive families who are in danger of breaking down as repeated confirmation that their current caregivers will continue as trustworthy and powerful containers. She recommends that much time be given to parents on their own to explore concerns, discuss practical parenting choices, and voice feelings of resentment, frustration and despair. All therapeutic actions in the child's presence should affirm the intrinsic value of parental actions. From the position of an adoptive parent Reynolds (2000) also a family therapist confirms the difficulty many adoptive parents feel about 'getting it right', describing the classic double binds adoptive parents often find themselves in which are intrinsic to the adoptive family situation. Gorney (2000) also an adoptive parent and a family therapist has found that recognising that the qualities, courage and resilience of adoptive children have been handed down, nurtured and inherited from their birth parent is a positive starting point for her own work with adoptive families.

Therapists also need to bear in mind that adoption issues relate to the future as well as to the past. Questions that young adopted people ask about themselves 'how may I become?' have a bearing on the question 'how may this relationship change?' for an adoptive mother or father, and 'how may this family change?' in the light of the young person seeking and finding the birth parents, or more usually the birth mother. For example, Jacky, now seventeen and adopted at two from a mother who had kept her first three children but found she could not manage a fourth, had a persistent feeling that she might not be the young woman she felt her adoptive family required her to be. Working with her adoptive parents in the therapist's room, the other mother's image was constantly invoked through the accusation from her parents of immorality, looseness and untrustworthiness. However, her own ideas about her mother included images in which the wish not to be confined in a family at the age of seventeen held positive values. Questions formulated around the strong images she held of her birth mother therefore positively addressed the differences negatively voiced by her adoptive family. When asked 'What are the kinds of things that you do which make you feel like your mother might have been when she was your age?', Jacky replied, 'My mother sounds exactly like me; she says exactly what she thinks, she's got an outrageous temper, to me also she sounds really strong and as though she knew what she wanted to do with her own life.'

In a family discussion it can be essential to tease out the distinction between what is feared by adoptive parents, and what is attributed by them to their child in relation to the idea of similarity to biological parents. Do adoptive parents believe a child is 'acting out' alone; do they see the child's actions as a reminder of an absent parent, or do they think that biological determination is making their child act as the biological parent acted a generation before?

As Gorney (2000) puts it 'it takes courage to acknowledge and understand our fears of bad blood, wobbly genes and negative influences. If they are intermittent flickering shadows across our adult minds then they are for sure magnified many times in the minds of our sometimes chaotic and confused children'. A crisis often arises when an adopted daughter reaches the age at which her mother gave birth to her. The time clocks of a biological mother and an adoptive mother are likely to be significantly different since adoptive couples, by virtue of their infertility, usually become parents at a later age. Discussion of the ways in which 'normal' developmental behaviour in teenage years is read by the family can help defuse tension: how do the adoptive parents view this behaviour; do they see it as an indication that the child is rejecting them, or acting like the biological parents, and so on? In constantly fearing that the child will grow apart from them, the normal rifts of adolescence can be intensified in the adoptive family's mind, or make the parents feel more than usually distant from or desperate about the child.

For children adopted at a later age who have had earlier negative family experiences or combined family and institutional experience, an important question is what kinds of earlier experience may make it possible for them to approach people and the environment as sources of learning and discovery? For all such children, lowered self-esteem, confusion and anxiety about themselves, their families of origin and why they were being 'looked after by the state' could all be expected to have some effect upon their ability to settle in a family and form secure emotional ties.

In a moving piece about her own adoption Buchanan (2000) writes of the tenuous sense of security and hyper-vigilance which continues throughout life. 'My behaviour for many years was a desperate attempt to do whatever I needed to do in order not to be left again. Life being what it is I was left again and again until finally I learnt that being left is not life threatening.'

Young adults who have grown up in second families

Interviewing young adults about their experiences of loss and transition in childhood has raised questions about the effects of family reordering that require further scrutiny (Gorell Barnes *et al.*, 1998, op. cit.). It is clear that the transitions many second families have been through affect the children because they require adaptations in intimate relationships and the processes of daily living (Dunn, 2002). At the simplest level this takes up time and mental and emotional space that might otherwise be filled by other kinds of learning, such as school work. The adjustment of intimate relationships requires time, and only through time, attention and constant negotiation do second and third families manage to create synchronicity out of dissonance. These adjustments have to take place at the emotional and cognitive as well as the behavioural level. When human beings from differing social systems first interact they bring different beliefs to their daily arrangements. Beliefs may be developed in one context and then transferred to another without revision, a key feature of the complexity of step-family life. Enduring beliefs founded in the context of former relationships often get in the way when examining the current relationship, and painstaking work is required in this area if things are not to be misunderstood and further breakdown to occur.

The long-term effects of being thoughtful about relationships as a result of going through changes in lived experience, showed in many of the answers about valuing family life. Social and family values were seen by many as more important than career achievement and interest in upward mobility. Things seen as contributing to adult well-being include having good connections with a supportive network, inner contentment or peace of mind, curiosity about others and the capacity to reflect upon and think about life experiences. The enjoyment gained from having children and the ability to nurture them and rejoice in their development was rated particularly highly. This was of particular relevance where a pattern of violence or negativity in a parental marriage had been replaced by a more stable relationship in a subsequent second 'step'-family.

Theories of child development

The widely different experiences that children live through, as discussed in this and the previous chapter, have long raised questions for me about the relationship between research based on normative views of life cycle development and the variety of lived experiences of families and children. Even now much therapeutic training is still rooted in assumptions of ongoing continuity of attachment to one set of parents (often primarily to mother); and family therapy theory has also been slow to change. Children who experience a number of life transitions are likely to have different life courses from children growing up in intact families. As therapists we need to take on board the variety of changes that many of the adults we see have been through and to explore with them the effects of these changes on their lives as they understand them. In addition we may need to bring some understandings from our own perspective about the potential effects of transitions and loss. Only by accumulating information about the common effects of transitional experiences can we develop 'normative' frameworks for theorising the effects of these experiences, frameworks that do not pathologise the experiences of those who have been through them. Given the radical shifts in couple and family form in our society over the last decade, we need to take on board the subtle as well as the gross differences resulting from different life experiences, and ask how we can adjust our theorising and practice to take account of these (Rutter, 1998, 1999).

5

FAMILIES, DIVORCE AND POST-DIVORCE FAMILY WORK: MOTHERS', FATHERS' AND CHILDREN'S PERSPECTIVES

Divorce has become a common experience in family life in the UK. However, the emotional effects of divorce on adults and children and the differential individual meanings people give to divorce require particular attention from counsellors and therapists. In the early 1990s, children under the age of sixteen in about 160000 families went through an experience of parental divorce. Of these children one in three were less than five years old; a further seven thousand children were between five and ten years old (Haskey, 1994; Reynolds and Mansfield, 1999). Approximately two-thirds of these young children were likely to experience further family changes in the context of one or both parents remarrying, so divorce is often part of a far more complex series of transitions. Research from many countries has shown how aspects of the divorce experience have short-term negative effects for many children. The long-term effects are much more complex to chart, since many factors other than the divorce itself are likely to affect children's lives. How well children adapt largely depends on how their parents manage the process, key factors being the minimising of conflict,and good day-to-day management of the rhythm of family life. Divorce itself may be associated with many other changes, such as moving house, changing school or leaving a childhood neighbourhood and therefore losing friends. In many cases, divorce is accompanied or swiftly followed by a parent starting to live with someone else. The term 'reordered' families is frequently used to take these wider changes into account, as well as to acknowledge the large number of children whose separated parents never formally married in spite of being together for a number of years. In this chapter, I will use the term 'reordered' to take account of the many changes in the child's world at the level of both family and social system that accompany parental break-up, and will focus on four key areas issues that are brought to counsellors and therapists for attention. These are:

- quarrelling and ongoing violence or acrimony between parents;
- secrets about the divorce that may add to a child's confusion;
- poor mental health in the parent who has residence;
- parental concerns about contact and the care offered by the non-residential parent.

There is always a danger of pathologising a life transition that adults may experience as intrinsically freeing. Men and women, but women in particular, may develop new aspects of themselves when freed from constraining or abusive relationships. In family life following divorce, families also develop new resources and solutions to the potential disconnections created by separation, in particular new rhythms in maintaining patterns of nurturant relationship. For example, children may see their fathers less frequently, but for longer, more intimate chunks of time. Closer relationships may develop with grandparents. Mothers may worry less about routine, but give more time to the quality of companionship. A clinician may be able to make an important contribution by focusing on these new developments and the increasing sense of well-being that often accompanies them. However, many studies conducted in different parts of the UK have highlighted the anger, conflict and bitterness that can accompany divorce. Walker and colleagues (Simpson, McArthy and Walker, 1995) in their study of 400 divorcing families in Newcastle, particularly cautioned against the danger of constructing an implicit 'ideal type' post-divorce family, which 'may organise professionals' beliefs and place too great an emphasis on a cooperative future'. One of the dangers of a middle-class movement, influenced by ideas of 'seamless' divorce and mediation, was that it placed too much expectation on agreement between ex-partners. For at least a quarter of the Newcastle families this was out of the question. The Exeter Study (Cockett and Tripp, 1994) also showed that of 152 children whose families were reordered, fewer than half had contact with the resident parent two years later. We must assume from these and other cohort studies in Australia, New Zealand, and the USA, that divorce is rarely easy for children and professionals need to understand the processes involved in detail rather than dismissing disruptive aspects as normative events from which children will recover in time. For systemic therapists the issue is not so much whether 'divorce itself' is harmful, but how the former patterns of shared problems and solutions have changed in the context of separation and post-divorce living. For children, the way their needs for dependence are met change as do their opportunities for independence. Questions should therefore focus on difference, before and after the household changed: what is worse for you; better for you; and what would you like your parents to keep an eye out for?

Keeping life predictable and maintaining self-esteem

How do the moves into post-divorce living validate or undermine the sense of self of those involved? Protective factors, highlighted by Hetherington (Hetherington and Kelly, 2002) in a review of her own three major research studies spanning 30 years, include:

- the ability to plan and to know what concrete steps to take in order to achieve recognised goals;
- the ability to regulate painful emotions, and not be swamped by them;
- adaptability and flexibility, particularly important in dealing with family reorganisation and contact arrangements;
- the ability to work on behalf of and alongside others (social responsibility).

Other personality traits cited are perhaps more obviously helpful, like 'autonomy' and a 'sense of being able to take charge of events' (internal locus of control). Religion, work, a socially supportive network, and a new intimate relationship also made a difference. What in particular helps children to experience divorce transitions in positive ways? Family work can be valuably connected to child development research and to what we have learnt about the meanings children give to parental interactions, both when talking with their brothers and sisters, and with their parents, and with outsiders such as extended family or friends. We can now think with some confidence about the way in which ongoing external experiences, what children witness and know about first-hand, and internal experience, what they feel, imagine, and think, mutually influence one another and interact reciprocally. We have conceptual frameworks for thinking about the relationship between sets of relationships and these provide a way of constructing ideas about the effects there may be for children who are developing in less secure contexts. A secure family base has many different forms, as discussed earlier, but in relation to the changes that follow the decision to divorce, it is the dissolution not only of the parental relationship and the daily rhythm of family life that has to be considered, but also of a number of overlapping social systems, each of which provides elements of a child's identity or ongoing sense of self. We also need to ask how many changes, and of what magnitude, a child can experience and still retain a coherent sense of self. When we consider divorce and remarriage, this frame of 'child in interaction with reliable sets of relationship' is valuable in developing questions about children's image of themselves and their daily lives. How much of their previously reliable daily lives are disturbed by the transitions of divorce? Which parent was favourite and which parent is now seen less frequently? How are the arrangements for contact being planned to take these attachments into account? How much of the larger family will be removed from contact? In short, how temporarily out of balance do children become?

Parents also need help in considering how the multiple adjustments required by changes in household structure, a parent living away from home, and the consequent reorganisation of weekly life, may for a time prevent other explorations or learning from taking place. In the last ten years, work within the NHS at the Tavistock Clinic (Dowling and Gorell Barnes, 1999), and subsequent work in the context of legally aided family court proceedings has engaged me in various projects of post-divorce family living. The conciliation of extreme differences in oppositional narratives in order to construct post-divorce stories about family relationships that children can live by remains a central task. This has expanded to include actively helping parents change the way they narrate each others' lives to the children, to minimise the negative descriptions and attributes. In addition, more direct educational work with parents, particularly fathers, in relation to creating safe contact arrangements and alternative home bases for children, has become part of my repertoire, as has initiating 'hostile parent–child' family meetings, and supervising initial contact parent–child meetings after lengthy breakdown of relationships.

Ambiguities in post-divorce relationships

When thinking about the ambiguities in relationships between divorced couples who are trying to continue a co-parenting relationship, I find it important to try to understand how each person is making sense of the inner images of the family life they are leaving behind. Each partner carries ideas of their 'family' in their minds, and there may be key constructs of family living as it used to be when the family was going well that both adults and children find important to identify as aspects of their own ongoing 'core' self. Sometimes a parent will hold fast to a fixed negative image of the other and the part he or she has played, and this may be detrimental to any future relationship between the child and the other parent. This is particularly important where violent behaviour has played a part in the separation, as the discourse about this can come to dominate and even obliterate all other aspects of a father's image once a child does not see him on a daily basis. Infidelity and pornography also complicate a spouse's views about their ex-partner, leading to narratives of blame that become paramount. An important part of the work therefore involves helping partners deconstruct their anger with each other enough to recover positive images of the other person as a parent with something to offer the children in the future. Parents usually struggle to become independent from the other, and to incorporate aspects of the tasks and roles previously held by a partner, but still find letting go of the 'couplehood' that is a part of each of them difficult. Some adults cling on to the image of themselves they constructed during the marriage long after it is functional in post-divorce life at the expense of developing new capabilities. There is often a system-maintaining period following a separation, when an adult gathers their resources, reformulates their guiding principles and reconstructs their own external networks; and then slowly they begin to follow separate pathways that lead them to being different people from the ones they were when they were living together. Differences extend and amplify, and may become increasingly divergent as each partner finds their own feet and picks up their lives unmoderated by the other. Part of the confusion in post-divorce communication relates to the move from shared meanings to the surprisingly different individual, subjective meanings that are often given to the same previously lived experience. What each of them takes into their own self-description from the marital and family system that has now been dissolved, and whether this transfer has been positively effected on behalf of their own subsequent self-esteem, are questions a parent seeking help in adjusting and adapting to post-divorce family life is likely to find useful to explore with a counsellor or therapist.

Residence and contact: parents and children in the post-divorce family

The relationship between parents and children is of paramount importance to the emerging individual identity of adults (as well as to the children) following a marital break-up. Parents find themselves painfully vulnerable to their children's views of them, tend to lower their thresholds of expectation of children, and routines become laxer. Researchers have commented that parents do more for their children, family meals become irregular, there are more TV dinners, and less formalised rituals for reading time, playtime and homework. Their children's observations about their own behaviour and daily living habits can pierce their self-esteem, where raw sensitivity is no longer protected by the shell of coupledom. In these early days, authoritative parenting can be extremely difficult, and preoccupation and emotional upset can often lead to parents ignoring their children or failing to treat them respectfully. Studies in the UK, the United States, Australia, and New Zealand have shown that, in the short term, children from divorcing families experience more difficulties at school, have increased health problems, including a range of psychosomatic problems, and are more likely to have negative self-image and low self-esteem (Cockett and Tripp, 1994; Ochiltree, 1990; Hetherington and Kelly, 2002).

Acrimony and hostility

Work in the United States and in the UK has shown that long-term quarrelling has a negative effect on children's behaviour and academic performance when families do not divorce (Jenkins *et al.*, 1988; Emery and Forehand, 1994; Cummings and Davies, 2002), or long before a divorce takes place (Elliott and Richards, 1992). Unfortunately the quarrelling may not end with divorce, and the ongoing acrimony many children have to experience during parental separation can remain a painful daily burden in the months and even years that follow – sometimes over much of their lifetime. Hetherington (Hetherington and Kelly, 2002) found that 10 per cent of her 30-year longitudinal study remained immobilised and still emotionally and psychologically mired in early post-divorce conflict ten years after the divorce conflict, whereas most parents make this move over two years. Couples who are fighting over finance or children can continue for much longer, five years being quite common in court proceedings. As the Family Law Act 1996 [5.11 (2), (4)] enacts the principle that in the absence of evidence to the contrary the welfare of the child will be best secured by (a) a child having regular contact with those who have parental responsibility for them, and with other members of the family, and (b) the maintenance of as good a relationship with the parents as is possible, the reduction of expressed hostility in post-divorce parental relationships is therefore key to promoting resilience in children.

Some of the aspects of pain and conflict after divorce in long-term marriages involving children work against cooperation at complex levels of ambiguity that defy simple analysis. Helping parents find continuity in promoting the competence in their children is a more positive future-oriented goal than a preoccupation with fighting about money and children. Garmezy's definition of resilience 'The maintenance of competent functioning despite an interfering emotionality' (1991, p. 446) has been a useful guideline in my own work.

Feelings of loss of primitive kinds permeate post-divorce interactions. Whatever language of theory we use to understand this, we need to recognise that we are describing important and fundamental areas of self that were previously connected in an intimate union at many complex levels. The major shock that separation entails can create disequilibrium at all levels. As one couple whose marriage was characterised by passion and violence said about their acrimonious contact disputes three years after the divorce:

Don: I feel the hidden agenda over Bob is from Jane to me. If I get involved in thinking with her about how to handle him it may open up something inadvisable. It may have reverberations which will lead us back into the mire.

Jane: It's not difficult for us to do things to one another... I become confused and start to fragment. I know I should have got over it years ago... I like Don a lot more now which makes it easier. It's been very difficult getting over him. I still feel very tied to him. I never had a period of saying 'that's over that's done'. I still have confusion when I see him or spend time with him.

Don: A consuming fog settles between us very quickly... it's a lack of instinctive information which becomes difficult. When you are together and having a bad time...there are still certain advantages in it...kinds of communication... codes which are set up so you are forewarned of things and can set up ways of sorting it out. If you split up but carry on with the kids you don't have those instinctive codes any more. People are having experiences elsewhere and the codes have changed. New codes therefore have to be developed on behalf of the children.

Ambiguities in post-divorce processes form their own self-regulating web. The relationship between spouses sometimes cannot be separated from their stance in relation to the children and one system of negotiations may be affected by the inequalities experienced in another part of the pattern, of access to money, housing 'goods' or children. Whereas women and children experience the most significant social and economic changes in the wake of divorce (loss of income and change of housing being two key factors that may amplify the emotional changes experienced in the separation process), men find it is the loss of daily contact with their children that is the most significant loss. The double loss of intimacy – the intimacy of home life and that of children – can create a profound loss of self-esteem when a man is setting up life on his own. This is often partially resolved by hastily starting a new relationship. This can intensify the experience of confusion and rage for the other parent, and children may also carry the unresolved feelings, or anger and pain. As Jerry, aged 8, said 'I can hear them rowing all over the house. I go up to my room and shut the doors and listen to my music, but I can still Mum downstairs yelling at Dad over the phone. If only they would stop yelling.'

Children may also begin to experience differences in lifestyle. Eight-year-old Bob, who was required by his mother to keep a regular school timetable, dress 'his age' and go to bed by 8 pm, was desperate to stay in touch with his dad, who had started cohabiting when he left home. His father, Rick, let him stay up till 2 am while he and his band played different 'gigs', did not worry about getting him up in time for school and often did not require him to bath for several days. Rick constantly 'badmouthed' his ex-wife for her middle-class values, claiming that she was trying to turn Bob against him. When she in turn planned to remarry, Bob became increasingly violent towards her, believing that she had abandoned his father, who still 'truly loved her'. Bob showed particular sensitivity towards the dilemmas faced by children with respect to loyalty:

I was watching this programme *Family Matters*, and in the year 2000 there are going to be about two and a half million parents split up and the children are going to be...could be told to choose, and then they could think 'Oh I'll want my mum', and then they could think 'Oh my dad will think I don't love him', and then they could go to the dad and the mother could think... And what I don't like is that they could go to the mother and then think maybe they should love their dad more...Or their mother.

For Bob as for many children the dilemma of 'which parent to choose' is a fundamental daily preoccupation. Lack of courtesy and respect for one parent by the other may become something the child feels she or he has to make up for; an injury done by one parent to another may be something the child feels she or he has to redress. To help the child understand, by getting a parent to explain that the divorce was not the child's fault, is a key principle to be established in the communication between parents and children – or at least by one parent if the other chooses to maintain a blaming, adversarial position. For Bob it was crucial to know that his mother still had affection for his father as his father, even though they could no longer live together as husband and wife.

GGB: Bob, what did you want to say just then?
Bob: Ummm...Yeah...Um um...I don't know if my dad still loves my mum...He's not in love with her but he still loves her like I love her.
Jane: [Bob's sister] He does still love her, yes?
Bob: I mean I'm not in love with my mum. [to mum] Do you still love him?
Mum: Probably, yes in a way.
Bob: You're not in love with him, but you love him?
Mum: In a way.
Bob: Like she's not in love with me, but she loves me.
Mum: [thoughtfully] Yes.
Bob: Or granny, or Tabby [the cat]. [There follows a long discussion about Tabby, the cat, and loving him and how he had to be put down and how Bob had specially cared for him.]

The nature of different kinds of love may be of particular relevance for children at a time when it seems as though love has disappeared from a family relationship that they believed to be secure. There may also be an explicit need for young children to know that parental arrangements such as divorce or remarriage are not their responsibility, and that a parent can manage the household and their daily lives. For five-year-old Pat, who we met in Chapter 2, his mother needed to tell him many times that the divorce and his father's ongoing violent behaviour towards her was not his fault, or his responsibility to manage. She also built up her own ability to show her competence to Pat by taking charge of his father's access to her own house with a Prohibited Steps Order, taking charge of the bad behaviour of her brother in her mother's house, so that Pat could visit his grandmother, made stronger links with her sister so that Pat could access his uncle and boy cousins, and subsequently began a part-time job which increased her own self-esteem.

Parenting alone

In looking at the different experiences of men and women learning to be parents on their own following marital separation, it is important to consider three interconnected levels. First, the macro level of socio-economic factors, including inequalities in former education, current job opportunities and income levels that can be expected through employment; second, gender roles as these have shaped the history and behaviour of either partner and interacted in the marriage; and third, perhaps the most complex to unravel, the subjective experience of loss and transition, and the different ways men and women describe this experience. In Sweden, when economic factors affected mothers and children less after divorce because high welfare benefits maintained family incomes at 85 per cent of pre-divorce income level, emotional effects for women and children have been reported to be much lower since the social and economic milieu for women, and therefore for children, remains much the same. Homes do not have to be sold, or new accommodation sought, schools therefore remain unchanged and peer groups also stay the same. The emotional climate of separation is not further clouded over with arguments about money (Wadsby, 1993).

Ochiltree, in her extensive Australian study (1990) raises the question of whether the bad effects so often attributed to fatherlessness in post-divorce families arise primarily from the absence of a male figure, or from the poverty, exploitation and prejudice that is frequently experienced by children living in a fatherless home. A combination of less money, poorer housing, overcrowding and more limited play space can create a powerful socially structured series of impoverishing events which can amplify the stressful effects of one another. These are likely to have as great an impact as more intimate interpersonal processes on the well-being of children. Young sons especially have been found to challenge the equilibrium of tired post-divorce mothers – children can become more whiney and aggressive, and boys increase demanding, aversive behaviours such as crying, hitting, whining and nagging (Hetherington and Kelly, 2002). Mothers in turn can be both more punitive, irritable and erratic, threatening but not carrying out punishment. Parenting programmes focusing on consistency, explanation orientated discipline and 'time out', have been shown to be effective in helping parents become less vulnerable to coercive cycles, and thus gain confidence. Working this way in family meetings can also be useful in reducing mutually escalating negativity and dislike. However, we also know that a good relationship with the parent a child lives with is the key protective relationship in relation to other stresses of post-divorce family life. Key issues to look out for include the parentification of children. Where a parent relies on a child for comfort, advice, and emotional support beyond that child's capacity, it can amplify a child's feeling that the divorce and their parents' state of well-being is now their responsibility.

The emotional and practical experience of parenting alone presents many challenges. It seems from studies of both twenty years ago and today that when a marriage has been based on stereotypical gender roles and a rigid division of labour there are particular tensions for parents subsequently living on their own. The ability of the care-giving parent to 'cope' is an important factor for children after divorce, and parents often benefit from the opportunity to rehearse solutions with an outsider to the home. Many women express surprise that in spite of greater freedom following separation from a partner who had become oppressive, they nonetheless have experience of depression resulting from the withdrawal of coupledom, and the task of living alone in intimacy and close proximity only to children. Work can have a protective effect, both by increasing income and self-esteem, and also by providing an alternative milieu for self-evaluation.

Ongoing worries for many women surround the well-being of children in relation to irresponsibility shown by fathers, and concern over how children thrive, or do not thrive during contact visits. Common concerns include drinking, watching late-night horror videos or sexually inappropriate material with their children, risk-taking around safety issues when children are young: Men's anxieties often centre around whether they will learn to parent successfully on their own, and on their own terms rather than on the terms of their ex-wives. Hetherington found that men are less likely to become involved in coercive cycles with their children, but are not too good at encouraging them to talk about their feelings and problems. She distinguishes between fathers who 'seek responsibility' and those who have it 'thrust upon them', in terms of their parenting success. She points to the importance of overnight contact as an opportunity to develop more relaxed relationships, and routines that draw fathers and children together. Regular 'overnights' make it far less likely that a father will drift away (estimated at 38 per cent of all post-divorce fathers in the UK (Simpson *et al.*, 1995).

Fathers; parenting in the context of 'contact'

Debate continues about the value for the child of maintaining contact with a parent who has left when an ongoing, acrimonious relationship exists between the divorced parents. My work through the courts with fathers in post-divorce emotional interactions with hostile ex-partners requires neutrality, compassion and persistence on my part. As a woman therapist I find that many of the emotions I experience reflect in small ways what the power of such interactions must be like for another woman who is trying to manage the two positions of ex-wife and current mother. At the same time I recognise that enraged fathers may be highly committed to the long-term parenting of their children. Lengthy outbursts, the reiteration of wrongs experienced and dogged determination to justify the self may characterise fighting paternal discourses in which 'woman' is often synonymous with 'wrongdoer'.

Hetherington (in Hetherington and Kelly, 2002, p. 34) quoting Gottman points out 'In disagreements men get aroused more quickly than women, as reflected by a sharp rise in blood pressure and heart rate. Men feel flooded, overwhelmed by physiological changes and afraid of losing control. Withdrawal acts as a safety valve for decreasing intensity'. Learning not to take the blame myself, and retaining empathy are key elements of this work, as is the ability to retain a focus on the positive intention behind the outrage. However, increasingly, precise research studies (Cummings, *et al.*, 2002, Hetherington and Kelly, 2002) have shown the negative effects of conflict on children. Three factors lead to more successful co-parenting: (1) minimal conflict, (2) trust in the other parent's ability to give good care, (3) parents updating each other on important issues. Young children whose parents do not meet these goals can become very disorganised and develop insecure attachments. Using such research in 'educating' parents about post-divorce behaviour and the outcomes for children is particularly valuable with fathers.

How do men and women develop the art of parenting once they live on their own? Former ideas of motherhood and fatherhood may constrain the inner capacity of either gender to visualise how parenting as a gender-neutral skill can develop. Many studies reveal how men may feel challenged by childcare, and doubt their ability to care for their children on their own. Kraemer (1993), in his ongoing review of fatherhood, asserts his belief that women continue to organise the context for the father–child relationship. In the wake of divorce, raw exposure to children can be both a privilege and a shock. However, Adams (1996), in a study of fathers parenting alone in an inner London borough, found that men manage well when they have had prior intimate contact with their children, and when they have models of other fathers who have involved themselves with their own children. This finding in a small scale study is replicated in the longer term work of Hetherington (Hetherington and Kelly, 2002). While the divorce debate and the effects of divorce on children continue to preoccupy society, the issue of post-divorce is often artificially separated from the issue of the quality of parenting prior to the parental separation. Hetherington reviewing 30 years of her own research, following the same couples emphasises the importance of active engaged fathering prior to separation. However, where a man has been psychologically absent before the separation, and a mother continues to parent competently following divorce, single family life has little enduring negative developmental impact on a child, especially on girls. Contact centres set up to further the development of relationships between children and fathers who have parted violently from their wives, have provided a forum for exploring the vulnerability of fathers who wish to maintain contact but do not know if they have the necessary skills to do so, nor how to develop these (Bratley, 1995). While few services are currently geared to recognise this need to foster the development and maintenance of new and fragile parenting skills, new contact-centre developments in the last 5 years have provided exciting models of what is possible with live observation and supervision of insecure fathers.

Experience of working with fathers in different settings, as well as the research into children growing up in step-families, suggests that disengaged fathers may withdraw for a number of reasons. Fathers may be faced with the requirement to learn how to parent on their own at a time when their self-esteem is low; they may be distressed by the effect on the children of moving between parents who live in separate places; and when their former wives re-partner they may find the pain of seeing their children living with another man too great to bear. Studies of divorced fathers have shown that many factors influence the development of the post-divorce fathering role, including men's own ability to develop flexible arrangements for looking after their children (Kruk, 1992; Hart, 1993). This was found to relate to their capacity to take on patterns of caretaking that include roles formerly construed as 'female', or more usually seen as within the domain of 'mothering' (Hart, 1993). Between 11–14 per cent of men have primary care of their children in the UK, a figure which surprisingly correlates with Hetherington's (2002) small group of 15 per cent in her USA based studies, who proved 'an exception to the general rule about male domestic incompetence. (Hetherington and Kelly, 2002). This group had a pre-divorce history of involvement in housekeeping, cooking, and grocery shopping, and enjoyed child care'. Simpson *et al.* (1995) showed how the contact that fathers have with their children is influenced by many factors, including the quality of their relationship with their former wives, and the post-divorce lives they develop with their children and subsequent partners.

It has been argued that in the social construction of paternal identity, a father's presence in the family is hard to define because he has no clear territories to call his own. What a father does is almost invariably shared with or dependant on the cues of his partner. Fatherhood behaviour may be essentially intertwined with his coupledom (Backett, 1987; de Singley, 1993). Current work suggests that such theorising only applies to some rather than all fathers, but that the degree to which a mother will 'allow' father to develop his own style of post-divorce parenting independent of her beliefs about 'correct' parental behaviour will make key differences (see Tom and Robert below). For fathers who are only allowed to parent under the watchful eye of a contact centre or a 'socially approved other' who has no official brief to let him know when he is doing well, the stress can be severe and potentially counter-productive. In practice, fathers voice diverse ideas showing that a man's own history, his childhood family experiences, and his relationship with his own father are important to his ability to take on a new role as 'parent'; as well as his own previous parenting of his children, and his current support network of 'intimate others' with whom he can discuss and construct his role as it develops.

After divorce, the loss of centrality that more traditional men experience in relation to their children's lives can reopen former debates about power and control in male/female relationships. The degree to which a man has seen control as central to the definition of fathering becomes crucial when adapting to post-divorce management of children. If the divorce agreement stipulates that the children will reside with their mother, he is likely to become significantly less central to day-to-day decisions about the children and more likely only to be consulted on certain agreed issues. Rethinking the change in image this requires may be an important therapeutically assisted process.

In one of a series of interviews with a father (Malcolm) and mother (Becky) who had been divorced for many years but were still fighting, the potential for a new construction of 'fatherhood' emerged from the exchange. Malcolm spoke disapprovingly about a friend who had also divorced:

Malcolm: He's completely pulled back from the patriarchal role.

GGB: Suppose you let the patriarchal role go for a year, what do you think would happen?

Malcolm: Well, first of all, I'm just not absolutely sure that I can. I don't know how one can pluck out 'dad' and replace it with 'parent'.

Becky: Do you need to pluck out 'dad'?

GGB: Why is 'dad' and 'patriarch' the same thing?

Becky: There's lots of aspects of your relationship that are 'dad' that are not 'patriarch' [she lists them] I think they're the majority ... But there's still that 'yck' area ... at least I consider it 'yck' ... maybe I don't like the word 'patriarchal'.

Malcolm: I suppose I've just got to give up the idea of being the boss [Becky laughs and Malcolm continues]. I suppose you effectively gave that idea up when you filed for divorce.

Becky: Yes, I just think 'boss' is not on any more – dated.

Following the idea that a person taking on another role, or developing a new aspect of self needs confirmation in that new role, I suggested that Malcolm bring his current partner, Bee, to the next interview.

GGB: [to Bee] One of the things Malcolm was saying last time was 'I'll just have to give up the idea of men being the boss'. How do you relate to that idea?

Bee: I think that's a very good idea. A very good idea.

GGB: Can you tell him why?

Bee: Because I think you [GGB] are right in what you said, that you do miss out on things if you feel you have to be in control all the time...or be the boss...You are building up barriers...you're building up blocks that don't need to be there...The easy flow is stopped when you start being the boss...do you understand what I mean?

Malcolm: I do, I do...it's the practical application that's difficult. As Gill [GGB] has seen, I have very little self-esteem for my own various reasons...somehow the less self-esteem you have the more you have to hang on to power and control...the more you have the more you can afford the luxury of going with the flow.

When working with fathers over the last three years, I have found that paying attention to the very small details of daily childcare, the relevance of activities chosen by fathers as appropriate to the age of the children, and support for fathers' low self-esteem have been the baseline for child-oriented conversations. However, some more extreme forms of parent–child interaction have also involved my paying attention to the effects of alcohol on childcare, promoting in my own orientation a more continual monitoring of potentially violent interactions. Children's voices can themselves be of great value in getting these messages across to parents. For example, children as young as six can tell their dads 'We like to come to you, but only when you're nice to us, not when you're drinking', and then go on to describe (with encouragement) how a father is 'different' when he's drinking 'You're scary, your voice is louder and you make horrible faces'. The use of physical comparison is explicit here, the size of the children in distinction from the size of their father: the loudness of their voice is contrasted to the loudness of his.

The misuse of children by treating them as adult companions often characterises post-divorce relationships with fathers who can use their children as vehicles for expressing their own distress and anger. Children have been encouraged to leave rude messages on voice-mail, or send text messages expressing (father's) hostile feelings towards their mother. Other fathers use bedtime as an opportunity not to read 'children's' stories, but to overwhelm their children with the sad story of their own ill-treatment, or their sorrow at not seeing their children more often. By allowing children the opportunity to tell the therapist what they find difficult in their home lives with either parent, these very specific examples can be used with fathers to create more appropriate child oriented interactions. The 'education' of dad takes place through the children (bottom up), rather than from the professional (top down).

Secrets and silence in post-divorce narratives

In the ongoing contexts of contact visits, children in The Exeter Study (Cockett and Tripp, 1994), reported that they sometimes had to avoid talking to one parent about enjoying time with the other, or had been asked by one parent to keep something secret from the other. Only one in five children said they were able to talk freely about one parent in front of the other. Many did not feel free to talk about the divorce and about changes in family life. The study of young adults who had grown up in reordered families (Gorell Barnes *et al.*, 1998) revealed that high degrees of silence often had to be maintained into adult life. Many of the respondents said that even now they felt the 'other parent' was a taboo subject. As one young woman whose mother had left said, 'I'd have to ask my father things, and I don't think, I should imagine if I ever asked about her, he'd just completely blank the issue, he wouldn't talk about it. Or he'd get very cross with me, I can imagine him getting cross about that'. Another young woman, for whom the inter-parental conflict still continued twenty years after the divorce, said 'I think a parent should never forget that the child has two parents, the original parents. My mother totally cut my father off from her and I felt she wanted me to do the same as well, but they were still my mother and father'.

In the course of clinical work in the divorce project in the Child and Family Department (Dowling and Gorell Barnes, 1999) we found that it was not only overt anger that makes communication difficult, but also deliberate silence, cutting the parent who had gone out of the memory. A key function of therapeutic interviews can be to challenge such silences, and to help the parent with whom the child is living to make it permissible and possible for the parent who has gone to have a legitimised place in the child's mind.

In the Ambrose family, for example, ten-year-old Andrew drew a picture of a 'proper' family where both father and mother were present and the family was white. This belied the current reality of his own family, headed by his mother Marilyn, who was black, and brought in the fact that he was missing his (white) father, who no longer visited them and to whom Andrew had felt very connected. His absence was a taboo subject in the family because of Marilyn's rage about her former partner leaving her. After four sessions, some with the boys on their own and some with Marilyn on her own, Marilyn was encouraged to draw up a list of aspects of life with her former partner that had been positive for her and which she was prepared to share with the boys. She was asked if she was happy to sign the list and say she would stand by it, before she met with her sons to share her thinking. Having activated some positive constructions of her former partner in her own mind, Marilyn was more open to the idea of sharing these than she had previously been.

Marilyn: He wasn't all bad. Daddy used to make me laugh, he used to be good at telling jokes. Do you remember any of the jokes he used to tell?

Andrew: Yeah.

Marilyn: Especially the one about Rover, that was your favourite, but we can't tell that here!...He used to make me laugh and he was nice and all that if he wasn't drinking or taking drugs. He used to help with the housework from time to time.

GGB: Let's just pause on that, because I know it was a thing that slipped out there and you are not sure if the boys understand about drugs.

Andrew: Yaah...

GGB: Tell me what you know about them.

Andrew: Well, some drugs like medicine is a drug, and if you use you got to use prescriptive ones like...And syringes people use for inject medicines and drugs into a particular place.

GGB: Right, and did you know that you can also use drugs in such a way that you end up not being able to live without them because your body really needs them?

Andrew: You get addicted.

GGB: Yes. Well, I think you need to talk a bit differently to Arnold about it because I think Andrew already has a very big understanding of what drugs are and that they can be dangerous if used in the wrong way.

Marilyn: They change people.

[Marilyn uses alcohol to explain to Arnold how people change]

Marilyn: What happens if people drink a lot of alcohol?

Arnold: They get drunk.

Marilyn:	And what do they do? They change don't they when they get drunk. Sometimes they are really really nice, aren't they?
GGB:	Can we remember why we were talking about it? Because I thought there was a very important thing...
Marilyn:	Because your dad used to take it, he use to take drugs and things.
GGB:	But the thing that I thought would be really helpful if you could talk about it, and Andrew obviously has a very good understanding of this, is that drugs can change a person, and so your dad may have been a very nice person when your mother first met him, but over time he went on using drugs and he also drank. And I think that led to changes, didn't it? In the way the two of you got on?
Marilyn:	He changed from being nice and caring, he used to show me that he loved me, he used to buy me gifts and that. He changed from being nice and caring and helpful and loving... Cos he was taking all these drugs.

In a family session two months later Andrew volunteered to give his mother a certificate of good mothering, telling her solemnly 'You are a good mum, you've brought up two boys who love you and you've done a good job'. His work at school had improved and he had moved to the top of his class. Since Marilyn wanted to stop coming in the light of this improvement, I encouraged both Marilyn and Andrew to think about hazards that might arise in which the change might be reversed.

GGB:	Given that this amazing shift has happened since we last met, what do you think might happen that could send it back to how it was before?
Marilyn:	Don't know...
GGB:	Using your mother's wisdom, what sort of things might give it that shove back to where it was before... let's ask Andrew, do you agree things are going better?
Andrew:	I do.
GGB:	So what sort of things do you think might send it back again?
Andrew:	I don't know.
Marilyn:	...[to Andrew] Do you think it might ever go back to the way it was before?
Andrew:	What you mean, when dad was here?

Marilyn: No, no, the arguing and that.

Andrew: It will not, it will not...

GGB: How old are you Andrew?

Andrew: Ten and five-twelfths.

GGB: How could a boy of ten and five-twelfths make that statement so absolutely definitely?

Andrew: Well, let's call it ten-and-a-half.

GGB: Do you think a boy of ten and a half can make such a statement, that he will never be rude to his mother again? It seems a big statement to me.

Marilyn: Let's have it in writing.

GGB: [persisting] Let's not leave it – Marilyn, what sort of things do you think it might take for the two of you to go back?

Marilyn: Like what you mean, head on?

GGB: Well, clashing. [long pause].

Marilyn: I really don't know, I have no idea, I suppose it might change when he goes to secondary school [Long chat about schools during which Marilyn expresses her belief that Andrew might lose his temper with her because she is 'thick'. GGB takes this up with her two sons]:

GGB: How much more work do you think we should do to help Marilyn believe she is not 'thick'?

Andrew: It's obvious you're not, Mum.

GGB: How is it obvious to you, she needs to know.

Andrew: She does a lot, she knows a lot, she is a lone parent with two kids who love her...I know, I should do a list.

Marilyn: I make great banana fritters as well, don't I?

Andrew: That's it...I should write a book...on good mothers.

GGB: I don't think you should think of it as going back but bringing up kids, there's always patches...

Andrew: Which need patching up.

For Andrew, the work that was done in including his father as part of the family story, who could at least be acknowledged as having played a good and important part for a period of time, was an important contribution to his own identity. The separation of the person 'father' from the 'drug trafficker' who was affected by his own wares meant that the negative descriptions that follow on from 'drug trafficker' were not the only stories about his father in the family. Equally importantly, the validation provided by the professionals, and subsequently by her eldest son, of Marilyn's abilities as a good mother and head of household contributed to small shifts in the family's ideas about its own story. A further important expansion of family life was the effort Marilyn was encouraged to make to reconnect with her family of origin, from whom she had deliberately separated herself during her time with her partner. Later drawings by the boys included a family with aunts, uncles and cousins in marked contrast to the isolated family unit they had drawn in the first meeting.

'Holding on to the bubble' – uncertainty about arrangements

Lack of clarity about the nature of parental arrangements in relation to the parents' uncertainty about whether or not their marriage has ended, has characterised the lives of a number of children, who show that their minds are taken up by other matters by failing at school. When a parent who has been left or is being cheated on is suffering deeply, he or she may prefer to leave things unclear for the children in the hope that the marriage will revert to how it formerly was. As Gita said when trying to decide whether to go back to her parents in Bombay:

I'm still holding on to a bubble which burst a long time ago...I can't go on with this kind of abuse...In the West we are breaking down as families but in the East we go to such lengths of deception....Twenty years ago we would have come to an arrangement, the woman does her thing, the man does, the women cheat, the men know, the men cheat but they don't let their women know...but they stay together because the family is the ultimate and most important thing...and now that's not possible any more.

The nature of the relationship between a separating father and mother can remain hazy for a number of years (in my experience, up to four years). The absence of explanation can lead to the children developing a wish not to think about the situation because to think might lead to asking questions, and to ask questions or display open curiosity is perceived as a threat to a precarious and unusual stability. As Louise, who like Gita had been left and was hanging on to a bubble, explained about her husband, who had been living with another woman for two years: 'When Andreas does come back...

he ... we, sort of fall into him being one of the family. He is like one of the family, you see. And on Sundays, it's like it always was'. In this situation a child may not only worry about the meaning or absence of explanation for herself or himself, but also for a parent whom he or she observes to be unhappy.

> He, Dimitri, says, 'You know I sometimes worry that you haven't had a very nice life, mummy', and I have to reassure him.... And I have to say to him, 'look we are very fortunate, and we've got a home and we've got enough money and we're really very fortunate. More than most people really and we, you know, see daddy twice a week, even though you know he doesn't live with us any more'. I know that it upsets him, and has upset him very deeply obviously, seeing me unhappy.

Working with the Charamboulos family, we saw each of the parents (Andreas and Louise) on their own, their son Dimitri on his own, and then Andreas and Louise together. They expressed their sorrow at having to face the end of their marriage and the intimacy of family life. 'It's a sort of feeling, like, the fall, from the garden of Eden'. Facing the end openly led to Andreas being able to talk more openly to Dimitri, who in turn was able to express his anger more openly with his father. I invited him to share his beliefs with his father.

GGB:	What's your understanding of where your dad is planning to live – do you believe he is going to come home again, or do you believe he is not going to come home again?
Dimitri:	Not going to come home again.
GGB:	Have you talked about that with him?
Dimitri:	He said I've got to accept the fact that he is living with someone else.
GGB:	Is it new for him to say that clearly?
Andreas:	You did say ... that you hadn't really understood that I was living somewhere else until you'd come here.... And he wished that Louise and I had been more forthright with him ... Because it would have helped him to accept it, and I think he's absolutely right. I think we both felt we were somehow making life easier for him by not involving him in it all, and I think you're right, I think we're making things more difficult for him.

Bearing the family in mind

Working with a family in the process of divorce, where one or more members is suffering acute psychological distress, requires attention both to the former family system and its ongoing bonds and loyalties, and to the disequilibrium and reordering of those connections in the process of post-divorce living. It involves drawing on what we know about couple work, individual work and family work and thinking about how to recognise and give weight to differences of view while balancing these with the children's need to have some reconcilable realities in their minds. It may, as I have indicated, involve working with different family members or subsystems at different times, including the couple, each individual adult individually and offering individual interviews and time to the children (Gorell Barnes and Dowling, 1997; Dowling and Gorell Barnes, 1999).

The use of whole-family interviews can be of particular value in sorting out conflict-laden issues in relation to contact; issues that may be as much to do with unresolved feelings between the adults as with the welfare of the children. Many of the points of view that need to be expressed reflect key differences that have resulted in the parents being unable to live together. Individual sessions with each adult, as well as individual sessions with the children, act as a precursor to bringing them together in the same room, and allow the therapist to ascertain what the potential flashpoints are likely to be. The therapist will have provided a secure space for each adult and can therefore redirect the session into a more useful frame. Such interviews are very focused – no open agendas – in order to address what the parents or children have said in relation to controversial aspects of post-divorce living, to listen to each other's views as distinct and sometimes oppositional. The paradigm of difference replaces the paradigm of right and wrong. The objective is a negotiated agreement of very concrete things concerning the children, in full acknowledgement of the affectively laden nature of the small details of family arrangements and the powerful personal meanings they can hold.

Whole-family work is then used to explore how the different meanings uncovered through working with the separate family subsystems can be woven together into new patterns that will allow the family to cooperate in the future. These meetings are powerful. They often prompt parents to work towards a better relationship. Following the idea that inter-subjective experience is created and experienced in conversations and actions with others, it seems that those same significant others between whom the problems were originally constructed may need to be regathered in some instances for new solutions to emerge and be developed. 'It's different talking now because we are all here and mummy is here, and it feels OK.' The original intimate social system in which misunderstandings were developed may need to be present for the misunderstandings to be re-experienced, deconstructed, and given fresh meanings and associations – and, as a result, changed. It is not only 'in language' that such changes take place but also at gut level. As one man put it, when 'surveying the battlefield over the bodies of young love and the carnage of the years between', the witnessing and participation of the therapists had been essential in moving from the trenches, or 'entrenchment', to fresh positions that included forgiveness and the ability to shake hands and plan for the future.

Separation when children are very young

Many children are now experiencing the separation of their parents at a young age. This means that in the generation of children under ten a small but significant percentage will never have the experience of their parents living together, or will not have memories of the family as a one household entity. Collaborative parenting where there is no parental acrimony may create successful infant and child rearing, but it is more probable that if parents have separated so early in the child rearing process, considerable acrimony already exists between them. Such feelings can lead to difficulties in contact, particularly if one parent, usually the mother, feels her intimate attachment to her young child is being jeopardised. The average accepted wisdom of the courts currently grants overnight contact on a fortnightly basis. However, current research poses wider questions about the value of overnight contact in very young children where there is conflict between the parents.

The first systematic investigation of the effects on infant attachment to mother and to father of overnight visitation was recently published (Solomon and George, 1999). This study related specifically to infants aged 12–20 months and their mothers and fathers. The study examined the relationship between overnight visitation with the father and the way in which secure attachments to a father were affected by (1) the conditions of handover and return, and (2) the degree to which mother felt under threat from father, and the effect that this had on her security and ability to calm, soothe and comfort the infant.

Three variables have emerged in the separation and divorce literature as a whole over the last 20 years as particularly important to a child's social and emotional well-being. These are (1) parent conflict, (2) parental communication, and (3) the parents' psychological adjustment to divorce. Any of these three variables may influence an infant's secure attachment to mother through the effect that they have on mother's sensitivity, on the infant, or through direct effects experienced by the infant and resulting in a change in their emotional state and behaviour.

Of the couples who had overnight contact on a roughly once a month basis, three features showed as indicators for particular fragility in the couple relationship. These were (1) the couple had no stable relationship at the time the child was conceived, or at the time of birth, or during the pregnancy, (2) restraining orders were more likely to be used, which suggests a high level of mutual threat and mistrust, (3) the degree to which a mother described herself as able to lessen or mitigate the child's insecurity or distress in the context of the father's visit was markedly less. This was in spite of mothers' own observations that the child was distressed, or their concern that a visit was psychologically harmful. Mothers described themselves taking action for the infants' benefit, but saw these actions as ineffective and experienced themselves as helpless.

I have now worked with a number of families (fifteen) where a father is 'fighting' for his right to co-parent very young children (under three). As with other situations where risk to children is concerned, the worker (who will usually be involved either as guardian, or in some capacity on a Family Assistance Order) (James and Sturgeon Adams, 1999), will have to consider how anxiety in one part of the system is affecting other members of the family. For example, in a family with a 4-year-old boy and a girl under 12 months at the time of separation, the boy is likely to have developed a secure attachment to his father, whereas the girl will have had her formative early attachment months (6–18 months) disrupted. A mother, worried about separating overnight from an infant, who she may still be breastfeeding, is also likely to convey her anxiety to the infant at the point of handover, and certainly to the 3–4 year old involved. In another family where father and mother have never lived together, but father continues to visit on a regular (weekly) basis, he will believe he knows his one-year-old intimately, but from the child's point of view he may only be one among a number of people they see on a weekly basis, and not be a person who is privileged with a special 'secure' attachment.

The Juniper/Rowan family: early separation, attachment issues, and the restoration of contact

Court work requires a particular focus, or clarity from the professional adviser to the court (as expert witness). It also requires us as professional advisers to ensure that the differing voices within the family are represented, that conflicts of interest are made plain, and that the point of view of the children is independently conveyed. I have found these dimensions coherent with further clarifying my work with divorcing families outside the court. I will represent some approaches that I have used in keeping a systemic family approach.

Tom and Larraine had cohabited for a number of years, but had never married. Larraine decided to end the relationship as she experienced that Tom was very disconnected from her although always showing himself a dedicated father. Contact had broken down some two years before I entered the proceedings between father (Tom) and his two children, Robert who was six, and Jossey who was four. The breakdown followed a complex interrelated series of events, an accusation of inappropriate behaviour from father to Jossey made by mother (Larraine), anger by father at the mother re-partnering, leading to a violent altercation at the home in which, during father's attempt to visit the children against mother's wishes, glass had been broken in the windows. Nonetheless, prior to this breakdown there had been strong, frequent, and affectionate contact on a weekly basis between father and his children over the eighteen months since the original separation.

My involvement with the family was an attempt by both parents to find a new resolution through the courts of what had become a very hostile entrenched situation. The children had close ties with their mother and Robert also had strong affectionate memories of his father. These were, however, in conflict with his observations of his mother's expressed anger with his father, and his own memories of his father being angry with his mother when he had come to collect the children but had been thwarted. He also feared that his father might have harmed his little sister because his mother seemed to believe this. Larraine alternated between agreeing that she 'may have been mistaken', but also insisting to me that Robert would not want contact with his father 'if he believed that his father had hurt his little sister'. Robert was thus in a continuous loyalty bind.

As already indicated earlier in this chapter, a model that has been found useful for working with divorcing parents who are in conflict about issues regarding their children is to see each parent separately, and understand the points in their narrative that distinguish their perspective from that of the other parent. In the Juniper/Rowan family, I saw Tom and Larraine separately and understood their differences regarding the resumption of contact. It is often the case that where a mother is taking a position against contact she may have fears for herself. It is therefore important to make any fears explicit so that they can be addressed. Larraine feared that her life would become circumscribed by Tom 'stalking' her, since she had already had several examples she could point to. She also feared his competence in handling her girl child as a lone male parent. However, she was able to acknowledge that she did believe Robert would have something to gain from contact with his father, 'A boy needs his father as he grows up.'

In my first meeting with Larraine, Robert and Jossey at a local contact centre, I began by asking the children what they remembered their mother telling them about why were all meeting here today. Robert said he thought we were meeting because of 'the court' having said that we should meet. However, he claimed that he could not remember what it was the court had wanted us to meet about. Larraine said that she had told them that 'the judge had asked me to try and get them to help it happen that they would see their dad again'. I asked each of the children if they knew what a Judge was, and Robert said he 'thought that a judge was someone who told people if they had done something wrong, and what they were going to do about it'. I replied that I thought this was a very good answer, and asked if he thought anyone had done anything wrong in his family. He shook his head. I asked the children about the different ways in which they might have memories of the court coming into their lives and Larraine helped the children remember how many professionals they had seen. I asked Robert and Jossey whether they had ever sat down and talked with their mum about why Larraine and Tom had separated. We worked out how old each of them was when Larraine had left Tom. I asked Robert whether he had any memories of how it was different after Dad had left the house, and particularly what he remembered of things that had been upsetting for him in going between Mum and Dad following the separation. He nodded his head vigorously at this, and described a particular incident on his birthday when he had not wished to leave his mother's house, but his father had insisted that the time was due to him and he had had to leave the house kicking and screaming. Jossey had not understood what was going on. He correctly dated this event. This precision of his memory suggested that an event that is highly laden with emotion can remain intact in young children's minds, in this case two-and-a-half years later.

I also discussed with Robert his sense of protectiveness of his little sister Jossey in relation to his father's care of her. We talked about the difficulties there might be looking after little babies and Robert made a short speech to the effect that 'in looking after babies it might be possible that Dad had been rough with Jossey and not meant to'. We then talked about whether Robert felt that his mother had really given him permission to see his father Tom. He said that he was not sure about this. Larraine said, 'You know we've talked about it and we talked about it coming here in the car'. I suggested that as this was a difficult subject, maybe we could talk about it again together. Larraine said very clearly that she 'knew that Tom loved Robert', and that she thought 'Robert should feel he could see his dad whenever he wanted to'. Ambivalence expressed by mother in relation to the children resuming contact with their father is a common feature of cases where there has been any show of violent behaviour, and in my experience this has been stronger where the children are girls.

Attachment

It was my hypothesis early in working with this family that Jossey was unlikely to have had a secure attachment to her father, whereas Robert had a secure attachment. Robert had lived with his father for three-and-a-half years before the separation. Jossey was under six months old. She used to go to his house for early contact visits while she was still being breastfed by her mother. Despite father's strong 'wish' to be a 'co-parent', the eagerness for the relationship was necessarily one-way. In addition, mother's strong anxiety about her girl child in this situation would have contributed to tension at times of handover (Solomon and George, 1999).

Using photographs and a letter to the children

Following meetings with each parent alone and two meetings with Larraine and the children, I encouraged Tom to write a letter to 'the children' and enclose a range of photographs of things which the children and he had formerly done together. The letter was to include an expression of sorrow and regret for any harm that he had done to the children, as well as an assurance of his continuing love for them. The photographs were intended to elicit memories of the times he had spent with them which I suspected would have been suppressed in the context of the acrimonious proceedings.

Tom had written a strongly emotional letter, but had managed to resist blaming Larraine in his wording:

> The reason why I have not seen you for so long, is that, because Mummy loves you as much as I do, unfortunately, we could not agree as to how long we could each have you for and to stop our arguing and to help us understand each other, I asked a Judge to sort it out once and for all. She then, did not know you and what you both wanted. She sent people to speak to you. This is what adults do if they can't agree on things. Mrs. Barnes wants to help us sort things out and its O.K. to talk to her and tell her, how you both really feel. Its all been very confusing and has taken a lot longer time that I had thought, I am very, very sorry about this and I am trying to fix things as fast as possible.

Tom had then included a number of specific stories about the children's lives and things he had done with them including details of the flat where they had visited him and pets they had. It concluded with thoughts and quotations about their own lives:

> I wonder what you are both doing all the time. How's the swimming lessons? Are you just getting confident in the water Jossey? I haven't been swimming since. Though I did go to that same school in Botham, in the evenings, to learn about computers, so I would be able to understand your homework and hopefully to buy one soon.

He also sent greetings cards and loving messages from his wider family. We looked at all the photos together and Robert made his own comments about what had been going on when they were taken. All evoked memories, some laughter and some wistfulness. At the end of our meeting, Robert said he would like to see his dad if I was there all the time.

Contact visit between Robert and his father

Robert myself and Tom met in the same family playroom with which Robert was by now familiar. Larraine, reassured by the process had made it clear both to him and to me that she wanted him to enjoy the meeting with his father, and wholly supported it. Robert was initially shy, as indeed was Tom. Tom had brought some crisps and lemonade, and some presents. The atmosphere was warm, and emotional. I curbed Tom's tendency to be more emotional than

I thought Robert could handle, and he followed these cues. He gave Robert his presents due from a previous birthday. After a while they began to be attuned to each other, and I suggested they look at the photos together. They went through each of the photos, establishing some shared memories. Tom described further work he had done on the house and garden. He had thought of some jobs that he wondered if Robert could help him with, and I suggested they turn these into a list.

Differences in work with Jossey

In a subsequent meeting with Jossey, who now wanted to meet her dad because Robert had met him, I suggested we look at the photos daddy had sent, which she was eager to do. Many of the pictures led her to describe what she currently saw in the pictures, rather than the pictures acting as a trigger to her own memories. However, there were some exceptions to this. She remembered herself in her own little 'princess frock'; she, like Robert, had laughed at a picture of Robert wearing Daddy's funny spectacles with a moustache attached, and she remembered her own doll's house, which was shown in one of the photographs. When it came to actual pictures of Tom, she passed them over the first time and I returned them under her gaze once we had seen all the others, asking her if she remembered him. There was one of him cuddling her as a toddler, and she looked at it in a thoughtful way. We talked about how I would keep daddy as a safe daddy while she got to know him again, and how we would then talk more together. I asked 'if I were here in this room with you, would you like to see him?' She said 'yes'. A few minutes before the meeting ended I asked her 'if I am talking to mummy and she asks me about whether you want to see daddy if I am here, am I still to say you said yes?', and she said 'yes'. I then asked her if she would like it to be with Robert or without Robert and she said 'with Robert'.

Comment – progress

Jossey's first meeting with her father took place with no embarrassment or shyness on either side. They kissed and greeted each other as though it was on the previous week they had met. It was difficult to focus discussion around the time that had passed in between, but we managed to identify some things that she saw as 'different' about her daddy. Following the success of the initial meeting, supervised contact continued for a number of months in the father's house. The following aspects marked progress in the children's and parents' changing positions in relation to one another.

Making sense of the question of whether Tom had hurt Jossey

I regard it as very important that fathers clarify any actions which have been perceived as damaging to children, and apologise for these. Tom told Jossey that if he had hurt her in any way he would be terribly, terribly sorry, but that he had never had any intention of hurting her. Following Jossey's second visit to Tom in his home she reported to her mother that she would like Larraine to know, and for Larraine to let anyone else who had been involved know, that she no longer thought her father had meant to hurt her. Larraine accepted this. Following Larraine's recognition that the children were happy in visiting their father, a joint meeting between the parents then took place in which a number of important points were made. Both parents at this point were prepared to be child-led, although Tom still became truculent about the fact that he did not have overnight contact.

Meeting between Larraine and Tom

I began with some introductory remarks expressing my pleasure that we had managed to meet together and that the parents had been prepared to set aside their grievances to focus on planning for the future. I stated my belief that we could make plans that would be the easiest and the best from the children's point of view, that avoided the children feeling caught in the middle, whether geographically or in their minds, and referred them to the time in my early meetings with Robert, when Robert had showed me a picture where a little child felt pulled in half on Christmas day. Larraine had prepared a list of issues she wanted to see resolved as had Tom. In summary the issues that we all wanted to resolve included:

1. how contact would take place in the future;
2. the amount of time that Tom wanted to be involved in his children's lives;
3. how communication could best established between mother and father;
4. how changes of arrangements could be dealt with;
5. how direct contact between the parents could be set up quickly in the case of an emergency or a need for information, and, as I put it, 'things affecting the children's lives where either of them might want the help of the other'.

Summary of key aspects of the progress of the meeting

Larraine created a positive track by reassuring Tom that she would always promote contact as she could now see that this was for the children's benefit. She commented that in the early days Robert had not wanted to go and this had made him anxious, but now he enjoyed contact and every time he had gone to meet his father had said that he had liked it: 'Initially it was a big step for him and now he has made up his mind.' She added that 'Jossey wants to do what Robert does.'

Tom responded that he 'did not wish to be inflexible'. Should Jossey not wish to come on any occasion he would not want to 'push it'.

Larraine in turn responded to Tom positively. She confirmed that she did not 'bad-mouth him'. She added: 'I never have and I never will.' Tom in turn confirmed a similar attitude on his part.

Larraine asserted that she could see how the children enjoyed and benefited from seeing their father. She commented that Robert was really happy doing his homework with Tom.

The build-up of mutually positive reciprocal influence led to a change in tempo. Larraine suddenly confided to Tom 'I have been thinking what it must be like for the children to pass your gate when they go shopping on Saturdays, and to feel that they can't go in. I would like them to feel that they could pop in at any time.' She said she hoped that such a point might be reached. Tom added: 'I would like to see a normalisation of our lives so that we can be civil to each other, then we could risk it'.

Following this comment I asked what a normalisation of their lives would look like. What, for example, would it mean in terms of changes of behaviour? Larraine and Tom agreed that the problem was that either of them could become intractable if there was a problem that they had different views about, so it was unlikely that too much informality would develop. Larraine expressed her underlying fear that Tom was trying to take the children away. She assured Tom that she was not trying to run the children's lives and that she recognised that what he wanted was more involvement. Tom reassured Larraine that he was *not* trying to take the children away from her. 'I'm there to be their father, it's part of their entitlement to know their father. All I want them to be is comfortable with me in my house.'

Continuing the theme of 'normalisation' I raised the question of holidays, commenting that I thought that we should proceed slowly. I recommended that we should have more overnights before progressing to a longer period of time with father. I reminded Tom that Jossey is two years younger than Robert and that the children might have different wishes about lengthy stays, and he would need to respect this always. We also discussed the freedom to ring one parent when with the other, and added this to a developing 'list of good parenting practice': 'When you are in one parent's house you can always ring your other parent'. We talked about overnight anxieties shown by the children on a previous visit.

At this point Tom and Larraine began a discussion about the children's plans for the following Saturday morning, and had a friction-free parental discussion about the various things that take place at weekends. I pointed out that they were now discussing issues together as parents do, and we talked about their usual difficulties in listening to each other's views. Larraine made a very empathic comment about how it must feel 'to want to be part of the children's lives, and yet feel powerless'. Tom concurred with her comment, saying 'I would like to know that what I say matters to them'. Larraine in turn said to him 'you used to talk so loudly that what I said was drowned out and I felt battered over the head'. Tom and Larraine then engaged in a long discussion about school issues which they agreed to resolve together. Larraine also raised the issue that if one of the children were ill and did not want to visit would Tom think that it was she that was trying to block contact. He might think this because of the past. She in turn felt that she was often criticised by him and given 'lists of things that she had done wrong'. Tom in turn said that he hoped that Larraine did not feel that he was 'steamrollering' her into contact. Larraine replied that she did not think that. However, she continued to fear that Tom would be 'nagging' her about a list of things that she was doing badly as a mother. Tom agreed that he would *not* do this. He said 'I am not going to catch the children in any crossfire. It is not fair to them'. Larraine commented humorously to me 'We will never be in each other's fan club!', and I responded that 'nonetheless you each need to hear positive comments from the other inside your own head'. Larraine concurred with this by saying 'it may be more important to have such comments inside one's head than to hear them outside'.

In a recent Judgment, Dame Elisabeth Butler-Schloss from the Court of Appeal adjudicating on four contact appeals, laid out again factors relating to contact applications. They were a summary of many previous Judgments, and drew out the principles on which the restoration of contact in cases where children have been affected by an exposure to high acrimony or violence are based. 'The Children Act draws attention to the centrality of the child, and the promotion of his or mental health and well-being as the central issue amid tensions surrounding adults in dispute. The purpose of contact must be clear, and have a potential for benefiting the child in some way. The risk of promoting direct contact includes the risk of increase of the climate of conflict around the child, which might undermine the child's general stability and sense of emotional well-being. Research indicates that even where children do not continue in a situation where there has been high negative emotional behaviours, emotional trauma can continue to be experienced from preceding high conflict situations.'

Summary

Key features for the maintenance of successful contact where it has previously broken down therefore include:

- the importance of parents being able to respond positively to the children talking about the other parent (positive connotation of the other parent in the mind of the child);
- the importance of being child-led with regard to developing positive mutual influence in the contact arrangements, rather than a parent pushing too fast for too much contact;
- the importance of keeping old patterns of involvement with each other, and old arguments and fights as a means of continuing a former relationship at a lower order of importance than the goal of promoting the best interests of the child;
- the creation of a context of safety for a new child-centred parenting pattern to be developed;
- the need to remain as a stabilising aspect of the newly formed post-divorce family system until parents are ready to maintain that pattern themselves.

6

STEP-FAMILIES

Family structures in the UK are changing daily. Approximately one million children were estimated to live in step-families in the early 1990s – 5.5 per cent to married couples, and 6.7 per cent to cohabiting couples (Haskey, 1994). The families are themselves of widely differing structures, with varying histories, losses, transitions and economic circumstances. Of the one in five children who currently experience family separation before they are sixteen, over half will live in a step-family at some point in their lives. Of the 150 000 couples with children who divorced each year at the end of the 1980s, a further 35 000 went through a subsequent divorce (Haskey, 1994). For some children, then, we need to think of step-parenting within a wider range of transitions that include relationship changes of many kinds (Dunn, 2002).

What is a step-family?

The context in which any step-family should be considered by a counsellor or family therapist will always include their previous lives and relationships within the current generation. Rather than identify a step-family as a 'distinct' family form, consideration of wider influences on the family should always take into account loss of former relationships, of transitions and disruptions and of the effects of these on all concerned. A step-family is created when two adults form a household in which one or both brings a child from a previous relationship. The new partner may become an important adult and parent figure to their partner's child, or may remain at best at the level of a 'friend' to the child/ren. Stepchildren may be full-time or part-time members of new households, and as children move between households created by each of their parents, they are likely to be required to accommodate more than one family style. Since step-parents are additional rather than replacement parents, the shared division of one same-sex parenting role between two people – mother and stepmother – father and stepfather – that arises from divorce is one of the particular adaptations a modern step-family and the children of the family usually have to manage. Children will have at least three, sometimes four or, in families that have reordered more than once, five or six 'parent' figures. Unlike extended kinship structures in cultures where these have developed to facilitate the rearing of children, these post-divorce kinship structures may not work in harmony, may well be adversarial and may be in competition for a child's attachment.

The focus on shared parental responsibility embodied in the Children Act 1989 infringes on newly forming step-family boundaries in many ways. It makes clearly visible the social belief that a parent is for life. This challenges emotionally preferred ways of forgetting old relationships and their importance to children which many parents involved in constructing new family lives, would choose. The Newcastle study (Simpson *et al.*, 1995) has shown that many women wish to sever all contact with their former spouse in the event of previous or ongoing acrimony and violence, or where they have felt oppressed by the relationship. When a parent wishes to continue his or her involvement with the child following a conflictual first marriage that has ended acrimoniously or violently, adversarial patterns of interaction between the former partners may not cease with divorce (as described in the previous chapter). If a former partner is actively disrupting current step-family life – for example by telephoning every evening and insisting on talking to the child during a family meal, or behaving erratically in relation to contact, thus engendering disappointment in the child and messing up arrangements for the family as a whole – the negotiations of daily living involve an active, external, third adult who is often not well disposed to the new family arrangements and may contribute to ongoing disequilibrium in step-family life. The pain and rage experienced by many men and women as they see their children in the daily care of other adults is an emotional force that receives insufficient recognition as a social phenomenon.

Following the death of a parent, the incoming step-parent obviously does not have the living father or mother to compete with, but the legacy they inherit and the roles they move into will already have certain preprogrammed expectations in the child's mind, with potential inbuilt loyalty conflicts. Precisely what a father or mother should be may have been laid down in the child's mind long before their arrival, and negotiating with these patterns of expectation will be a continuous part of the family reorganisation (Gorell Barnes *et al.*, 1998).

The loss of intimate relationship with one parent and the introduction of a new adult into family life as a factor that may be stressful for children in the long-term received relatively little attention in the step-family literature, until the publication of analysis of the 1958 child development cohort (Kiernan, 1992) and the publication of *The Exeter Study* (Cockett and Tripp, 1994) which looks in detail at current transitions in family life. Hetherington, probably the most influential researcher in the step-family field, emphasises the diversity in children's responses and ability to cope (Hetherington and Kelly, 2002; Dunn, 2000, 2001) has emphasised the importance for children of honouring their biological relationships, and the relatively low level of importance accorded by children to step-parents.

Our own research study (Gorell Barnes *et al.*, 1998) of children who have grown up in step-families, found that as adults their accounts echoed one of the findings of *The Exeter Study*: that adult relationships disrupted by divorce do cause grief to many children over time – through economic change, through the transitions and losses involved, and through the reordering of intimate relationships and the pattern of daily life. While a good step-parent can bring many strengths to a family that has been through disruption, including emotional stability (Golombok *et al.*, 2002), and the possibility of keeping the family above the level of the 'poverty' trap by providing a second income (Glendinning and Millar, 1987), many children are emotionally content living in lone parent headed households, where they experience a strong bond to their care giving parent. Hetherington (Hetherington and Kelly, 2002) has emphasised the dangers for step-parents in assuming that marriage is a form of parental entitlement. Step-parents often assume an intimacy and authority that they have to earn. Even in long-lasting step-families tight-knit relationships are not the norm. For many post-divorce families the patterns of parenting include an ex-partner who is living in another country or another continent. Contact with distant biological parents, and issues of authority and related views, are then balanced even more sharply against proximity with a step-parent with whom the children live. Step-parents therefore often have management responsibilities for long periods of time, without being accorded authority by the children.

Boys' and girls' ways of dealing with family distress: similarities and differences

Let us contrast two girls and two boys of the same age who are confronting a common situation for children: their mothers are taking a new partner after a period of living as single parents. Each reacts violently in different ways, but the girls' verbal violence is an open expression of their fear that they will lose their relationship with their mothers. The boys' behaviour, while involving a similar fear, involves more open acting out of hostility and is more physical and less verbal. Louisa (aged 11) rang a clinic to say that a crisis was threatening her family. It transpired that she did not like the fact that her mother, after nine years of living without a partner, had now found a man with whom she was planning to set up home. Louisa's sense of panic and fury at the idea of another person entering her mother's emotional world was expressed by her as being 'shut away from her mother'. As the interaction between mother and daughter developed in the room, it could be seen how important it was for Louisa to look after the mother who looked after her and her little brother for nine years. 'I've always been grown up. I had to grow up quickly because Daddy left...I'm used to being responsible.' She said that in her life nothing was as important as 'looking after Paul and Mum. You've always needed me, and now you don't need me and I still need you.' She said to the counsellor, 'She's always looked after herself and Paul, but in a way I've sort of looked after her too.' Catching on to how important this job was to the girl's sense of self and identity, the counsellor said, 'and it's very sad to think of giving that job up, isn't it?'. Louisa replied, 'It's because I've been so used to it, it's me, I'm so used to it...and then this man comes along and says "Well, I'll take over that job, thank you".' However, Louisa came to trust her stepfather once her resentment and fear of losing her position was acknowledged, and she saw some of the advantages in being 'allowed' to be a teenager.

Anna, aged 7, described a similar sense of exclusion in another way. When describing her mother's current boyfriend, she said 'It's bad stuff from him...it started when he started to be nasty to me, tell me what to do and stuff...it felt like he was pushing me away.' Anna's fear was triplefold: fear of another person threatening her autonomy in the home fear that she would lose the important position of looking after her ill mother, and fear of being separated from the person to whom she was closest in the world, her mother. She was also suspicious of the quality of relationship offered by men, having herself been abused by her father on a contact visit earlier in her life. A boy may be just as closely connected as a girl to a parent when he has been encouraged to be so, or has had to 'look after' a lone parent and is just as anxious about this connection being severed, and it is likely that the display of 'connected' behaviour will be tolerated less well by an incoming stepfather than if he had been a girl, as it may well be construed as deliberately trying to keep the incomer away. Unlike a girl, a boy may be responded to aggressively, as a rival, by a new male partner. Sean, aged five, came with his mother and stepfather following a crisis line call initiated by the latter who feared the violence of his own responses to Sean's 'possessive' behaviour towards his mother. 'He will not leave you alone, he follows you around like a little dog ... he pulls and pulls at your arm until it's sore, and it's "Mum, Mum, Mum".' Sean's mother had been left by his father when Sean was eighteen months old and had subsequently been in hospital three times for overdosing. His concern thus had at least two levels of meaning: how his mother would fare with a new man in her life, and how he himself would fare. The arrival of a new man raised other questions. Would a new man coming in mean that he was displaced? Was there only room in the family for one man at a time?

Dave, aged ten, was furious not so much about the loss of his mother (who had decided to remarry), since he lived with his father most of the time, but that the decision offered further proof that his mother was not going to return to his father, even though they had been living apart for over three years. He had attacked his mother on three occasions, and had also hit his father's girlfriend in the face. 'She pisses me off ... I just found out that he was having an affair with her and I don't know if he would have told me or not.' The question of where primary loyalty and the 'proper' path of communication lay in his family – between the adults, or between parent and child – was for him, as for many children living with a lone parent, a very important question. However, during the discussion Dave was able to note some differences in his mother's relationship with her new partner that he found reassuring: 'You and dad were always quarrelling, you and Jim haven't had a single row.' Over a number of sessions his preoccupation that his father and mother would stay connected, in spite of each of them having a new relationship, was talked out more openly.

First and second marriages differ around issues of how a satisfactory marital relationship develops. In a second marriage, establishing some kind of workable relationship between step-parents and stepchildren and resolving those conflicts may be the key to a happy marriage. Remarried families cite children as the number one source of marital tensions and stress. Research assures us that what helps is for the biological parent to continue to serve as the principle parent while the new step-parent gets to know the children slowly and supports their partner in discipline. In Hetherington's cohort, only one-third of stepfathers and one-sixth of stepmothers, in comparison to 60 per cent of parents in non-divorced families ever become authoritative. To quote Hetherington (Hetherington and Kelly, 2002) 'The average new step-father behaves like a polite but wary stranger trying to ingratiate himself, seeking areas of common interest like sports, movies, and music, rarely criticising the child, but feeling little emotional closeness or rapport' (p. 195). Children recognised step-parents as more marginal and often preferred this. Only 21 per cent of children said stepfather was the 'boss', in distinction from non-divorced families. However, as our UK study found (Gorell Barnes *et al.*, 1998) stepfathers were accepted if they brought in income, were a support and companion to the mother, and proved a long-term friend to the child. A good relationship with a step-mother was most likely to occur when the father was an actively involved parent who supported stepmother's authority, where a first wife did not act as a rival, or when a biological mother had disengaged from the child's life while the child was young.

Lesbian and gay partnerships

When a woman forms a second relationship with another woman rather than a man, many of the preoccupations a couple bring are to do with whether the children are reacting to the lesbian relationship and are showing 'homophobic' attitudes, or whether the anger the children are showing is a feature of post-divorce family behaviour and step-family life. Beth and Mary, a white British couple of different cultural backgrounds, were living with Beth's children from her fifteen-year marriage. Initially they were particularly concerned about Paul, who at fourteen was anxious about how to describe to his school friends the relationship between the two women in a way that would not lead to a show of disrespect. When at home, Paul got on extremely well with Mary, consulting her about his homework and watching TV comedy shows with her. However, outside the home he was much more wary and specifically asked his mother not to put him in positions where he felt she would be made vulnerable. Paul went to a large boys' school and his anxiety about homophobia at school was probably realistic. Beth and Mary decided to honour this above their campaigning zeal to have lesbianism accepted as a family form by Paul's friends. Samantha, at eleven, was more problematic to Beth and Mary, playing her father (Harry) off against the couple as being able to offer her more material goods and give her a nicer time. She also seemed to be picking up and bringing home a number of 'attitudes' that Beth felt were coming from Harry's new partner, Dolly. These, while not overtly homophobic, were emphasising Samantha's 'girlie' qualities in ways that Beth experienced as a hostile attack on her own presentation of female self. Furthermore Harry continued to treat Beth as his 'ex' in sexually intimate ways that Mary found intolerable, such as patting her bottom or calling her 'old girl' while he pinched her cheek. Beth and Mary negotiated the transitions of gendered partnership and adolescence by insisting on as much open talking within their household as they could manage within the constraints of their both working full time, by making clearer boundaries with Harry, and by giving each other recognition that they each needed time on their own to continue habits of living built up during their former lives, only some of which they wanted to share with each other. Paul and Mary also found a number of things they enjoyed doing together that he did not do with his mother, mainly centred on his hobby, fishing.

However, another fourteen-year-old, Robert, living with two sisters and his mother Jane and her partner Rose, found that living in an all-female household was too much for him to manage in terms of carrying too many remarks aimed at disqualifying men and men's attributes for him to handle successfully within his peer group. Jane and Enrico, Robert's father, had separated bitterly and with a lot of violence, and Robert found himself constantly on the receiving end of remarks about male aggression; particularly, as he saw it, whenever he stood up for himself in a 'house full of women'. He became progressively more marginalised from his family and more connected to a peer group who used drugs on a regular basis. When Robert's school excluded him, his mother finally asked his father to take over his care. Enrico, who ran a cafe, was dismayed at having to take charge of a son with whom he had not lived for four years, and he had to rearrange both his working life and the two rooms he lived in over the cafe in order to accommodate his son. He also had to rearrange his freewheeling sexual activities to take account of his son's presence in the home. Robert initially found the transition to an all-male household both difficult and surprising because his father demanded far more of him in the household and in relation to his school work than his mother had done. The use of his aunt's house and his grandmother's house as alternative weekend homes helped him adjust to the new gender balance in his life and to build up a new, more extended family life. Recent research from the West of England (Golombok *et al.*, 2002) has shown that co-mothers in lesbian mother families smack the children less, play with them more and show a tendency towards less frequent disputes with them. The authors conclude from this and other studies of lesbian co-parenting that it is the presence of two parents irrespective of their gender, rather than the presence of a parent of each sex, that is associated with more positive outcomes for children psychological well-being.

When fathers choose to leave the family and adopt a gay lifestyle the problems for a new partner are likely to depend largely on the responses of the children's mother. Women struggling with the loss of their husband to another person of the same sex (as with men struggling with the loss of their wives to another person of the same sex), have additional complexities to handle when it comes to helping their children make sense of subsequent family arrangements. Whereas research has shown that children themselves suffer no disadvantage in lesbian step-parent households, there is no research available on men as 'co-fathers'. Concerns that have shown themselves important to the mothers of sons relate to the influence of a homosexual household on a child's subsequent choice of sexual orientation. Questions around what may be displayed as homosexual love in front of children themselves, as well as more subtle issues of whether a son will be influenced in adopting attitudes of misogyny, have to remain open to be kept on a running agenda discussable (where possible) between parents themselves. For a boy approaching adolescence the meaning of 'dad being gay' and the implications for his own identity is also crucial and may affect his relationships with the new couple. The integration of the households, heterosexual, gay or lesbian and the children, for events such as birthdays, school events and religious festivals, all play a part in how the child processes the experience and feels permitted to make his or her own choices in relation to sexuality.

The extended family

Research findings differ on whether children are likely to lose touch with the parents of their non-residential parent and to maintain contact with the parents of the caretaking parent. *The Exeter Study* (Cockett and Tripp, 1994) suggests that the more often families reorder, the more frequently children lose contact with the two sets of grandparents, so that the 'core' family has less support from the extended family. This was in contrast to our own study of children drawn from the 1958 National Child Development Cohort (Gorell Barnes *et al.*, 1998), which showed a high degree of grandparental involvement while the children were still growing up, and ongoing extended family involvement in spite of increasing family mobility throughout the UK. Dunn (2002) confirms the importance of grandparents to children in the ALSPAC study. The Children Act principles and practice document (1989) emphasises that wider family links matter, with particular reference to brothers and sisters as well as grandparents, and it may be of great importance for clinicians to remember the roles that extended family members can play in ongoing lives.

One dilemma arising from the emphasis in the Children Act is that step-parents are by implication potentially relegated to a less central role in relation to post-divorce child rearing than either of the child's biological parents, and can be less important in child-rearing terms than grandparents. While this may be appropriate in relation to children's need for intimacy and continuity, it is not always recognised as appropriate by new step-parents, who feel they ought to be doing a particular job in relation to the children who have become part of their lives. The models of family life that many step-parents hold in their minds and put into practice may not recognise others who were previously involved, or may actively set themselves up against earlier models of family life. The Children Act also allows members of the extended family to apply for varying orders in relation to children, and when this happens step-parents have less legal authority over the children until they too apply for parental responsibility. A step-parent's growing connections to the child over time are likely to require changes in the balance of power in the family, and when this becomes overt it can create disruptions. The Children Act does not take this complexity into account, since the child's 'best interests' may not be reconcilable where two 'parents' of the same gender are in clear opposition.

Maxine, Joachim, Ked, Anna and Rusty

Joachim and Anna, of French Caribbean and British mixed race background, had been separated for over seven years at the time I met them. After the separation Anna had become depressed on a number of occasions, leaving her son Ked with Joachim and his mum and dad. Ked had suffered from meningitis at three weeks and had a number of disabilities, which meant he required full-time attention. Within three years Joachim had re-partnered with Maxine, and they subsequently married. Maxine became devoted to Ked, taking increasing time off work to look after him and take over the routine previously supplied by Joachim's parents. Anna, when recovered from her depression, began to grow jealous of Ked's attachment to Maxine, and returned to court a number of times to increase her contact with him. This was resisted by Joachim, who felt that Ked needed the stability that the existing arrangement provided. Anna had a number of relationships that did not last, partly it seemed because her co-habitees found the care of Ked, even on a part-time basis, too demanding of her time. In addition her preoccupation with having 'more of him' meant that 'less of her' was available in a sexual relationship. However, Rusty, her fourth partner, took warmly to Ked and inspired Anna to believe that she could gain custody. This prompted Maxine to apply formally for parental responsibility, which she had previously not been concerned about as she had respected Anna's need to regard Ked as primarily her responsibility. The situation escalated into an increasingly adversarial and rigid pattern, with each set of parents claiming that what they had in mind was best.

Following several interviews with different combinations of the extended step-family system, a whole-family meeting with both sets of parents was arranged. Much attention was paid to the difficulty each of the participants might have in talking in front of those who had previously been seen as 'opponents'. Each parent was asked for their view of the ideal future arrangements, as well as what they realistically thought would be best for Ked. The enormous amount of work Maxine had put into Ked over the last three years was acknowledged. Rusty expressed his belief that Maxine and Joachim should take more breaks and look after themselves. Joachim was urged to recognise Anna's grief at not being able to look after Ked during her depression. As the atmosphere relaxed, Joachim freely acknowledged Ked's love for Anna. In turn Anna was able to say that she did not want to upset Ked's life in spite of her great desire to be with him. Gradually the adversarial atmosphere was replaced by one of cautious optimism that it might be possible for the participants to work out something between them.

When parents place huge importance on continuing to care for their children, this inevitably requires adjustments both in daily life and in the minds of all concerned. The capacity to share the care of children and the adjustments to daily life that this involves often stretches parental management abilities and reserves of patience to the limit. A non-resident parent may continue to behave in ways that complicate the smooth running of the daily life of a child (as the mother sees it) by insisting on involvement in the small details of daily life. Such intrusiveness may continue long after the child experiences this as 'care'. Fathers who are having to learn both living skills and parenting skills post-divorce, at the same time that their ex-wives are trying to build new lives without them that may include new partners, may sometimes focus more on trying to disrupt those lives than on developing new ones for themselves. A child entering a step-family and managing the social and emotional adaptations that requires, may be exposed on contact visits to a parallel experience of a 'helpless' father who is reconstructing his life unsuccessfully, which then becomes a significant emotional burden (see the Marley family below).

Economic tensions

The post-divorce housing activities of many families often involve frequent moves and more crowded accommodation. On average step-families have more dependent children per household, are more likely to live in local authority or terraced housing, often in overcrowded circumstances, and have a lower average income. Depleted economic circumstances can in themselves exacerbate already stretched relationships between parents and children.

Liz, Frank, Tom, Bill, Dan and Sheila

When Liz and Dan separated after cohabiting for five years and having two sons, Dan took the eldest son Tom to live with him, while the youngest son Bill went to live with his mother and her new partner Frank, whom she subsequently married. Bill was very devoted to his father and visited him every other weekend, even though they lived quite a long way apart. Difficulties arose when a new baby, Roddy, was born. Dan and his partner Sheila, Roddy's mother, began to argue every time Bill visited as she said that he took up too much space. Bill was very distressed by these arguments and felt responsible for causing so many rows. The situation was 'resolved' by Bill sharing a room with Roddy, who woke him up, as babies do, at all hours of the night and this affected his performance in the school athletic programme at which he had been excelling.

The privileging of the baby above Bill in Sheila and Dan's home was accentuated when one half of the boys' room was redecorated for the baby while Bill's half was left, on the basis that as a teenager he would prefer to decorate it himself with posters or other wall coverings. Bill described this as quite a rejection, but was keen not to make a fuss about it as it had reduced the quarrelling between his dad and Sheila about his visits and he placed family harmony above baby-blue walls. However, the subtle disqualification of himself as a significant person in their household began to show in other ways, so that he allowed himself to be bullied in situations where he had formerly felt in charge. His older brother Tom, who was in turn fed up with the amount of attention now being lavished on baby Roddy, also began to bully Bill when he visited, complaining that he was always hanging around and being a nuisance. As Liz said to Tom, 'We need to build up Bill's confidence, to make him feel strong about himself and that's difficult when the person he is closest to doesn't really help him.'

Work with this family took place over a number of years, in intensive bursts interspersed with long gaps, as has much of my work with step-families. I first met Liz and Dan when they were breaking up because of considerable violence in their relationship. This was the second long relationship Liz had severed, and she had children by each partner. Subsequently I met Liz and her new partner Tony, then Liz and each of her children and then the new step-family together on a number of occasions. It has been important for many families going through the tumult of unclear transitions – in which matters only become resolved for new ones to emerge – to have a place where they can safely return to examine developments without necessarily feeling they are embarking on 'therapy'. I see much of this work as consultation to ongoing transitional disturbances, whereby overburdened parents are provided with a place in which to reflect on 'how to manage the next bit'.

Stepmothers and mothers: trying to get it right

Step-families formed after the death of a partner are less common than other forms of step-families in the UK today. However, family construction in the presence of mourning carries its own loading. Mourning the dead person will inevitably be very different for the different members of the step-family. On the one hand the death may have created the space within which the second marriage could take place, but on the other hand everyone involved is likely to be highly ambivalent about the space being filled. Sometimes, as in the Clarke family below, the parents may have already divorced before the death of one of them, and the children then join the other parent and their new family. The processes of mourning, both complex and long-term, will have a rhythm and timescale that is different to the pace of a developing step-family structure, which has its own daily pressures and emotional demands.

The Clarke Family

Dave and Simone brought their family of four children for family sessions sometime after the death of Dave's first wife in a car crash. Within a couple of months of the funeral, her two daughters by Dave had joined their father, stepmother and two step-siblings. In between they had stayed with their maternal grandmother, whom they dearly liked. Dave had chosen to make his issue of concern the fact that one of his daughters was not taking her school work seriously. As an Irish family living in an English community they were very determined that their children would do well, but they were somewhat isolated in terms of having other families with whom to compare their required standards of hard work.

Ffion, the younger daughter, was refusing to conform to the new family rule about getting good marks and behaving well. She was failing consistently in school, and showing what they saw as 'bad adolescent behaviour' by staying out late. She had been kept in for three months for not doing well enough generally. The family seemed to find it difficult to think about the relationship between Ffion's lack of interest in school work and her mourning of her mother; indeed Dave found it hard to express his thoughts and feelings in the meetings at all. He held himself separate from the women in the family, between whom emotion and passion flowed volubly.

I encouraged all the children to draw a genogram together, looking at the different sides of the family and the ways they had overlapped before they came together. I had previously encouraged them to create a family photoboard in which friends, aunts, uncles and their grandmother back home in Ireland were portrayed. However, the girls had 'decided' not to put their mother on the photoboard, because in their stepmother's opinion their father would have found it too painful to have a visible reminder of the woman with whom he had had an acrimonious post-divorce relationship. I asked the girls 'how in this family is your mother to be remembered?', and Ffion replied 'I remind them of her by the way I act.' This statement can be read a number of ways, one being that her mother had been a fun-loving person and she was holding out for a different family ethos:

fun-loving rather than serious and hard-working. Another might be that she was saying 'I remind them constantly that there is something wrong for me – I have a loss that they don't want to know about.' The long shadows of the post-divorce wrangling between the girls' parents was tearfully reported by Simone, their stepmother. She believed that Ffion and Marie had been consistently misinformed by their mother that their father was a bad man who had gone off to England with another woman and left her to bring up her kids single-handed, and that he had never paid for their upkeep.

The two sisters talked about their need to keep a boundary around the memory of their mother. I asked them how long they thought they would feel they were lodgers in the household, or whether at some point they thought they would actually join the family. Marie, the elder sister, replied that although she did not wish to give offence she did not really regard this family as her family. It was particularly difficult for these two teenage girls – who had grown up in another culture and had been developing a lot of autonomy in a small community – to move home and join a second family with very firm rules that had been developed around life in an alien urban culture. Many tensions had arisen as a result of mourning their mother and entering a family who were saying 'We've got to get together and be a close family and reorganise around our way of doing things.' Ffion added, 'I don't think I will ever feel really comfortable. If I was younger I probably would, I mean I can have fun with this family sometimes, but I feel like a real outsider.' Her older sister joined in, 'I often think how difficult it was for Francois and Florence (their step-siblings) to accept us in their family'. When I asked, 'Do you think they have been able to accept you?', the step-sister burst in, 'I feel really strongly about this whole thing: I don't think it is fair at all ... I just feel we are being completely rejected, and we're trying so hard.' Ffion replied, 'We didn't say you weren't trying', and in the face of her step-mother's mounting tears said, 'we didn't say anything against you'. At this point the father was able to join in. He said, 'I think Simone and I have different goals about what is good for the kids. I understand how she feels, because she has invested lots of time and energy into trying to make things OK for everybody ... I think she spends too much time trying to do the right thing. I think she tries to take care of too many of the details.'

When thinking about work with this family a therapist might ask her-or himself how the members of this family could together create a new family that honoured the different sorts of family they had been before. Useful questions might be 'What sort of family would you like to become; what is the nature of the family you want to move towards; where in the family do you think important conversations need to take place in order for the things that are going wrong to change?' I took two ways forward simultaneously: ascertaining how the girls' mourning for their mother would be taken into account in the larger family conversations; and following the father's idea that his wife was too central in sorting out the details of everything that went on between the different subsystems of the family. I set the two sisters and their stepsister the task of thinking of ways that Simone could be relieved of some of the household responsibilities. Ffion was put in charge of reporting back.

Three weeks later Simone reported that there had been a transformation in terms of the emotional alliances and daily patterns of behaviour in the family as the act of talking in different generational groupings had changed the affect within the family. It had allowed Ffion's competence to emerge. The question of not being disloyal to her dead mother was moved to a different space in which she and her sister came to talk about their mother. Representing her no longer had to be held in the idea of 'failing' in school; and the family responded by encouraging her success and returning her free time. In talking with Simone it was agreed that her role was not to replace the dead mother nor to be super-stepmum, but to find a more comfortable way of allowing the girls to remember their mother. The question of how in any step-family everyone is able to tolerate each other's different positions is ongoing, complex and often not resolved. In this family it was important for the daughters to get to know their father as well as for each family member to move towards recognising and accepting one another's very different positions in relation to the dead woman.

Stepfathers and fathers

Many years ago I was struck by a comment by Mavis Hetherington that however hard stepfathers try to be nice, stepdaughters just go on kicking them. Since then I have been highly sensitised to the dilemmas of stepfathers. Chapter 5 touched on the issues of men creating post-divorce parenting situations on their own while witnessing their children relating to another man in a step-family context. The Marley family created an unusual solution by welcoming the children's father, Frank, into their home for weekends so that he could continue to be in touch with the girls, who had left with their mother at the ages of four and six. For about five years Frank came down from Newcastle once a month and stayed with the family, being warmly welcomed by Jerome, the girls' stepfather, and Melissa, their mother. Frank was white Geordie, Jerome was black British African–Caribbean and Melissa was second-generation Lebanese British. Both girls resembled their mother. At around the time of puberty Sofia, the eldest daughter, revealed to her younger sister, Paula, that Frank had sexually abused her while she was visiting him on post-divorce access (as it then was) when her grandparents had been supposed to be looking after her. Frank had been through a period of severe alcohol and drug abuse and had often taken her to his room, where he had 'interfered with her'. News of this seeped back to the family, and although it was not openly discussed Frank's visits were stopped. Jerome said privately that he would kill him if he came near the girls, but was not 'allowed' to discuss the abuse with Sofia. He became intensely protective of her, watching over her every movement so that later in her adolescence she felt quite suffocated. Knowing of the love behind his watchfulness she left home to go to college without any major rows taking place. With Paula it was a different story. Unable to compete with her sister's brainpower Paula became progressively more sexual, provoking the same watchfulness in Jerome, but using it to fight him through every second of her adolescence.

The family came to therapy in order to try to sort out the fights, which had become serious enough for Jerome and Paula to consider (1) splitting up, (2) having Paula looked after by the state (although this was only a threat), (3) sending her to her grandparents in Wales or (4) having themselves removed to psychiatric hospital for a rest 'cos I'm very close to cracking up. Her mum's very close to cracking up ... but people don't realise that because we keep it all straight ... I could just go ... her mum could just go and just never be seen again.' Together we worked intensively for a year. There were whole-family interviews, interviews with Jerome and Melissa, interviews with Sofia on her own, interviews with Sofia and Paula together, and interviews with Paula on her own. The only aspect of this that threatened Jerome was the idea of the women in the family meeting to 'share' their life story:

GGB: I really do respect the way you think about family ... you teach me a lot, but I think one of the things that Paula and Sofia need is some time to put things together themselves, to talk about the history together ... [To Melissa] So many things that happened before you came to Jerome need putting together for the girls.

Jerome: Obviously they've got things that they've got to talk together, it's obvious ... but if you ask me whether I like it, well, I don't – I feel left out.

GGB: [to Paula] I think you've got the most unusual family in that you've got parents who both care very much and that's a blessing that at fifteen you may not realise, and they watch over you more than some parents may do ... Sometimes its very difficult to think how to find a way out of the family when you know how much they think about you ... so perhaps you cut yourself off.

Jerome: I think she tries to do bad things so that she hopes that we will say to her 'piss off'.

Melissa: I think Jerome is right because I've often thought that.

Jerome: And then it's 'Oh, you don't want to know me' ... we've talked about that cos after rows I used to try every different way, be quiet, be angry, be violent, be reasonable, and it didn't make any difference and then I thought, 'Oh well, Paula's just winding me up here', and then it gets to explosion point so you say, 'Go on, do your own thing, we're not bothered about you any more.'

Later we explored Melissa's terror that Paula would leave before she could manage and would not be 'allowed' back through the door. I ask the family, 'What channels can Melissa establish for being in touch with Paula when she goes?' Talking with Paula about her terror that she would lose touch with Melissa continued the thread of the disrupted lives she and her daughters had together earlier:

GGB: It's also to do with your particular history ... you've got two girls that you had in another place in another time and you've survived all these live transitions together. Now you're about to embark on another transition – your girls leaving home and [to Jerome and Melissa] it marks a passage for you two doesn't it, you do have life outside the girls to think about. [To Jerome] There's something here that's much more painful, which is whether you think its alright for Melissa to have her own relationship with Paula.

Jerome: I've never said different.

GGB: In as much as Paula is the child of her womb...this is something that the two of you have never been able to share and that is a very particular aspect of your relationship. We've talked about that and how it has a lot of sadness attached and I think the fact that Paula is not your daughter is also quite painful – it may be a relief but it's also quite painful at times.

Jerome: It's never a relief.

GGB: Never?

Jerome: No, and she is my daughter. I'm her father, it's got nothing to do...

GGB: [quietly, knowing it's something Paula feels strongly about] You are her stepfather, Jerome...

Jerome: Well, I may be her stepfather, but as far as I'm concerned a father or a dad is someone who's there when you're crying, when you're happy, who picks you up when you fall down, who takes you to school, who feeds you, who fights with you, who cuddles you, who talks to you, who doesn't talk to you, who's there. This other man who gave birth to her through sperm is nowhere near her father...the only influence he must have on her is a genetical influence.

GGB: [checks with Paula] do you know what he's talking about?

Paula: He's talking about what he's done and my father hasn't done, so he's trying to say that he is my father because he's done all those things.

Jerome: There will be things from Frank that affect you whether you know this or not...you will move certain ways, you will act certain things...the bits that he's handed down to you that you have inherited...that to me is private and separate to them...they can come and talk to me about that and ask me my opinion as an outsider...but I am her father, full stop.

GGB: However much you are her father, there is also another father there and I think that has been something that Paula has never quite made sense of. There is a lot more talking to be done about that. Also [to Paula] you feel quite angry with your father – your Frank father – because you think he messed your sister around...so the whole question of fathers is quite a complicated one in your family and I think you take a double load a lot of the time – you know, Jerome...

Jerome: I didn't know that till we talked about it before...I just thought it was personalities, mine and hers that wasn't getting on.

Melissa: I think it's happening too, I've thought about it a lot and I think that is right.

Step-family experience always needs to be understood in two other contexts than that of the family in the room. The first is all the previous transitions and the associated hazards to adult well-being and children's emotional development that the family have been through. The second is the extended family network and its patterns of relationship with the family over time and in the present. Communication in step-families, and the way the shifts and transitions have been discussed and explained, continues to be of importance to children who need to process information by repeating conversations over time, not through a single 'telling'.

The wider extended family may have been of crucial importance in supporting children and lone parents during transitional periods, and may therefore remain a presence for good or discomfort in the event of subsequent family formation. Such kinship networks may hold more importance for the children than caretaking adults realise. It is important to bear this wider network in mind when working with the child or family. Negative patterns in relationships during childhood do not necessarily go away when children grow up. Sometimes the same patterns continue into adult life and become part of adult experience, as when the two original parents continue to row. The effect of such patterns in all families who have experienced adversarial divorce may be an important component of inner disturbance in an individual presenting for psychological help. Young adults may experience relief in reviewing these childhood experiences in the light of their own maturity, or at the point where they experience relationship difficulties with a partner.

7

THE FAMILY AND MENTAL ILLNESS

Cultural and family factors affecting descriptions of illness

The story of the family in relation to mental illness, the part that family life is seen to have played, has had a convoluted course. It remains one that is highly culturally determined. While the full scope of psychiatric debate on the aetiology and onset of various forms of major mental illness are outside the scope of this chapter, an understanding of the social and political antecedents of modern-day formal psychiatry, and the researched evidence of the physical causes of illness – 'the virus, enzyme, hormone, toxic substance, gene, organic deficiency responsible for schizophrenia', for example – still contribute to oppositional contemporary debates (Asen, 1986, p. 32). Cooklin *et al.* (1997) have commented on the way in which British psychiatry developed within a belief system that takes as its core the individual and the illness, independent of the social context or culture in which this occurs. The impact of the illness on the family and of the family on the illness has only recently received formal attention at the level of health-care planning and policy. Cottrell (1989) demonstrated that the training of junior psychiatrists has led to little or no family history, and less cultural history, being taken from patients admitted to acute psychiatric wards other than that which emerges by default when 'taking a past history'. Both Cooklin and Byng-Hall, in their role as training psychiatrists in family therapy, have described the impact that requiring all admitting doctors to ask about the children that a patient may have at home has had on the practice of the psychiatrists they have trained. Bishop *et al.* (2002) recount children's dual experience of, on the one hand, being explicitly blamed by parents for their own mental illness, and on the other being ignored by mental health professionals when the parent is in crisis.

As discussed in Chapter 3, culture and ethnicity raise many questions about 'who may be the family to be enquired about'. Taking culture and ethnicity into account in the treatment of mental illness also raises many questions about what good mental health care may be. As Cooklin puts it, 'Is it a set of principles, practices and services which can be transported from one country or culture to another, or is it a culture determined set of ideas beliefs and practices in which people are helped, treated, diagnosed and the like, within the frameworks of that culture' (Cooklin *et al.*, 1997). Comparative work among different cultures on responses to schizophrenia demonstrate considerable differences in both family responses to illness and patient relapse rates (Leff *et al.*, 1987; Xiong *et al.*, 1994). Different studies in the UK show the highly negative impact of a dominant culture on a minority ethnic group, as evidenced by reports that in Britain, black African–Caribbean men are far more likely to be diagnosed as schizophrenic, admitted to hospital on a compulsory basis, placed in secure units and given large doses of medication, than white men who present with equivalent behavioural symptoms (Fernando, 1991; Collins, 1994; Littlewood and Lipsedge, 1988).

In the early history of family therapy some theorists of mental illness asserted that there was no such thing as mental illness (Laing and Esterson, 1964). In the 1960s the literature on family therapy training often described and discussed mental illness as an interpersonal phenomenon resulting from the confusional ties created by certain kinds of family living and the confusing and conflicting demands that can arise in some families (Bateson *et al.*, 1956). Since that time much research, while taking the phenomena associated with mental illness as having their own reality, has also identified particular aspects of family relationships as important factors in the onset and outcome of certain major mental illness. Two key areas have been those directing attention to positive factors in relationships: the protectiveness derived from intimacy in relationships in relation to the handling of stressful life events (Brown, 1991), and those scrutinising the negative effects of family attitudes in relation to some aspects of mental illness, in particular schizophrenia and depression. Relapse rates can be reduced to levels as low as 15 per cent by helping sufferer and family consider the mutual influence of each on the other (Leff *et al.*, 1994; Lam, 1991). Research is also prompting us to pay further attention to genetics, brain science and biological influences (Cody and Hind, 1999).

Many autobiographical accounts of mental illness offer powerful testimony to the alternative and cruel realities that can be created. For example Kay Jamison, Professor of Psychiatry at Johns Hopkins University, describes the two positions of illness debated within her family, where both she and her sister were periodically overcome by manic depressive cycles, as being the debate between illness as 'family related' and illness as an 'alien force with whom battle has to be done'.

> Not surprisingly perhaps when both she and I had to deal with our respective demons, my sister saw the darkness as being within and part of herself, the family and the world. I, instead, saw it as a stranger; however lodged within my mind and soul the darkness became, it always seemed an outside force that was at war with my natural self (Jamison, 1995, p. 15).

These two different positions of illness located within the self, or external to the self, has characterised the difference between therapeutic approaches to sufferers and their families: on the one hand focusing more explicitly on family interaction one in which members of the family are helped to collaborate around developing less intrusive, more effective problem-solving techniques, and on the other focusing on a narrative approach by externalizing the problem and mobilising alternative 'subjugated' stories in the sufferer to help defeat the problem (White and Epston, 1990).

This chapter describes some of ways in which family phenomena surrounding mental illness and its effect on both sufferers and their families are likely to be encountered in everyday practice by counsellors and therapists. The growth in community care has meant that a working knowledge of the effects of major mental illness needs to be part of a therapist's repertoire. Illnesses, or alternative views of reality encountered (if not always usefully 'labelled'), are likely to include:

1. anxiety neuroses, which include such features as fear, alarm and the feeling of imminent danger, sometimes including panic attacks and sometimes chronic anxiety states;
2. forms of imagined illness, or hypochondriasis and psychosomatic illness, in which emotional disturbance plays an important part in causing, aggravating or maintaining the physical symptoms;
3. phobias, including irrational fear of objects or situations and obsessional neuroses, repetitive thoughts or images that force

themselves onto the patient's mind even if he or she recognises them as nonsense at another level; and

4. depression, both at a minor level and at a level that can become disabling.

Professional approaches to family work with major mental illness

While psychotic disorders are more likely to be held within the domain of formal psychiatry, many clients may come with beliefs or thoughts that they do not regard as irrational or absurd, but which appear so to others who surround them. The psychotic person lives in a world that has its own logic and rules and may be inaccessible to others (see the story of Tess this chapter). This may include delusions or hallucinations. Of the four major categories of psychosis – schizophrenia, manic depressive psychosis, paranoid psychosis and organic psychosis – the first two are most likely to be encountered by family therapists either in the context of children with parents who are ill, or adult patients and their families. The effect of any of these conditions or states of mind on other family members who come for counselling or therapy may form an ongoing part of family work in all forms of practice. As drug treatment for psychotic conditions becomes more effective and hence the damping down of other aspects of personality is reduced, the need for family work has increased. The emphasis in family work will be less on the antecedent factors in the illness and more on the current stress factors between family and patient that are exacerbating or ameliorating the illness.

From long association with the phenomena surrounding mental illness, both in my personal and my professional life, I also find it useful to conceptualise what happens within people as relating to a unique sensitivity characterising the person who is suffering. This may filter their perceptions and their constructions of life events in ways which make them temporarily or chronically closed to receiving and assimilating the alternative perceptions and ideas of others (Scheflen, 1981). Thus the process of being mentally ill can be both painful and lonely. It involves not only the loss of the usual arrangement of family and friends who can be relied on during periods of being well, but also a loss of mind, a reliable sense of self. To quote Jamison again:

I was used to my mind being my best friend, of carrying on endless conversations within my head, of having a built in source of laughter, of analytic thought to rescue me from boring or painful surroundings. I counted upon my minds' acuity, interest and loyalty as a matter of course. Now all of a sudden my mind had turned on me: it mocked me for my vapid enthusiasms, it laughed at all of my foolish plans; it no longer found anything interesting or enjoyable or worthwhile. It was incapable of concentrated thought (Jamison, 1995, pp. 37–8).

Living with a parent who has temporarily 'lost their mind' is likely to be confusing and sometimes traumatic for children (cf: Wilson, 1999: 'The Illustrated Mum'). Children have described how they do not know how to read the signals for the turning point when they have to start caring for a parent, and can no longer rely on a parent looking after them. Bishop *et al.* (2002) have shown that the way a child construes the illness can have a significant effect on the child's psychological health. Place *et al.* (2002) have described the development of a resilience package for children which includes education about the parents' illness, sessions with the child and family focusing on dynamics in interactions, and looking at the interaction between illness and family behaviours, and skill development for the child's self-esteem, and social and problem-solving skills. Early results suggest that positive changes can be made in the children's lives, and new patterns of improved mental health for the children initiated.

Work focusing on patterns of communication

In the last decade, the work of Leff and his many colleagues in the development of understanding potential negative effects of family communication patterns on mental illness has been of particular value (Leff *et al.*, 1987; Xiong *et al.*, 1994; Leff *et al.*, 1994). Attention to the family's style of speaking and behaving, what is going on around the person who is ill, as well as psychotherapy that addresses what is going on in the person's mind are therefore both likely to play key parts in facilitating an ill person's return to recovery, just as medication may be essential in keeping them functioning. The Family Project team at the University College Hospital in London have developed some guidelines for working with families in the context of major mental illness, placing the accent on the positive development of problem-solving skills rather than on pathology, and helping the family to adapt to a pattern of life in ways which allow the expression of needs of all members, not only the patient's. Different solutions are tried out in family sessions in response to problems identified by the patient and family together. All solutions are aired, however absurd, and are rated by family members. This offers a non-critical 'playful' approach in which differences of opinion are addressed in a less emotional manner. In addition the use of multi-family groups addresses the social context in which patient and family experience the illness and its sequelae, particularly social isolation, stigma, self-blame, and mutual recriminations. These groups also help parents to develop skills in specific child-related issues, such as responding to a child's anger when a parent is ill; helping a parent assess when they can be called to account by a child for irrational, or inappropriate behaviour; helping children know what they can continue to count on in a parent when they are ill, and helping parents be explicit in exonerating a child of any responsibility for the illness (Cooklin and Gorell Barnes, 2002; Bishop *et al.*, 2002).

In my work with couples or families where a parent is the one who is 'ill', I try to gain an understanding of the family processes that are helping to maintain the ill person's position in both positive and the negative senses. These are likely to include processes that are intended to protect the person who suffers most, but may also act to keep that person a 'patient'. There are also likely to be processes in the family that mediate the differing realities created by the needs of the patient and the demands of the rest of the social world. Long-term mental illness, for example bipolar disorder, creates extreme patterns that over time both shape the development of the family and become incorporated into its ongoing life (Moltz, 1993). Patients remit more clearly, or alternatively frequently switch into depression following a manic period. Thompson *et al.* (2000) following extensive research have commented that it may not be as useful to ask relatives about the effect of the patient and the illness on the family, as to obtain an actual sample of their interactional behaviour in the session. The most difficult 'to help' families showed the most destructive forms of personal criticism. Effective treatment centred on practising or implementing communication skills and problem-solving training. In families with a manic depressive parent who is being highly critical themselves, any decision to confront them, and treat them as 'well enough' to behave as a parent may be hazardous for children from whom the parent demands services and attention, since, for example, a father, told to make the tea himself, may 'accidentally' pour boiling water over himself. A mother told to go away until homework is completed, may slash her wrist with her nail scissors and then appear dripping blood instead of showing off the outfit she was trying on. Such situations can be the regular experience of children whose parents live with bipolar disorder. When the parent then gets 'better', as they usually do, the patterns of responsibility, with all their delicate checks and balances, have to be subtly and sensitively re-attuned to take the altered state of 'wellness' into account. All this can be discussed, negotiated, and written down in the context of a family session, and a 'charter' drawn up around the rights of the patient, and the rights of the other family members. Adaptations required of the family in taking the implications of the diagnosis into account are also important. For example, in the recovery phase of schizophrenia it is important that the patient is not put under pressure to achieve more than he or she is comfortable with. Family members may need help in building 'positive privacy' for the patient as a substitute for 'negative isolation', and also in protecting them from excessive intimacy which can be experienced as over-stimulating and intrusive. On the other hand, a patient who has been depressed may crave greater intimacy, and see this as a crucial reinforcement of his or her worth. Other disorders, such as phobic states, or obsessive/compulsive disorders, may require a particular mix of respect for a patient's experience, coupled with an appropriate challenge to the reverence often imposed by the symptoms (Cooklin and Gorell Barnes, 2002).

Family descriptions and self-description

An important influence on the processes of illness and wellness is the language that people who are ill use to talk to themselves about their illness: the degree to which they see illness as an overall description of themselves, and the range of alternative descriptions of themselves and their own functioning that they have been able to keep open, both in the family and within their minds. When a person's self-description is characterised by low self-esteem, which is often the case with mental illness, it is particularly valuable in therapy to address other constructions of the person than those associated with the negative effects of the illness (White, 1986, 1987; White and Epston, 1990). A particular negative self-image is likely to have become 'fixed' and dominant, so that the descriptions of the person arising from this fixed image rule out other possible ways of seeing and describing the self. In families, because of their 'familiar' and habitual ways of relating, a limited descriptive frame may become a cage, so that other descriptions of the self cease to be available. As one young woman, Rosita, said of the experience of seeing her mother come home after ECT treatment, repeated many times over ten years, 'They would tell me it was my mother, and tell me to be glad she was home, but I knew and they knew it was just a mad person'. For this young woman, the image of 'mad person' had become the dominant image of 'mother', which ruled out other ways of seeing her and thinking about her.

When seeing adults whose images of parents have become fixed in rigidly negative ways, I may invite them to bring in photographs of the individual who is now ill in different relationship contexts within and outside the family. Several images then become available for description and discussion. This leads to clearer experience of anger with the *effects* of the illness, rather than with the person as a whole, and also assists the process of mourning the person who was once functioning well in different social contexts. This contributes to the freedom to relate to the parent in more than one way, both in daily life and in the mind. Where a parent is no longer accessible I may also encourage a young person to write letters to other family members to elicit new descriptions. Rosita, for example, wrote home to her father and her elder sister for photographs of her mother and received images of her when she was a young woman, when she was married, and while she was still an active mother. This led to a different series of conversations in her mind about her lively, intelligent mother whose questioning of the political regime in her country at the time was testimony to her active mind. In turn this fed back into her own image of herself as a person who could be more free to question and challenge. When negative images are held by the ill people themselves, such inner descriptions or ongoing monologues, constructed around a negative image, can be invited into conversation with other more positive views of the self displayed in other contexts, such as being a friend, a daughter or a mother: 'OK, so let's see what the depressed voice is saying about you today and then we'll find out how we can answer him/her'. If alternative descriptions are accepted in conversation with the therapist, they may be incorporated into the language and interactional habits of the individual and subsequently into the family pattern. I also extend the idea of developing a different 'voice' in other contexts in which a depressed person may feel disqualified. I encourage clients to think about what they would actually say the next time their father (or a senior male colleague) puts them down, how their mother would react to this new 'voice' (or how a senior female colleague who does not feel threatened by this male colleague would react). Introducing irreverence can be valuable. In rehearsing these small sequences, the goal is to harness positive ideas (or deviations), and see how the new potential can be amplified to move the client in the direction they want to go, in order to feel more effective the next time a similar situation is encountered.

White and Epston (1990), drawing on the ideas of Foucault, suggest that these positive descriptive processes can be central to the diminution of negative dominant voices (those by which the person feels themselves to be largely described and defined). By reintroducing marginalised voices (other possibilities for definitions of the self) new repertoires of thinking and feeling about the self can be made available. In my experience the very process of 'playing' with these ideas of alternative descriptions and other ways of thinking about reality begins to create a less rigid and more hopeful framework for client and therapist.

Family relationships and different illness processes

Four areas of influence that connect family relationships to illness processes and are important to address in relation to images of self are:

1. the person who is ill and their partner if they have one;
2. the person who is ill, their family of origin, and their extended family;
3. the person who is ill, their child and any significant caretaking others; and
4. the external realities outside the family that may be having influential effects.

The way in which ideas about the illness from any one of these areas is reinforced, balanced or disqualified by ideas from another can make a significant difference to the available pathways to recovery.

Liz and Jim, a depressed person and their partner

Liz was suffering from a severe and immobilising depressive condition in which her only activity was incessant tidying of the house. Her current immobility in the face of her husband Jim's criticism of her housekeeping was amplified in her mind by earlier 'annihilating' scolding from her mother, whose high standards had been developed in the context of a household of seven children in a small, fiercely well-organised Catholic home in Northern Ireland. In this context, as Liz said, 'All Catholics were at risk minorities' and, in her mother's eyes, 'had to be seen to be right'. Any infringement of standards was an infringement on behalf of the community and the church and might be seen as 'letting things go' or 'losing face'. Her current achievements as a working woman were undermined by her draughtsman husband who, in his accounts of her competence, subjugated her skill as a dressmaker to her incompetence at home, constantly criticising her lack of attention to detail in household cleanliness while also expressing his concern for her apparent fragility. In situations where one member of a couple is severely depressed I find hypothesising useful, as it helps me generate curiosity in a context where energy and curiosity are likely to be low. Hypotheses about Liz and Jim and the role of depression in their lives which led to useful exploration included:

- depression as a communication to her partner that she needed to be more actively involved in the life outside the house
- depression as a gendered discourse of 'loyalty' to her mother
- depression as a way of maintaining competence in her husband

Talking with a woman therapist who could value her achievements, as well as taking a broader gendered deconstruction of the way she was continuing to lead her life as a 'minority voice', led Liz to a different view of herself as a woman who had a right to speak and be heard. This involved deconstructing a gendered family discourse (her mother's views about a woman's role), a political discourse (the position of women in her community in Northern Ireland) and a religious discourse (a good woman is a woman who stays at home and has babies), all of which were playing a part in keeping her disempowered. Gaining a temporary empowerment in which she tried out her new and stronger voice, she told her husband of her hatred of her own symptomatic behaviour:

Liz: I'm sick of being the wife, the mother – of always being the caring, responsible person, which of course I am but I'm sick of only being that... [shouting] I'm sick of it!

Jim: [Surprised at her passion] Well, that's absolute nonsense... when I'm busy trying to fix things so we can have a nice home; do things together without, say, you having to go out to work, so you are not so stressed all the time.

GGB: Can I put it another way? What alternate views of your life have you put to Jim – not 'What I don't want', but 'What I do want'.

Liz: Well it's very difficult to talk because Jim does not like to talk, and if he does it's in the very very short term like 'next week let's be doing this'.

GGB: But if we just talk now, just for three minutes, what kinds of ideas did you have about what you might like to do?

Where a situation has become frozen, questions which invite a hypothetical conversation, to proceed 'as if' a change might be possible can be specially useful. Feed forward questions (Penn, 1985), invite the couple to consider change, or the lack of it, at future points in their lives. This can also be used to highlight the absurdities in the current situation. In this extract the shift from impassioned outburst to developing some new constructions of coupledom while the emotions were high on both sides, created the beginning of a new trajectory in which Jim's increasing anxiety that his wife might break down altogether if she were to do anything extra outside the home could be seen as 'fitting' the concern she had taken on from her own mother about the political and social disaster inherent in 'letting things go'.

The pathway into depression can be constructed along interactional lines in which the effect of one thing amplifying another can be seen. There is often a precipitating stressful life event (the death of one of Liz's close women friends in an accident) that requires a new adaptation – internal as well as interpersonal factors and patterns of behaviour have to change. Liz could no longer rely on her friend for social and childcare support; and particularly missed the voice of another woman. Lack of adaptation may be connected with falling back onto old patterns that are no longer a resource, keeping the house tidier in order to ward off feared disaster. In this case the idea of her husband doing more with the children was dismissed as not being man's work, leaving Liz feeling more alienated and resentful and without the solace of her best friend. Jones and Asen (2000, op. cit.) have written a comprehensive and humane account of working with clinical depression, offering a variety of ideas and interventions.

A gendered deconstruction that takes apart the traditional roles still allotted to men and women in the new millennium, independent of class or ethnicity, remains a central feature of the work I do in relation to many of the different depressions, over-controlled behaviours or obsessive states that women may present themselves with. Lack of recognition for what a woman has achieved remains core to many marital and family relationships that still values male success as a measurement of happiness in family life.

Working with the person who is ill, their family of origin and the extended family

The way in which illness behaviour can be seen as functionally related to or 'fitting' the wider organisation of relationships in a family emerged during two years of working with the Struther family. Following her grandmother's death, Tess, then a thirty-two-year-old mother of two, had felt as though she had been left alone to take care of others in a way that replicated earlier events in her childhood. Her grandmother had acted as a key support to Tess when her own mother had become severely incapacitated by brain damage inflicted in a car accident. Tess, as the elder sister, had been instrumental in bringing up her three brothers and sisters while helping her parents maintain the illusion that mother was still in charge. Following the loss of her grandmother she became acutely depressed, started drinking heavily and was admitted to several psychiatric hospitals, on each occasion discharging herself and refusing to take medication. After her third discharge she and her husband came to see my partner Alan Cooklin and myself. Their first child, Dot, was present at the meetings for most of the first two years of her life. For a long time in Tess's inner discourse, it appeared that she could only listen to a single negative voice telling her of her inadequacies and incompetence; and when other voices – her husband's, the therapist's – told her of her good qualities and strengths in caring for her child, they met a kind of rubber fence from which they bounced back. Therapist persistence in asking continuously about the possibility that other voices in her head might have a right to be heard eventually met with indications that minimal changes were taking place. Tess and I delved into aspects of her negative imaging of herself, taking them into the wider social domain, 'woman in role as housekeeper', in which we could both participate in a subversive female discourse in which another aspect of her ongoing resilience and competence could be recognised and constructed as an alternative voice to her 'illness' discourse with herself. Her positive healthy parenting capacity could be seen in the way that Dot continued to thrive; the house was kept at a reasonable standard, and Tess herself remained outside the hospital.

As time went on, and in the context of great perseverance by her husband and by the therapists, she began to enjoy aspects of the therapeutic conversations, in which much teasing and humour would go on, introducing a number of other frames through which her dilemmas might be considered. However, her continued obsessive preoccupation with 'the four walls' that she described as trapping her, suggested to us that the choices she saw herself as having would need to be contextualised in a wider family arena if she was to believe that her position could ever change. We invited the couple to call together both sets of grandparents and all the siblings. This took several weeks of preparatory phone calls. The reason given to the extended family for the therapeutic 'clan' gathering was that this was a family consultation aimed at exploring together the way in which people carry into marriage the traditions, cultures and influences of the families from which they come, and the way in which these cultures may form part of the difficulties any couple are having. This construction was particularly well received by Tess's father, who had himself lived through the adaptations made by the family after his wife's injury. Throughout the meeting his behaviour was highly eccentric and self-referential, as he continued an uninterrupted stream of talk that at first seemed unrelated to the current family discussion. However, he also interjected messages that suggested he had a better understanding of his daughter's dilemma than anyone else. He stated that he and his wife also had problems, and that while the focus might be on the young couple today, it might more appropriately be on the senior generation tomorrow. He commented on how 'Tess has had to evolve by herself over the last twenty five years since her mother's accident'. He described how he saw himself and his wife as actors, playing the part of normality, with himself acting as his wife's memory (the young adults confirmed that her memory was lost).

During the course of the conversation, Tess revealed that she thought she would never make the transition from being a Gurley, her family of origin, which she visited each weekend, to being a Struther, the family name of her husband. This came to be used as a metaphor for the two different worlds of experience she was contending with: the world of her brain-damaged mother and illogical, eccentric father, and the world of healthy child development that she saw herself as having lost following the loss of an actively participating 'mother' in her own childhood. This world was now represented by her husband's family, as her husband's sisters had many small bright, neat children, and Tess did not always feel that her own child was welcome in that world. To join the 'normal' world was experienced by her as a potential betrayal of the realities of the world of her childhood as well as the current world of her family of origin, as constructed by her father on behalf of both her parents. Confronted by the power of her father's rambling and random stream of interruptions, her husband challenged her more directly with the dilemma. 'Your father's world is more real to you than my world'. She denied this, but went on to show how compelling the reality of the world of her family of origin was for her. 'Every weekend when I visit, I feel I am going back into a Gurley world. I have this hammering in my head to become a Gurley again'. Her husband engaged her in an intense conversation about his family's readiness to have her 'enter' their family, although he had not yet picked up on the connotations of disloyalty outlined above. In the middle of this, and seated on her other side, her father began to talk at the same time in a compelling, low-key voice. Gradually her head turned as her attention was drawn back to her father, who was saying without any logical sequence, 'I don't worship any family. Tess and Peter have got to find their own way somehow. They got married in the Scilly Isles. Where do you want to be on Friday, Saturday and Sunday?'

At the point when her head turned, both therapists, her husband and her father engaged in a lively and direct critique of the brief and intensely packed sequence that had just taken place. The taboo against discussing the interconnection of Tess's behaviour with that of her father, the Gurley world, and the pain of transition from her father's domain of logic (in which as the keeper of his wife's memory he held the power of two parents) to that of a more everyday reality, was vigorously debated. Her father, accepting both his power and the necessity of its overthrow, cheerfully said, 'I'm older you see... some weeks I accomplish nothing, other weeks I write to Washington, I write to Moscow.' His inability to achieve much in the 'everyday' world and Tess's competence in surviving in it were highlighted in the relevant context of the wider family.

Many constructions could be made from this densely packed text, but those that overtly showed themselves as freeing Tess began with the open highlighting of the power of her father's voice in a context where other voices – her husband's and her own, the next generation – could be heard in a new way by the whole family. This allowed the beginning of the development of new constructions of how she herself could be a parent; differences both of generation and of gender. These could develop because her husband, far from 'holding' her memory during her 'mad' episodes, as her father had done for her mother, had always taken the position that the speeches she made during these periods had meaning, although their meaning was not yet revealed. Once Tess ceased to be afraid of her voices she was able to play with them in a different way, until she could decide which were the appropriate ones for the context she was in. We continued to see Tess and her husband for a further two years, but with less and less frequency. Their family grew in size and both of them grew in confidence as they developed their own ways of being parents. Tess had no further episodes of illness.

In working with the extended family in this way the goal was to help Tess and her husband to view the ill behaviour in a broader context; to see new constructions of meaning for her symptomatic behaviour and the utterances emerging from the larger grouping of the family. Current patterns may be linked to patterns from a former generation, and in identifying such connections a new understanding of how this is contributing to paralysis in current situations can emerge. In considering the progress of work with this family, the tenacity of the therapists and their affection for the couple both contributed significantly to subsequent change. The main pointers to defining new meanings that validated Tess and her husband as a parental couple included:

1. challenging them to accept the control of their own definitions of good and bad parenting;
2. encouraging them to view Tess's repetitive utterances and complaints as having potential relevance to their own family life, even though neither had achieved a new definition of how a family should be; and
3. challenging the absolute definitions of 'truth' expounded by Tess's sensible in-laws, while connecting to and redefining the apparently 'crazy' world of her own family of origin.

Parents who are ill and their children

The pattern of finely tuned anticipation and responses within a family has to be scanned as widely and sensitively as possibly by a family therapist in a therapeutic interview with young children who have a parent who has been or is currently more ill than well. Murray's work with mothers and their infants (Murray and Cooper, 1997) shows powerfully how even a relatively short depressive episode can affect the fine tuning between mother and child. Murray's work extends Stern's earlier work on the 'dance' between mothers' expectations and stimulus of their babies in everyday life and the children's difference in responding to their mothers (Stern, 1977, 1985). Murray shows how a child who does not get a response because its mother is depressed can in turn become lacking in expectation or disturbed by the lack of interest on the part of the mother. If the fine tuning upon which communication in families is progressively based starts from the earliest days of an infant's life, then we could hypothesise that any discordant notes are amplified by inappropriate parental responses to the child that develop in the course of the parent being mentally ill. The child will learn to manage many of these, but at certain moments the discordance may be too great to manage and her or his sense of inner coherence will be thrown into disarray (Downey and Coyne, 1990; Schuff and Asen, 1996).

Parents and children often have very different views of the point at which a parent moves from 'behaving well' to 'behaving ill'. It is important to listen to children's own accounts of these periods in family life, and help them define what resources can be called in. It may also be important to ensure that parents explicitly absolve their children from any guilt in relation to 'causing' the illness at a time when they are well. The alternative 'reality' created by some mental illness is that others are to blame; and children often are the 'others' most actively present during periods of illness. Creating joint systems for managing the onset of florid illness with parent and child together provides reference points in the relationship that can be used in subsequent conversations. 'How do you know, Kevin, when Mum is having one of her stress periods (Mum's word)? If I were there what would I see that was different to Mum now?'. Kevin embarks on a tentative, but lively description of changes in Mum's behaviour that build up over days. Mum (Alice) says 'No, I don't, do I, really?'. Kevin says 'Yes, you do; don't you remember when you swept all the plates off the shelf?' Alice says 'it was only two plates'. Kevin (in his story now) describes her face 'staring' and how she comes up very close to shout at him. Alice says 'But you know I don't mean to scare you, don't you?' Kevin says 'Well, I know it now 'cos we're here in this room talking to Gill here, but I don't know it then.' We go on to work on how he and Alice can 'remember' next time that she does not mean to scare him, and plan what they can do instead.

Children of parents who have manic episodes remember this as a vivid, painful and sometimes unmanageable aspect of their own experience. The girl whose mother roams the house all night, putting on bizarre make-up and waking her up for company whenever she manages to go to sleep, or the boy whose father invents and reinvents the machine that will save the world, are coping with experiences that may later need to be unpicked with a calmer adult who can help them process the emotions that have been stirred up. When such a person is not available, as is often the case, it may be a counsellor, or therapist who needs to listen carefully to the details of these narratives – both at the time it is happening if the child comes the way of a professional, or, as is more likely, when the child becomes an adult and, in a therapeutic context, raises these earlier experiences as part of the stress he or she is *currently* experiencing at moments of high arousal. Such events may also be troubling when some aspect of their own current security is removed, for example, by breaking up with a girlfriend or boyfriend, or losing a valued job. The emotions being experienced in the current anxiety-arousing situations may need to be located more precisely to these earlier bizarre behaviours to make sense of the levels of insecurity experienced at the disappearance of a relationship trusted as reliable.

Mental illness and external realities: social factors

For many people mental illness is associated with adverse social factors such as poverty, job insecurity or unemployment, and being on state benefit, together with the family hazards of marital precariousness and marital discord. These social disadvantages create their own weight. When surveying the research on factors that amplify the adverse effects of mental illness, it is difficult to tease out which factors relate to social disadvantage and which to mental illness (Brown, 1991; Jones and Asen, 2000; Patel and Fatimilehin, 1999). We also lack detailed information on how different family structures within different cultures moderate mental illness for children. Whereas Eurocentric studies show the importance of the presence of a second parent in the home and an understanding of the relationship episodes that maintain the child's own positive concept of self, these are not specifically related to different key relationships in different cultural family groupings. In many families, for example, the relationship with a grandmother could make a crucial difference, but this is rarely reported on. We know that the chance to talk to a reliable adult outside the home, contact with peer groups through school or sport, and a reliable and continuing social life that includes the opportunity to maintain a world away from the home milieu are all described by children as important, but therapists need a better understanding through enquiring of each family who else can be called in within different kinship networks.

As I see an increasing number of families for whom migration has been a major transition in their lives, I now pay much more detailed attention to how the migration story is told. For example, Naomi, an African–Caribbean woman, saw her recurrent depression as linked to early feelings of 'aloneness' in England. She had been sent to

England by her aunt to join her mother two years after her aunt had married a 'very angry man': 'she sent me away so that I should not be affected'. She found her mother unloving, in the sense that although her mother cared for her, she was unable to cuddle her; and she found her school unkind. Naomi worked extremely hard and became a successful administrator in the civil service. Her current fear was of retirement from the relatively 'safe haven' of employment, where she had made a life for herself. When she was 'down', her fear was of death, or of not feeling that it was worth being alive. She was frightened of pain, of any money problems, and of being a burden to her children in her old age. Her husband had protected her by 'putting her in a glass cage', but this had broken up after his death. She feared therapy, because a hospital psychiatrist had told her it might lead to her having a 'breakdown'. I suggested that there might be a 'number of conversations' that were not 'therapy' that we could have together. I commented on the number of transitions she had had in her childhood and that the transition of retirement might be resurrecting some of the anxieties she had experienced earlier in her life. Perhaps we could explore some of these as they came up in her daily life; or at least feel free to talk about them, as she felt she had to hide them from her family 'because they are bored of them'.

Over the next year, we had meetings with two of her five daughters and her sister, and she managed to construct some more positive images of herself and how other people regarded her as still having a purpose in their lives. Nonetheless a missing part of herself remained unlocated until a chance opportunity arose for her to return to the island she had left when she was twelve years old. We planned some of the conversations she might have with people there who had been part of her childhood. The outcome of this journey was moving, powerful and surprising to both of us, since she got in touch with a much more joyful image of her childhood than she had previously carried around as part of her own story. More than the 'story' however, was the medium: a whole way of living out in the street, in interaction with many of those who had formed part of her childhood community. This experience of being with others who were also part of herself, rather than feeling she was in a fragile 'glass cage' looking out at others, freed her to approach her relationships in this country with more zest. A long-standing study group who have recently begun to publish and teach on the results of their research have given significant meaning to the experiences of loss and reunion for Caribbean people (Arnold and Adams, 2000).

Children of chronically ill parents: protective factors and 'being alright'

When considering the impact that ongoing parental illness has on children, it is useful for the therapist to consider the social and emotional factors that buffer children against stressful experiences in other contexts (Beardslee *et al.*, 1998). Where the family acts as the context of care for the ill person and simultaneously as a child-rearing milieu, factors that mitigate the negative effects of illness on the developing child are important. More severe illness, as distinct from mild episodes of illness, may involve acute or erratic and unpredictable behaviours of moderate to high intensity as well as indefinite duration. Random interaction that may at times include violence or inappropriately abusive behaviour towards children, require a child to be clear about who else they can go to make sense of the process. This may need spelling out with the child(ren) and their mother when she is well, and at that point the child will likely need to be given explicit permission to be in contact with others, rather than this being later construed as 'disloyalty', or 'betrayal'. An effect of the illness can be that a child is not perceived as a child, a developmentally dependant being in the process of growth and change, but is construed as an 'object' that is hostile to the ill person. Illness in a mother may be of particular difficulty for a child if the father is not prepared to act as an alternative intimate and safe base, or if there is no other adult in the household to take this role, which is often the case. Practical arrangements, such as lists of telephone numbers on the wall, or built into the mobile telephone memory system, can be very reassuring to younger children.

For Renata, born in Colombia, looking after her mother was second nature, since her father had decided that the only way he could both endure her mother's long, complicated and deteriorating depressive and psychotic illness, and ensure she had regular care, was to take long business trips abroad and leave his wife with Renata, the housekeeper and a nurse. Although he visited daily between trips, it was Renata who organised the housekeeping, helped the carers to plan her mother's day, and provided continuous companionship after school and at weekends. Every moment of her life for the ten years between eight and eighteen she had to think about her mother's needs before she made any plans for herself. She also had to manage an inner negotiation of loving and respecting her mother with an intense despising of her. Her inner voice told her 'I'm the real mother round here'. This secret scorn, which often appears as an inner voice in children who have to look after their parents, developed in Renata a capacity for seeing relationships in polarised ways, in which although she was overtly in the social and family world, the compliant one, she secretly believed that she was always in total control of all relationships. In her teens she entered a sexual relationship with a man who both dominated her and depended on her utterly. Taking control of her relationship with him, with her mother and, in her mind, of all the other intimate family relationships of which she was a part, she reached a state where having imaginary control of everything meant she could complete nothing. She entered a state of helplessness and panic from which, in weekly work, she slowly began to reconstruct a version of herself in which her inner voices could become more congruent with her outer life. The only sign she gave of needing me or anyone for the first year that I saw her (with and without her father) was to say 'I have never had anyone who could tell me that it would be alright'.

What, then, helps a child like Renata to 'be alright' in spite of so much appearing to be 'all wrong'? I have already mentioned the presence of a second parent, but many children live within lone-parent headed households. For 'parent' we should also learn to read all the other types of reliable intimate adult others that families can include: in her case cousins, but for others grandmothers, aunts, older sisters, grandfathers, uncles and older brothers. She also had long-term friends. As a young adult her work environment was constant, and her therapist/friendly 'other' was continuous over the years, even though later meetings often did not take place for several weeks. As long ago as 1966, Rutter indicated the importance of interactions and discussions with a reliable adult outside the home for children. Therapeutic interviews may therefore include friends as well as family, where such a person is seen as offering an intimate protective relationship.

It is important to emphasise that while a child may cope resiliently with a parent who remains ill over a long period, the experience of caring has its own limitations and constraints. This is also the case for adult carers, but children, being both dependent and in development, will need to have other opportunities provided for them to get on with their lives outside the limitations of the illness context – 'go out to play'. Place *et al.* (2002) have developed groups in centres outside the family home to facilitate such developments, and make specific links between children, community groups, and support groups. Mental illness can be accompanied by a self-focused preoccupation in which patients can only think of themselves and their needs. Where there are several children in a family whose needs are in competition, their lives may be disrupted in ways that can become both predictable and dreaded by them.

In the Gordon family for example, the father's manic–depressive illness had been accompanied by loss of business, loss of income and a severe and persistent disqualification of both the mother and the children as females for 'sucking him dry'. When ill he would sometimes refuse his medication, sleep all day and stay up all night, often going into their bedrooms to complain of not being entertained and demanding that they sit up and watch television with him. He would often resort to violent bad temper in order to have his way, and although he did not damage either child, Susannah, the eldest daughter who loved him dearly, found it hard to tell her mother how furious her father's behaviour made her. Work with the family involved the use of gender-specific genograms, 'men's stories' and 'women's stories', which helped the women to develop a very positive story about the women in their immediate family, as well as drawing on strong traditions handed down from the mother's family of origin. Paul, the father, was encouraged to begin to put some of his strong views about women into a storyline, as this related to his family of origin. This led to him getting back into contact with his family and discovering some very positive things about the traditions of men and women, which enlarged his repertoire of ideas about women to include a recognition of care-giving, nurturance and independence and led to a diminution of both his unreasonable expectations and his violent behaviour towards the women in his current family.

Dementia in the elderly

Dementia in the elderly has been brilliantly documented by Margaret Forster in her book *Have the Men had Enough?* (1990). The pain of watching a loved one deteriorate is experienced by all members of the family in different ways, but it is felt most acutely and sometimes unbearably by the spouse or partner, who may well be the one that the ill person most often turns against. It is carers who most need the support and understanding of professionals during the months and years of dementia, and in order to keep going they may need to have the best constructions of the ailing partner recreated for them as part of the everyday conversations they have with others. Boss *et al.* (1988), in their study of families managing dementia, note how painful it is for all members of the family to see the person they have known and loved being replaced by a person they do not know, who does not know them, and who is often hard to like. Family members, and particularly the spouse – the carer – may find comfort in a light-hearted notebook or account, kept by someone who has ongoing contact with the person with dementia, in which anecdotes of what is still gentle or humorous in that person are captured – since it is these features that can be lost by the carer in the battle to keep daily life going.

Since the caring person may be elderly too, his or her grasp of reality may be deeply shaken by the delusions of the partner, and he/she may need regular discussion of these. Such delusions can be persistent and complex, involving the carer in attributed behaviour such as stealing money or sexual license behind the ill person's back. Conversely, on the sufferer's better days his or her stories about other people can contain heroic features that surprise the relatives to whom these acts are attributed. The degree to which family members join in the delusions must be judged by them as in the best interests of the patient; but this should never involve collusion to take sides against the patient's carer. During such times old unhappy marital or family quarrels are likely to be resurrected in new forms, so that it is hard for carers not to try to justify themselves by answering back or becoming combative.

Too little is known by most of us about how to work with the acute anxieties of elderly people with dementia, but it is probably safe to assume that the anxieties reflect in greatly amplified form earlier anxieties from different parts of the patients' lives. They may need reassurance that these are now in the past rather than debate about their current 'truth'. They may well be concerned about past sexual or other behaviour of which their spouse (carer) is unaware, and it is certainly unhelpful to bring such things to the carer's attention for verification if they are told to another family member in confidence.

It is also important to mention here the deeply intimate relationship, often based on fantasy or illusion, that may spring up between patient and professional carers such as nursing staff or helpers in the home. If not contextualised by the illness, and understood by all concerned within that framework, this can cause great distress and resentment to marital partners and even to adult children, who see their parent behaving in strangely inappropriate ways.

8

VIOLENCE IN FAMILY LIFE

Work with families where violence has been a regular component of the ongoing pattern and 'balance' of family life – part of the family 'modality' of being together – throws open questions about the degree to which the privacy of family boundaries and the maintenance of inequality and power within them should be respected by others outside the family. The Children Act 1991, by replacing 'parental rights' with 'parental responsibility', put the conduct of family life in relation to children within a legal framework and under broader public scrutiny than ever before. However, scrutiny does not in itself afford protection to vulnerable family members, and ways of effectively and lastingly changing violent patterns remain some of the most problematic concerns for a family or a therapist to face. We know relatively little about how to stop violence between men and women and between adults and children, and the alternative care systems offered by the state have themselves proved open to similar forms of abusive behaviour. The degree to which violence in childhood may carry forward into violent adult experience, and what a family therapist can do to mitigate such experience, needs to be continually debated and tested. Browne and Herbert (1997) reviewed the direct and indirect effects on children of witnessing their fathers assault their mothers. They concluded that children may become less sensitive to violent behaviour and also learn aggressive styles of conduct (Sroufe and Fleeson, 1988). They also show increased arousal to aggressive situations and have pessimistic views about conflict resolution. Other work (Cummings and Davies, 2002) has shown how children discriminate between different forms of marital violence, and find threats to leave the marriage, or experience of fear during marital conflicts as particularly distressing. In their work with men in prison and their partners Vetere and Cooper (2001) emphasise the importance of routinely asking both couples and children about violence in the family, commenting that therapists often avoid this issue. They focus on a dysjunction between explanation (which is often presented as an excuse) and the necessity of acknowledging responsibility for violent behaviour on the part of the perpetrators. Failure to do this is a contraindication for success for rehabilitation (Goldner *et al.*, 1990). At the outset of their work they take the position that violence is a criminal offence, and negotiate confidentiality on a continuous basis telling clients that if they judge there is a risk of harm, they will, following discussion, inform the appropriate statutory and legal authorities.

In this chapter we will look in detail at three different examples of work with families where violence has included children and adolescents, offering examples of how it was possible to make a difference to the violent patterns at the time of working. For me, how violence is constructed at different levels of our society and how these levels influence one another are always important questions to discuss with the family. Different families see violence represented in different ways: some see it in the street, some in the economic market place, some in the ways government policy affects families, and some in relation to wars, for example between England and Ireland or India and Pakistan, Israel and Palestine, as well other parts of the globe. The relationship of the UK to these external wars (for example, the ongoing sale of arms) is also crucial to many families. The ways in which small but unbearably intense episodes of violence in intimate life between couples and within families can contribute to larger violent episodes, and the way in which larger ones act as isomorphic representations of what goes on inside each one of us, continue as a series of questions. Opening up violence as an issue at a number of levels of context offers different positions from which to examine and discuss phenomena associated with violence. For example, violence can be presented by families as having historical origins, carried by families over generations and therefore justifying its existence in the present – 'it's the way we are in the Barnet family', or 'children have always been beaten in the Taylor family' – or less explicitly as simply part of what has always happened and will therefore always continue to happen in relationships between men and women: 'We Greeks treat our women like that.' As I became more confident about what I could tolerate and challenge as a psychotherapist and a family therapist, I became more curious about what I could do to (1) change the interactional experience of violence while it was still occurring, or (2) change it before it became a formalised part of the mental representations of relationships of the children in families

I was working with, and (3) help people recover from the trauma of violence.

The 'carry forward' of patterns

What contributes to the carrying forward of patterns of violence, and the replication of aspects of these patterns within new structures of family living? Replications can occur either in the same generation – for example when families split up and form new families, and then individuals find they are responding to the new relationships in similar ways to the ones from which they had freed themselves – or in subsequent generations. When violence recurs in a family, a professional can enquire of themselves and of the family: (1) what other behaviours or aspects of relationship can be brought in to act as protective factors for children in buffering them against the effects of what is going on, and (2) what may allow them to develop sufficient flexibility in their own ways of responding to violent behaviour so that they are not trapped by it and are able to respond in alternative ways in a new context? A number of research studies have looked at violent patterns in relation to women and children carried across several generations and considered the ways in which young children experience and acquire positive and negative adult interactions. These studies use the concept of 'internal working models' (discussed in Chapter 4). Such models are defined as 'affectively laden mental representations of the self, other and of the relationship derived from interactional experience'. In relation to violence, held in the mind as an aspect of a 'working model of relationship' the children studied were seen to learn complex patterns and carry them forward into other contexts in their lives, where they could be seen repeating aspects of violent behaviour towards them or violence they had seen taking place between their parents. In other words they were able to play the role of both abused and abuser. Emde (1988), when discussing the relevance of research to clinical intervention, addressed the question of individual meaning and the way in which experience that is lived through or witnessed becomes transformed into represented relationships in children's minds. How do repeated interactions influence the formation of represented relationships, including ways of looking at the world, thoughts and feelings about it and social value systems? In addition, how do patterns begun in families connect in the child's everyday experience with other social systems with which the family interacts? Do these other systems offer the opportunity for more flexible development and a variety of options, or do they reinforce negative lessons already learnt in the family? At what point does a child's way of viewing the world become relatively inflexible and self-perpetuating? At what point, for example, might we say that violent interactions that have carried on over time impact on a child in such a way that it becomes an intractable part of his or her way of construing and responding to the world because he or she has been offered no other experience. Cummings and Davies (2002) in a review of the effects of marital conflict on children's adjustment have shown that children's distress is diminished as a function of whether conflicts are resolved, and the degree of resolution. Children benefit, as in many other family contexts discussed in this book, from good explanations. As they are affected by both the emotional and informational content of what they hear, explanations need to meet their anxieties. An important finding from this series of studies was that children do better where conflict is resolved behind closed doors, that is, where they are not caught in the middle.

In my experience violence in families is often accompanied by a degree of social isolation which has a number of self-reinforcing effects. Children and adults often do not have third parties they can discuss things with, and women and children often get together in a context of fear which they are reluctant to disclose to others. This makes it important to consider the family networks of which children and families are a part, for as Gelles (1987) observed, families where violence takes place are often characterised by a lack of participation in wider social relationships that could offer children alternative ways of relating and problem-solving.

The Wade family

The Wade family were a 'close' family, running a business from home. They were referred by their General Practitioner for a number of different, but related, family tensions that were reflected in constant rows and violent episodes between husband and wife and father and son. Both father and mother drank heavily. The pattern was usually one in which the father, Terry, would verbally attack the mother, Sheila, whereupon their son Dean would defend his mother, and father would then attack son either verbally or physically. Daughter Emmy was the peacemaker and generally sided with her father. An alternative pattern was that the father would attack the son, the mother would defend the son and then the father would attack the mother. Terry expressed the view that his wife, Sheila, and son,

Dean, were locked in a *folie à deux* that was preventing him from looking after his own wife Sheila, and that he could only handle his anger by 'drinking himself into forgetfulness'. Sheila expressed the view that Terry's unfulfilled wishes for himself were being verbally attacked in his son, and that he wouldn't recognise Dean's good qualities. The Wade family were characterised by many of the features that have been identified in relation to violent families. Firstly, the presentation of right and wrong in the family was dominated by patriarchal views voiced by Terry. Such male 'voicing' had also been a feature of Sheila's childhood, so she felt doubly disadvantaged in the attempt to oppose him openly. Although Terry would never have agreed that he saw women and children as legitimate objects for attack, this pattern was dominating family life at the time when we all first met. Secondly, the amount of time the family members spent with each other was considerable. Their normal family closeness had been intensified after Sheila had had a car accident. She became even more confined to the house, and concomitantly more central to the family business. Thirdly, the degree of engagement and intensity with the family interactions was higher than those outside the family.

Families where violence occurs exhibit a disproportionate amount of negative behaviour towards one another in the face of what may be relatively small differences. Many interactions are inherently conflict structured, with winners or losers. This experience will be re-enacted with professionals. There may be an insufficient range of social skills to manage differences of opinion. If coercion has been used to resolve conflicts, children are unlikely to develop their own voice in initial professional interviews, and space, as well as safety, will have to be made for them to speak. Therapists will have to have a clear idea of when it is safe for a child to do so, and invite the children to work with the adults in the session to let them know how they and the children can be sure that this is the case. Much of the initial work therefore involves agreeing definitions of safety with the mother, father and children and exploring the likely effect of the therapist asking open and specific questions about violent behaviour or episodes.

In the Wade family, Terry would scrutinise everything his adolescent children did and comment on the manner in which they did it. They each reacted in different ways. Rows would flare up over very small things, such as the way Dean spoke in a 'London vernacular', or the exact amount of time he spent on his homework. These rows would proceed with intensity and rigidity of pattern, and were set up so that winning and losing became the primary objective, rather than any new agreements or contracts being negotiated.

Dean:	The week before term started, I did two hours everyday revising for my exams.
Terry:	Sheila, do you agree with that?
Dean:	It's perfectly TRUE.
Sheila:	We had our worst rows in years during that week.
Dean:	I don't agree.
Sheila:	You didn't do enough revising for your exam.
Dean:	I did two hours every day.
Terry:	You did NOT...you did NOT.
Sheila:	Well, you did two hours some days...
Terry:	Three days you didn't do anything AT ALL...YOU WERE WATCHING TV and then you went off to Ben.
Dean:	That just isn't TRUE.
Terry:	It is TRUE...THREE OF US WILL TELL YOU.
Emmy:	[quickly] Two of you.
Terry:	Well, two people...I had promised your mother I wouldn't say a word to you, and let you get on with it on your own; and you did virtually nothing.

In this extract, shifting alignments, and interruptions of any attempt by one family member to gain support from the others are demonstrated. Terry tried to get his wife, Sheila, on his side, but Dean, her son, answered for her. Sheila therefore couldn't answer without letting one of them down. Her diplomatic answer leant towards her husband, but did not directly challenge Dean. Terry tried to bring his daughter, Emmy, in but she did not allow it, challenging her father's dominating discourse by not allowing him to speak for the whole family.

Five minutes later I commented on Terry's loss of faith in his son and asked him, 'Does your lack of faith mean that he is likely to do better or worse in the exams?', since I could see a self-fulfilling prophecy developing from Terry's continual bad-mouthing of his Dean. This was further shown in the way he picked on Dean's speech, his choice of friends, his misuse of his pocket money and the way he would not adopt his father's upwardly mobile aspirations. The meaning of 'loss of faith' was explored by the family for a good half an hour as a key shift in opening up a discussion by the adolescents of their parents. Here Emmy joined sides with Dean, but urged him not to adopt the same 'grudge bearing' attitude that she saw her father holding. I commented on her usual protectiveness of her father and she described how she felt a need to side with him as she saw him as being very alone. She said to her mother, 'Dean generally goes to *you* out of loyalty so that leaves Dad out on his own...if you three have got different opinions and you want someone to say out which is right, then I think I would tend to argue along with dad.'

My goal with this family was to promote an ongoing deconstruction of the violent episodes that took place two or three times a week and to tease out the meanings embedded in these, so that there could be some reworking of old family stories. This included some mutual exploration by the family of past events in which one or the other person felt themselves to have been unfairly blamed. It also included getting each of them to listen and to hear explanations that they had previously cut out, and for different individuals to understand that regret was being expressed for wrongs done even if forgiveness did not immediately follow. It incorporated ongoing work with Terry and Sheila as a couple over a year. The work also included regular detailed discussions of the amount that was being drunk, liaison with the GP, and one joint interview with the GP, Terry and Sheila in which the GP spelt out implications for their physical and psychological health if they continued to drink.

A year later Emmy, Dean and Sheila were more able to express opinions that were different from Terry's without a fight ensuing. Terry had not curbed his tendency to go for Dean, but the others in the family were less prepared to let him continue if they thought his attacks were unfair, and he was much more prepared to listen to their views. Ordinary bids by Dean for more autonomy were still taken by Terry as a challenge to his authority as the man in charge of the house. In the session outlined below, Sheila challenged Terry's opinion that it was Dean who was making life in the house difficult (as a prelude to tackling him more directly about his own behaviour).

Sheila: I don't believe that it's Dean's presence that is making my life difficult.

Terry: No, but Dean's told you that he deliberately intends to have rows, he deliberately intends to be difficult, and that is not a relief to any of us.

Sheila: He didn't say that.

Emmy: I think you're twisting his words there, Dad.

Sheila: He didn't say that.

Dean: I didn't say that.

Emmy: He didn't say that at all.

Terry spoke about Dean in the third person, as 'he and his intentions', and his sister and mother came in on Dean's side to defend him. Emmy tried to share some of her experience of being 'picked on' when Dean was not in the house. Dean then challenged Terry about the way he picked on people, including Sheila:

Terry: Ask your mother and sister, whether in your absence I pick on them.
Emmy: [trying to deflect from her] not me, on Mum.
Terry: [deflected] Sorry, on Mum.
Dean: Well, I was told very much so.
Terry: Were you, by whom?
Dean: [to Sheila] When was it Mum, that you got hurt? [She doesn't answer. Terry turns to Emmy.]
Terry: Do you think I had arguments with you that I need not have done?
Emmy: You did – you did put a lot more energy into concentrating on whether I was doing the right thing at school – what I was doing, what I was doing wrong.
GGB: Terry asked your mother as well as you, Emmy, – so [to Dean], do you want to ask your mother?
Emmy: [continues] you put a lot more attention on me and my life.
GGB: [focusing] Dean...
Emmy: [continues] ...concentrating on it...
Dean: [to GGB] Ask her what?
GGB: Whether she thinks that Terry does pick on her when he's not picking on you – ask her.
Dean: Mum, does he?
Terry: I'm just trying to show Dean that it isn't...
GGB: Just a second, you asked him to ask her.
Terry: Sorry.
Sheila: Yes, well, I wouldn't say Terry picks on me very often and I can usually handle it when he does or...or... avoid it.

This led into a painful account, involving all the family, of a recent fight when Sheila had got hurt by something being thrown, which had followed Terry attacking Dean for the way he had tied his shoe-laces and then blaming his wife for not bringing him up properly. However, Sheila had become much stronger and insisted that while her management style was not confrontative, the fears her son held for her were inappropriate. She believed he was still working on old models of how things had been in the family. Dean expressed the view that he should move out in order to help peace to be developed within the home, but his mother did not think he would be able to manage. This doubly enraged his father, both because Sheila was 'protecting' Dean, and because he felt it put him in a bad light in his wife's eyes. I asked Sheila what Dean would have to do to convince her that he could manage if he lived away from home:

Sheila: I haven't really thought about this before. I just thought that protectiveness is, it's one of the qualities of loving someone else. Mothers are supposed to feel that way aren't they for their children? Even such big blokes as this one. I'm not sure I'll grow out of it, but perhaps I can tone it down a bit. [To me] do you think it's necessary?

GGB: [inferring she should ask her son by nodding and looking his way]: Do I think it's necessary? Ask him...

Sheila: [to Dean]...to tone it down a bit?

Dean: Yeah, it does annoy me when you treat me like a mummy's boy. You're a little too soft on me.

Sheila: Too soft on you!

Dean: Yeah, when I'm down about Dad or he's carrying on, you sort of make such a fuss and then I think 'Oh, it must be worse than it really was' rather than, you know, laugh...I mean 'shoelaces'...It makes me feel worse about it.

Emmy suddenly volunteered at this point that she was frightened that Dean would be able to manage on his own, because if he moved out much more attention would be focused on her. I constructed a frame that was intended to allow the young people to view both their parents as deeply concerned about their future:

GGB: I want to say something which is in a slightly different frame to the one you've often used in which Mum is seen as loving and Dad as angry. I think the two of you, Dean and Emmy, have got the disadvantage of having two extremely loving parents, not one unloving and one loving, but two very loving parents and growing up when you have two such loving parents can be quite complicated – because that loving can feel like a bit of a burden. But one of the talents you have inherited from them is to have your own voices and speak clearly, it's something they have taught you. Now given that talent, is fighting your way out the only way to grow out of the family or are there other things you should be speaking about and using your voices for?

Sheila: [Because of the nature of the family business] we're too claustrophobically focused in on each other. Since I've been involved in running the business, life has been much more family centred and that makes the whole thing more of a hothouse and I can quite see that Dean and Em had more attention than they either want or need.

GGB: Well, another thing we might see together is that, following the accident, when you now get tired, it's very difficult for people to give you the proper amount of attention...perhaps in not thinking enough about your need to rest as an important issue for the family, people focus more on their anger about each other, and less on your needs. It might be better if the family could take it on board that the effects of your accident is something they are going to need to work out how to manage in the next few years.

Dean suddenly exploded at the idea of actually being confronted with his mother's becoming less competent than she had been.

Dean: [violently] NO!

Terry: [surprised] Hey, wait a minute what do you mean, no?

Dean: It's just one of those things, you can't, you've got to channel it elsewhere, you can't think of that; its much too upsetting.

Terry: I think that's bloody right, it's upsetting, but I think personally it's something we should talk about and I would be happy to make another appointment to do that.

In disentangling the different descriptions and getting the individuals to speak more clearly for themselves, I worked towards illuminating some of the shadowy alliances and re-establishing husband–wife solidarity in a situation where a strong protective alliance between mother and son had begun to develop negative effects. Further shifts in the family over the second year included a move from oppositional behaviour between father and son towards more curiosity, turn taking and greater equality of participation in family conversations. In the language of families, particularly when they are angry or 'mad' at each other, certain conversations and ways of talking about (languaging) problems may come to dominate the overall pattern of relating at the expense of other kinds of conversations about the family, which become marginalised. The family then do not develop the opportunity of seeing themselves in other ways: loving rather than angry, protective rather than aggressive, connected rather than disconnected. The introduction of these missing aspects of family emotionality by the therapist, if they are accepted, can allow marginalised areas of concern to be brought into the centre and made part of the family repertoire of what is given attention and airtime. Focusing on love and protectiveness and the power of intergenerational attachment and rivalry to perturb a marital relationship, as well as examining sequences of violence and aggression in detail, expanded the emotional vocabulary of the family away from the narrow and rigid reactivity illustrated in the first session. While expanding emotional language may not always be a component of successful therapeutic work with violence, it often plays a part in achieving a shift in mood and a change of position in the family exchanges, from which other issues can be examined.

Three things have to be taken into account when considering the likely effectiveness of working with a family where violence is part of the modality of exchange:

- Can the violence be stopped for long enough for the people who constitute the family to become safe?
- Do they know how to stop it themselves with the help of other people, or do they know how to achieve safety by leaving the home?
- Will the violence stop for long enough between sessions for any positive changes in ideas or feelings developed in the course of the session to be amplified?

This issue is key to family therapy since any changes achieved in a session are useless unless they can be taken home and worked on there. Vetere and Cooper (2001) have usefully suggested the use of the worst and last episode of violence to problem-solve around the safety in couple work.

In that my work has formerly been a child focused context, I include questions around the modality of violence in the family, and ask each parent to consider how they take responsibility for the safety of their children. However, in the following vignette, which is illustrative of a number of families I have worked with, the father who is violent will not accept this definition of his own behaviour, and other frameworks for thinking about his behaviour have to be found. The additional problematic dimension is that an aggressive style of behaviour has become a part of the son Ray's repertoire, a core part of his own experience of himself within a modality of family violence.

The O'Rourke family

Ray (9) had to learn to manage both his father's anger and his own urge to respond aggressively, as he moved between two volatile parents with widely differing expectations following their separation. His father William's violent temper had existed for years, and had intensified towards him in the context of a deteriorating marriage. The disciplining of his son was never called 'hitting' but was known as 'giving him the hand', or 'a clout', 'a box', a 'whack' or a 'thwack', never a 'smack' or a 'hit'. Ray was passionately attached to his father but frightened of the hitting. He had not learnt to read the signs that meant he was in for one of these episodes, labelled by his father as 'corrective teaching'. On contact visits he had to manage his father on his own without recourse to his mother's vigilance. A short statement by Ray's mother gives the flavour of the kind of random violence that Ray had to learn to manage:

> His father grabbed him by the neck, twisting his collar while he felt choking, that he was almost choking, lifted him into the air and then started hitting him while he was in the air, at random and he said fifty times just absolutely hitting out at him, shaking him up and down and then threw him to the ground....

The use of language

One of the difficulties for Ray in finding a way of dealing with his father's violent behaviour was that when we first met, his parents had started to use 'police' language to describe it. Punching, kicking, hitting and strangling had begun to be referred to as 'incidents'. The first thing that seemed to be important was to deneutralise the language and unpack the incident into details of what actually happened, then to link the behaviours to feelings of bodily hurt, upset, tears and sometimes blood. Having broken down a particular episode, 'deconstructed' it, we could then think about specific ways of breaking down the violent spiral so that it did not escalate. Vetere and Cooper (2001) have drawn particular attention to the use of language and focusing on how a man rather than 'losing it', can 'restrain it' and regain control. Mr O'Rourke initially denied that the incidents had occurred, but was nonetheless prepared to have serious discussions about what good parenting involved, which included learning 'new ways of how to be a parent', and abandoning 'inappropriate discipline'. He accepted that children could only manage 'so much' of this and that activity, or time spent doing self-improvement tasks, and that 'parental home teaching' would have to be modified. Attempts to disentangle 'truth and reality' in this situation, as with others involving ongoing denial, may be unproductive in that truth is likely to remain hidden. An 'as if' frame was more productive for scaffolding change. For example, if such things might be demanded by a good parent of a child of nine years old, how might the process be thought about? With Mr O'Rourke contributing from his store of beliefs towards the advice given to a hypothetical parent of a hypothetical child, considerations of 'appropriate discipline' could be more usefully reworked into another frame of better parent/child interactions, which he himself had constructed in debate with me and therefore believed in more readily.

A key feature in reducing the father's violence also involved working with him to allow the expression of his loving and protective feelings towards his son to be validated by me, who as a woman and therapist showed she did believe that as a man he could manage the job of parenting his son on his own. Mr O'Rourke's ongoing commitment to his son was a vital part of his life, and he welcomed the brief and intermittent but focused opportunities to discuss these in the explicit context of 'developing what is best for Ray':

> I mean, to me, a father's role, from the sort of society I'm from, was the tough, bluff, let the mum look after the kids sort of thing, you know, and I'll go down to the ale house, and that's not the sort of role that I'm playing now, or have played. It's mum and dad role that I'm playing. You know, I find that instead of saying 'Now look, get up, you're going to be okay, be a man', I've got go over and cuddle him.

Kerry James (2001, p. 44) from her extensive work with violence in Australia, has noted 'you can't just ask men straight up about whether they came from abusive backgrounds because their experiences are probably not something they understand to be abusive. Abusive treatment of boys over generations has been so taken for granted that they don't see themselves as having experienced abuse. Often this contributes to them not seeing their own actions as abusive.'

Many studies have noted how a good relationship with one parent may ameliorate the negative effects of the violence of the other. Working with Ray's mother was therefore a vital part of providing an alternative context in which he could build up some self-monitoring reserves and belief in his own abilities, both to protect himself sensibly and to develop and maintain ways of communicating other than those learnt from the moments when his father 'lost it'. In order for Ray's mother, a Chinese woman who believed deeply in family harmony, to feel that she could provide an effective alternative milieu for Ray she had to overcome her long-felt shame about having lived in a family situation that was far removed from her ideals of what a family life should be. When I first came to know her she had already been to five agencies of different kinds to try to talk about the violence in the family, but the only people who had taken her seriously were those in the domestic violence unit run by the London Police in her area. All the others had somehow blinkered themselves to the difficulties she was trying to describe. She explained her own part in the maintenance of family violence as follows: 'The thing is, you tend to keep a front up which is to hide everything...I actually used to go round and say he was a nice person and that it was a happy marriage...you know, to admit failure to anybody was bad.' The first challenge for any professional may be to make a space for unspoken experience to gain a voice. However, once people who are being hurt start to admit this to themselves, they often feel worse unless they can find some allies who will help them maintain strength in their new identity as injured persons who have found the strength to admit to and tackle their own situation. Andersen's question (see p. 45) 'who will affirm the person you are trying to become' is relevant here. Of equal relevance is the question of how a person can protect themselves once they find the determination to face a partner with the fact that the violence has to stop. 'I actually felt that getting out of it would involve being pursued and being either destroyed or being killed...or having Ray taken away...he had already taken him away across the water once and prevented me from having access to him'. The fear of abduction of a child can also provide a threatening alternative strategy of control.

The crunch point for Mae in determining to change the pattern was when she began to see her son repeating the violent patterns of his father:

> I would cook a meal, I would prepare everything, and then he would just take everything and throw it out...and it would come that Ray would say 'You do that and I'll just throw all your cooking out' and he would take a dish and throw it across the room...that was the crunch point I think...I thought, first I thought that he would benefit from having two parents. You know, a boy needs

a father's input and I actually believed it, because I didn't have my father's input – he left when I was three.

In the relative calm of the new home Mae had created for her son after the separation, she discussed with Ray how he saw the story of things going wrong. 'He said "six was when things began to go bad", and I said "why" and he said "because that's when dad began to teach me"'. Three things helped Mae with her own developing self-esteem, following the separation: Ray's improved performance in school, his improved relationship with her, and the fact that her ex-husband started to listen more to her opinions about Ray's care than he had done when they were living together. His realisation that Ray was now doing better in school contributed to his willingness to lessen his old style of supervision of his child's learning, and to proceed with more relaxed parenting behaviours.

Post-divorce issues

Following separation, Simpson *et al.* (1995) found that for one in 4 of the fathers in their study, violence between a father and mother increased for the first year. This normally erupted at contact handover. A child who has to coexist in two separate households after a divorce, where each modality carries emotional power due to the child's loyalty to both parents, is placed in ongoing conflict, internal and external. Either parent may also actively disqualify, or 'badmouth' the other. Children exposed to couples that fail to resolve conflicts over and over again are more likely to predict that future conflicts will not be resolvable, (Cummings and Davies, 2002). Couples who resolve, or constructively handle, disagreements give a different message. It is therefore important to attend both to the inter-parental behaviour in resolving rows, whether pre, during, or post-separation, as well as to developing skills with parents and children in handling parents' angry behaviour. Ongoing disturbance expressed in violent behaviour, which may have been contained to some degree in the marital relationship, will have to be handled in a different way as the child confronts two parents, each with their own separate constructions of reality, and each with their own acute and possibly rigid version of how their child should be. What may also happen in this situation is that the child becomes temporarily annexed to form the 'other person' in the mental representation of each parent whose self-definition as 'good' or 'capable' has formerly required the other person in the 'couple' to be assigned the function of 'bad' or 'incapable' person who has to be punished or shaped correctively. When a parent has resigned from this ascribed role through divorce, the child may take up the understudy position in the other parent's mind. This can put the child at additional risk. New signals and communication skills have to be developed between parent and child, since the child can no longer rely on the other parent being present to defuse or divert an escalating conflict.

Ray also had to be helped to think about how he could 'bring down' his father's escalating zeal for 'correction', which once triggered off seemed to have 'a life of their own'. On the basis of information now shared by Mr O'Rourke that these tempers had originated in his own childhood experience of being disciplined by his father, we developed some ways of breaking into his temper when he saw it coming. When thinking of ways of responding that would lead to his father curbing his anger, Ray's original idea had been to argue or fight back. However, this had instead served to intensify the anger. Ray's subsequent idea was that he could just slide to the floor and show how small or helpless he was. In further work with him and his father, routines for stopping violent escalations were ritualised into agreed codes. Since Mr O'Rourke was now in touch with his more tender parenting side, words to emphasise Ray's smallness and his youth were used to break into his stream of thought: small, little, child, too much. This happened in work at the clinic and as recommended 'ideas about children' to take away. An important gender move for both father and son was to shift from patterns based on violent action and reaction to ones where feelings of tenderness could be evoked and built on. It is probable that Mr. O'Rourke also took away images of 'working alliances' with other watchful but caring adults who had Ray's interests at heart, since he wrote several letters of gratitude for the help he was receiving. James (2001), from her extensive work with violent men in Australia, comments that men who have a more controlling paradigm may fit much better with socio-educational models, whereas others may be helped much more by therapy. In my experience an educational model is always of value if a child's well-being can be constructively brought into the process.

Family violence and traumatic effects on children

Violence is often brought to the attention of a therapist through the surfacing of an earlier violent experience that imprinted itself on the mind of a child or adult. Something in the mind that has been formerly experienced as emotionally unmanageable may take a number of forms for showing itself subsequently: the replaying and re-enactment of the event 'flashbacks' triggered by reminders, spontaneously arising as a result of a smell or a sensation, during play or through dreams or nightmares. Traumatic experience can induce a state of alertness, or arousal, or irritability, and can affect sleep and the ability to relax. A man of 32, remembering a violent childhood, put it this way: 'The mind is like a video recorder, and it runs, you know, just constantly running and every now and again you get images, and every image is...too painful...you have to block that part out.'

Traumatic events that take place in families characteristically accumulate in their effect over time. It is more likely to be the repeated rather than the single event that creates a traumatic legacy. Such events are frequently associated with secretiveness, or minimisation, and denial. In Chapter 9 we will look at how such intimate processes requiring subordination, or violation of a childhood self, may be associated with subsequent subordination of the self in relationships in adult life. Where the effects show themselves in the same context in which a trauma originally occurred, a parent can then act to protect the child from further exposure to the precipitating events, and heal some of the earlier effects. Professionals can help them think about how to do this.

Clara and Pat for example, who we met in Chapter 2, had to deal with male violence in their home. Clara had brought Pat (aged 5) to the clinic because she was concerned about his night terrors following an incident in which his father had broken down the front door in a rage on an occasion when she had withheld contact with Pat because of his father's drinking. Clara had decided to take action to stop this happening again but also ensure that Pat could continue to see his father with relatives elsewhere, thus dealing with some of the frightening effects of feeling helpless in the face of his violence. Pat on the other hand had continued to feel helpless in relation to the 'break in', and the incident had rearoused memories of previous fights between his father and mother. Clara describes his dreams: 'He's bed-wetting as well. The dreams, he screams. Sometimes he scares me, one night he screamed and screamed, it was if he had been murdered in the bed, and his eyes are open but he doesn't realise that I'm there – he is still calling out for me. He is petrified'. I asked her if she talked to him about his dreams and she replied:

He says he can never remember. The dreams seem to take an awful lot out of him, that he just wants to go straight back to sleep and he will lie in till late in the morning. They are not as bad as they used to be but sometimes they can be. A while ago they were bad and I was thinking that maybe it had something to do with him seeing his daddy hitting me when he was three.

I then asked Pat what he remembered.

GGB: [to Pat] Do you remember when big Pat used to hit Clara? A long time ago?

Pat: Eh, no. [He is drawing at a little table, and while he is talking he is drawing the fight we are talking about.]

GGB: Do you remember shouting and fighting? Perhaps you used to watch it sometimes or did you run away and hide? Where were you when they were fighting?

Pat: I was standing near the door.

GGB: Right, so you could run away?

Pat: Just watched so they couldn't get me.

GGB: When they got very angry, were you afraid they might hit out at you as well?

Pat: Yeah.

Clara: It always used to be when his dad was drunk. And he used to be frightened as to what might happen.

GGB: Was your dad different when he was drunk?

Pat: Yes.

GGB: What was it about him that made you think 'Oh, Dad's been drinking'?

Pat: They were just rowing. [Pat shows GGB a picture he has drawn of the fight.]

GGB: It is a very, very good picture, tell me who is who so that I don't guess wrong.

Pat: That's Dad and that's Mum and that's me.

GGB: That is a very very good picture. [pointing to the drawing] And did Dad used to grab Mum sort of by the neck or just push her around?

Pat: Push her around.

GGB: Right, and did she push him around too? Was he big?

Pat: He is a little bit bigger.

GGB: But did she push him around anyway? Because when mums get very angry they sometimes push back.

Clara: I could never do that because I knew that would make him a hell of a lot worse.

GGB: Yes.

Clara: Like I knew what he would be like, I know the temper there so I couldn't fight back. Before I was married, when I was single I used to fight back, but then after I had Sean (2nd son) I just got a bit scared for him.

GGB: Did you get hurt?

Clara: Yes, bruises and scratches and he used to strangle me, pull me around.

GGB: Just because (to Pat) you've drawn it like he is sort of holding Mum round the neck.

Pat: No, by the hair.

GGB: He used to pull her by the hair? Because she has long hair I can see … did you ever try and stop them?

Pat: Yeah.

GGB: What did you try and do when you tried to stop them?

Pat: I tried to shout but they couldn't listen.

GGB: Yes, it's a horrible feeling when you're trying to stop someone and they won't listen.

Pat: Yes.

GGB: Did that happen quite often, do you think?

Pat: Yes.

Clara: He's never mentioned it at home.

GGB: Children often do remember frightening things, you know, especially if it's happening to people they are fond of. [To Clara] And did that happen very often, are you able to remember?

Clara: Yeah, too often. It was every weekend and sometimes during the week.

It seemed that at age five, Pat had only been able to dream his terrors rather than talk about them. His mother had not thought of talking with him about his father's violence, partly because the events he remembered were events from which she had wished to protect him, and partly because of the hurt of remembering them herself. Many parents also fear that by talking about an event they will make it worse rather than better. However, his mother did not wish to conceal from him what had taken place once he had begun to talk about it, because she wanted things to change for all of them – herself, Pat and his father. She actually wished for a new resolution. We ended the first interview with the agreement that any time he had a dream he was to go straight to Clara, to tell her about it, even if it meant waking her up. Pat asked his mother, 'Even at midnight?', and she confirmed that he could. Two weeks later she asked to come on her own, saying that there had been no more nightmares or bed-wetting but there were things *she* wanted to discuss.

For Clara an additional powerful meaning of Pat's drawing lay in its intergenerational repetition – she too remembered just such fights in *her* childhood and her own sense of impotence. Going through the meanings embedded in this intergenerational repetition was very important to her. After her own mother's divorce from her father she had not continued a relationship with her father, which she bitterly regretted. Because of this her wish was that Pat should be able to continue to see *his* father after the separation. Her goal was to become strong enough to feel safe enough to allow Pat's relationship with his father to continue in spite of the former marital violence. As we saw in Chapter 2, she was able to be clear with her son that the separation was not his fault: 'You're too little darlin', it couldn't be your fault in no way'. She handled his father's recent attempted violence by taking out a Prohibited Steps Order to prevent him from coming near to the house and negotiating further contact between him and Pat outside the house until she felt safe. She also decided to tackle some of the ongoing violence in her family of origin by taking charge of her brother, who was currently terrorising her mother in her mother's house, blaming her and 'punishing' her for 'breaking up the family home' some twenty years before. Over three sessions she became progressively more empowered to take charge of situations in both families, and over the following year she transformed her view of herself to one where – as a result of different kinds of affirmative action, including getting some job training – she felt in charge of the family and the risk of violence that that involved.

For adults who remember violent experiences in their families of origin, questions of a larger family text about what may be remembered and what must be forgotten may still operate as a powerful constraint on the telling of their own stories and on how they think about changing the text for their own children (Gorell Barnes *et al.*, 1998). When people's lives have been characterised by quarrelling and discord, and in their childhoods they have had to listen continually to oppositional viewpoints that were not reconcilable, the way they later think about their own lives and the lives of their children is likely to reflect this. Whether it is a woman who has been continually exposed to the threat of violence, a man who has had his points of view scornfully opposed and disqualified by a parent or a partner, or a child who has been in the middle of parents who argue or fight, the many contradictions of these experiences may well be reflected in the way they present both their difficulties and the story within which these are embedded. As therapists we need to attend to fragmented memory and confused accounts of original experiences and look out for ways that other adult strengths offer opportunities to amend or overcome these. Parents who are looking for better experiences for their children than they had themselves may need this goal to be kept in the forefront of the therapist's mind, at times when it becomes submerged by more persecutory childhood experiences in their own minds. The therapist's voice becomes an active ally in moving to and maintaining different positions as a parent on behalf of children. As Franklyn (see Chapter 4, pp. 84–6) reported about the earlier experience of working on the effects of violence in his own childhood and its relationship to his own parenting dilemmas, 'by you looking out for us and what we could do different, it made a difference to how we thought about ourselves'.

9

SEXUAL ABUSE IN CHILDHOOD AND SOME EFFECTS IN ADULT LIFE

Boundaries of trust in therapeutic work

It is not only families that break boundaries of trust in relation to sexually abusive behaviour, but also counsellors and therapists. Aspects of professional behaviour relating to safety between client and professional need to be addressed before any of us attend to abusive behaviour in a man or woman's personal life. While it may be hard for anyone practising under a therapeutic title to recognise that their own practice may have abusive elements, these can range from abuse through oversight and unintentional overfamiliarity, to the open infringement of physical and psychological boundaries that is taboo within ethical professional codes.

Marcella, for example, a young Italian woman who had been referred from a training course to an experienced practitioner for therapy as part of the qualifying requirements, found that the therapist swiftly moved from comments relating to her account of abusive experience in childhood to comments relating to her attractiveness, accompanied by an ongoing disqualification of the way her husband had failed to appreciate a 'woman so attractive'. Subsequently he took her out for a drink and offered her extra sessions at a reduced rate 'to help her with her training'. Responding to his interest in her she began to see him at a reduced rate with more frequency, in hours after her own work, which led to the possibility of sociable time together. Her attraction to him and to the intimacy of understanding generated between them in the therapy sessions led her to look less favourably at her husband, and the excitement of the conversations in which she explored her more intimate feelings with her therapist contrasted with the dullness of the conversation at the kitchen table at home. Marcella came to see me following a referral from a colleague, her friend, who recognised that she had become highly emotionally enmeshed with her therapist. In the months that followed she began to allow the passion with which she described her therapist to overlap with accounts of an experience in her early teens, when a teacher had favoured her above all the other girls in the class and given her extra maths tuition after school. This relationship, which had become highly eroticized, was itself embedded in a childhood in which she had lost her father, whom she believed had loved her more than her mother did. Her mother remarried a younger man who, while never 'actually' abusing her, had teased her sexually and harassed her for many years, forbidding her to mention it to her mother.

How do we account for the effects of the behaviour between the therapist, the trainee and the trainee's earlier family relationships, and what does it teach us about exercising caution when working with sexual abuse? Sexual abuse represents the extreme end of a spectrum of male – female relationships in which power, coercion and the assumption of 'female compliance' constitute the assumptive base. The way in which women share habits of submission or of subordinating their common sense to men differs dramatically, and variations are created by class, education, poverty, race and culture as well as by particular family patterns. Obedience and compliance from an early age usually characterise relationships that are also sexually abusive, as does an inbuilt wish to please in the context of what will probably have been experienced as a failure to do so.

Built into any culture – whether of family, class, neighbourhood or religion – are different degrees of gender awareness and ways of 'double dealing' in relation to 'respecting' the authority of men. Each culture contains different sexual arrangements, in which for the most part men's power is privileged above women's. However, different cultures have different ways of detoxifying this so that women have alternative ways of responding to and dealing with the overt cultural requirement for obedience. (Obviously there are exceptions to this in some countries and in some aspects of some religious belief, but this is outside the limits of what most therapists will be helping clients to struggle with.) For young girls in many cultures, there also remain socially prescribed ideas about compliance, especially to older men and women. Also powerful in many cultures is the specific idea of women being pleasing to men (rather than each gender being pleasing to the other). Thus the idea of cooperating in acts that may be abusive to the gendered self in order to please men were instilled, for example, in my own Anglo-Greek childhood through school, church and media, as well as through the more powerful distillations peculiar to my family. In our pre-adolescent days in the 1950s, most of my friends and I had sufficient opportunity to giggle or whisper with each other about the peculiarities of men and their daily sexual oddities ('flashing' at church fetes; coats over the knee on the top of buses with invitations to stroke penises underneath; men in raincoats and indeed sometimes in uniforms you were supposed to trust, wanting to see your knickers in the park and so on). The giggling gave us a shared sense of being different from them and immune to the impact of these behaviours. Nonetheless many of us did expect and accept that men behaved like that, however much we disliked it, and we had extremely ambivalent feelings about how we were supposed to respond to such behaviour from older people (men), to whom we had also been brought up to be polite.

This phenomenon continues for both boys and girls through such institutions as school and church, and has painfully been revealed through the public exposure of 'care' systems specifically set up to 'look after' children. For a young person like Marcella, locked into an intensified, eroticized relationship with an older man in a position of authority, there is a potential sense of being favoured, singled out as someone special, which offers a potentially invasive role for 'compliance', carrying, as the relationship does, implicit messages of special intimacy, embedded in the context of abuse of a position of authority. Such powerful messages are easily rearoused in subsequent contexts in life, especially within the intimacy of therapy. The way in which subsequent male figures fit or do not fit into these early experiences and influences on the gendered self are likely to influence all anticipations of encounters of men in authority, including therapists. These are some of the normative social dimensions of sexually abusive behaviour which can deprive women of whatever age of their capacity to think freely, to trust their feelings and to believe in their right to take charge of their own bodies.

Therapy with a man: some considerations

Identity, and particularly sexual identity, does not develop in isolation. The young girl develops in mutual interaction with the males and females in her family; and it is in relation to the male and female images that she constructs her identity according to her experience. The erotic sensitivities of the child's body are interpreted through the meanings the child attaches to her body through early experiences in a sexed family world (Jones, 1986). The question of male power and the constraints it imposes are determined not only by a daughter's direct experience of her father but by her perception of her mother's experience or her sister's experience of her father; as well as by her own direct access to her mother or other important senior women in her life. These will all contribute to her own systems of self-perception and self-valuation (Sapphire, 1996).

In families where sexual abuse by the father is an ongoing and regular part of the family life, not only will the father play a disproportionate part in the family power structure, but access to the mother will be either prohibited or confused by virtue of the role the daughter is taking on 'for her mother'. Access to other adults who might offer different conceptions of the female child is likely to be blocked, because of fear, loyalty, protectiveness, secrecy and shame. Nonetheless many women report on the vital part played by an aunt or family friend who, usually in teenage years, offered another perspective on the family and therefore provided an opportunity for at least some reappraisal in the adolescent mind. Sometimes this leads to the beginning of being able to say 'no', although 'no' usually begins with small areas outside the sexually abusing acts themselves and may or may not be amplified depending on how the voice of defiance is elaborated within other subsystems in the family or, very importantly, in school. The struggle for many women who have been abused therefore includes the question of not only how to get out from under the father, but how to get out from under the father-subjugated mother. The challenge is to find a way of being female that has a newly self-defined centre, not a male-dominated centre with the power and abusiveness that has entailed. The 'mind' has to free itself from a series of abusive encounters and their interconnections with other networks of collusion and distortion (Gorell Barnes and Henesy, 1994).

In an earlier piece of work shared with a male colleague (my partner Alan Cooklin) the client, Linda, defined the limits of her work with him in the developing context of her understanding about her earlier relationship with her own father. She believed he (Alan Cooklin) would laugh at her for her stupidity; not only for 'making a fuss' about her sexualized experience, but also because of her 'incompetent' way of expressing herself. To develop a voice in which her own language was heard and valued would not have been possible within the therapeutic context she had with him, however 'safe'. The ten years (from the ages of four to fourteen) in which her own father had taught her to enjoy her mind, laughed at her for its products while at the same time engaging her in powerful and violent sexual activities had led her to mistrust both intimacy and the use of her intelligence with a man. In describing the therapeutic process she said:

> In therapy sessions we seemed to spend much time talking at one another – like radio towers trying to transmit signals but trapped by too much interference. As a result, I shifted my focus from the topic of abuse to holding onto a buried and well-protected sense of my own abilities – in order not to feel entirely responsible for the lack of communication. I would hint at my intelligence and even reveal my ability to grasp his ideas when I was feeling brave but did not feel my efforts were recognised.

The therapist as another woman

As well as the deconstruction of events specific to the therapy, a different continuity can develop between a female family therapist and an adult female client. This stems from a joint scanning of the many small tasks of daily life in which oppression may be actively experienced, such as childcare, cleaning, household finance, domestic administration and the confrontation of male belief systems. The conversation draws on a joint legacy of female experience of growing up and forms an ongoing critique of life and its daily hazards. This component of the therapeutic conversation is interactional and egalitarian, based on genuine mutual influence, often leading to new insights for both participants and a movement within the conversations that are more specific to the therapy. A paramount consideration in this painful but liberating work is facilitating the unique experiences of each woman that gives meaning to the events that have shaped her life and the voice that will shape her future. Words have to be given new meanings so that she can reshape and redefine herself. As Bakhtin (1984, p. 202) has put it:

> When a member of a speaking collective comes upon a word, it is not as a neutral word of language, not as a word free from the aspirations and evaluations of others, uninhabited by others voices. No, (s)he receives the word from another's voice, and filled with that voice. The word enters her context from another context. Her own thought finds the word permeated with the interpretations of others.

The therapist, in her ongoing presence and conversations, begins to detoxify the words and the thoughts from the abusive contamination of others, so that feelings that have had to be disowned by the client because they are too permeated by 'others' may be reclaimed within her own body and mind. As Linda said:

> I chose to put my analytical, intellectual self to the side for awhile and set free my trapped emotions. I made a commitment to...allow the ideas created in therapy to be my primary influence. I was able to do this in therapy with a woman because she 'allowed' for my intelligence. The struggle to prove its existence became unnecessary.

Traumatic, formless and perverse events

It is well known from other fields, not only that of child sexual abuse, that in order to function in adult life a survivor may have to make a division or compartmentalisation between their memories and their so-called 'normal' life (Bentovim, 1992). They know that the world can be dangerous, randomly cruel, and contain unbearable pain under the facade of everyday behaviour. Keeping this in mind may always be a necessary part of their personal integrity. Finding meanings from traumatic experience that allow it to be resolved, cannot easily be done and may never be done. The growth of an alternative experience of perceiving the self as strong and valued in different contexts may be built in the context of therapy, but at times of acute life stress, this stronger self may well collapse, leading back to an experience of crisis (see Maeve below). The therapist therefore should never be too speedy or too hopeful. Negotiation between the private truth and what the client thinks the therapist can accept or stand, the 'public truth', may take place many many times. Bringing such hidden knowledge into shared consciousness is essential and painful. How an idea that is half there becomes something that can be expressed is one of the intangible but vital parts of the therapeutic exchange.

Early work in therapy: the written word

In the early part of therapy I have found that one of the most important tasks for women is to discover their own way of reaching into memories about abuse that can be managed within the context of current daily life. Such current contexts include children, relationships, households, financial problems and work structures. The experience of memory returning is both exhausting and frightening, since the reality of that earlier experience can become temporarily more powerful than the current reality in which the client's adult self lives. The memory of the abuse of the child's body may bring such pain to the mind that the adult body is re-traumatised. For the client to find ways of containing the experience so that they are not immobilised is thus of key importance.

In the work that I have done with both adult women and adolescents, writing inbetween sessions has played an important part in negotiating the move from a remembered abusive reality to one defined and more contained by the writers and the writing itself. Writing has included fragments of memory, sequences without context and whole episodes of behaviour. Sometimes it includes descriptions of the abuse itself, or of things connected to the events that were particularly upsetting in the opinion of the child concerned. These might not have been seen as upsetting to the people to whom they have previously been recounted. Prose, poetry and letters have been used in different ways. Writing provides a medium in which powerful feelings can be kept separate from the body, containing the fear that the body may once again be overwhelmed or obliterated. By having the words on paper they can be viewed and managed in a safer way, creating a story of which the abused person is the author and not the victim.

For example when Linda began to remember the experience of her father climbing into her bed when she was a child, and was consequently lying awake all night in terror, I suggested that she wrote down her memories. This was the beginning of a long stretch of continuous writing. The form in which she wrote changed. First she wrote on scraps of paper whenever a memory assailed her. In these early days she could not look at the words once they were down, but passed them on. It was necessary to keep herself and the words separate, and for the therapist to keep them safe. Then she began to write in an exercise book, and gave me a copy. By calling this her journal it became of key importance as her own pathway to the truth she was seeking. 'I can refine and edit the journal, check it for lies or hints of subterfuge, go over it with a magnifying glass as if it were my own skin. I am honestly here in these pages'. Two years later she added, 'for a long time the journal seemed to write itself. I followed it through its often terrifying course until I felt I could take charge of it and write about the truth instead of relying on reading the truth as it was uncovered in the journal'. In the later part of the work this writing was connected to the writing of others, particularly to feminist writers.

Another woman, Maeve, preferred to write in poetry, struggling to capture the essence of particular childhood experience in a form that was tightly defined by her adult mind. Having never written before, she was timid about her poems, which were extremely powerful, and constantly critical of her inability, as she saw it, to convey the rage and terror they did in fact show. Determined to find a public voice in which she could express the outrage of abused children, she published some in her church magazine. A young Greek woman, Melina, who had still not freed herself from the family in which her brother had abused her for many years, wrote small scraps of description of the exact moments she had experienced the sexual encounters, still disbelieved and dismissed by her parents as 'making a fuss'. She gave them to me as 'testimony' of what had taken place, since her own mother did not come to believe her story for many months.

Confronting the voices of others in therapy: parents and children

Taking charge of traumatic events also means changing the subjective feeling of being the passive object or recipient of the abusive behaviour of others. In the process between two people, one of whom has been abusive to the other in the past, gaining even a small amount of control can make a significant difference to other contexts. However, it may not be the single relationship only that needs attention. There may have been others where the client has experienced aspects of misused power. When this has happened in a marital relationship over years, aspects of the pattern may have carried over into the children, so that the client experiences in her relationship with her children some of those same aspects of control that she felt in relation to her father. Brief extracts of a session between a client and her mother and a client and her children follow. In the session with the mother, the focus of the therapy was simply to ensure that Meg retained the focus that she herself wished, in the context of exploring the triadic relationship in which she had experienced herself as interchangeable with, but organised by, her mother in relation to her father:

Meg: [strongly] Mother, I need you to recreate for me.
Mother: I am trying.
Meg: Try – really hard; you're over here and I'm here and Daddy's there, please [showing with her hands].
Mother: I'm trying to do that...

Meg: Do that.

Mother: But do you understand [shouting] that you were never alone with him?

Meg: Then when you were there, try and see how it is [showing with her hands] him and me and how it was.

Mother: He hated his daughters – it broke my heart – I overcompensated like crazy with you all, with my attention.

Meg: I know...

Mother: He didn't like you. When I tried to get him to, he said, 'I can't get interested in girl's things'...he wouldn't read you stories.

Meg: He played baseball with me.

Mother: I didn't even know that; but do you know, he didn't want to do things with you and so he...I could write this in a sequence of events for your therapist.

GGB: takes up idea of the mother making a tape and 'going step by step in your own time'.

GGB: [to Meg] You find that what your mother said about your father fitted with your mental representation; because you have often talked of feeling there was a lot of love between you and your father?

Meg: I do find that it fitted...I think that as a child I can see lots of shifting roles and memories...in the past couple of years I have seen things I thought was mother and things that were father the wrong way round. Do you know what I mean? [turning to mother] I know that you loved me...there have been times when I thought we have not communicated in the right way, but I always get back to knowing you love me.

Mother: Oh, sure.

Meg: But there's a great uncertainty about Daddy – so rather than accept the hate, it was easier as a child to remember something that was an illusion [the mother tries to interrupt].

Meg: Please [the mother persists].

Meg: Mother, please, this is really important. Can you let me finish please.

Mother: I wanted to give you the whole picture.

Meg: The process is far more important than the whole picture. If you have given me something to put things into perspective in my mind – the process is far more important.

Mother: [tries to interrupt]...than what you have to say.

Meg: This is probably what made me feel I couldn't turn to you...that you can do this to me...completely just taking it over and not letting me talk.

GGB: You're not doing badly.

Meg: [laughs] No, I'm not.

GGB: As long as you know your mother is doing it with love, and not because she is trying to take your mind away.

When reviewing the interview Meg commented on the memory of:

Myself as an aspect of my mother – the madness of not being separated from her, the truth she speaks is that we were not often separated. To that truth I add that I was where I should not have been because she felt me to be part of herself. My vision of a real physical space, is suffocating space where they fitted them between me. I wasn't there yet I really was.

Maeve: using workmates and children to create alternative voices

Maeve, a white woman of Anglo-Irish descent, was in her forties. Following a divorce from a man to whom she had been married for twenty-five years, she made several suicide attempts that led to her referral. As she described it, the precipitating factor was that she had begun a love affair with a man to whom she had initially felt very close, but it had become increasingly violent and controlling. One night she had boarded up the windows of her flat so that he could not see her shadow from his watching place across the street, and she had begun to believe that she would never again be able to have a relationship in which she was not in someone's control. Between the ages of four to fourteen she had been 'required' to let her father into her bed at weekends to have intercourse with her. The arrangement was that the mother would go down to get breakfast and he would then tap on the door of her bedroom as he went to the bathroom, whereupon she would be expected to prepare herself for him to join her for different kinds of sex that were not fully penetrative. Three other aspects of abuse in this relationship were particularly powerful in her memory. First he would try to control her in everything she did – for example she was always expected to take empty bottles back to the pub in the dark. Although she hated doing this, and had two elder brothers for whom it was an equally appropriate task, it was part of a ritual of submission in which she had to do what her father said. This was one of many rituals designed to show his total authority over the women in the household. Not to carry out the task would have led to her mother being chastised for 'not bringing her daughter up properly'. Secondly, he would denigrate her and tell her how ugly and skinny she was, and he would laugh at her attempts to look pretty. Thirdly, he would shout abusively at her mother as well as her. She described feeling as though she could not tell her mother about what was going on, because what she was doing was to please her father so that he would not shout at her mother.

Mothers, in the accounts of women who have been abused, are in my experience themselves described as overloaded, devalued or powerless. Responsibility is handed down to the next female in line. However, none of the women I have worked with have felt their mother was 'justified' in her failure to intervene. This 'sharing of responsibility' has horrifying ramifications for all, like a highly contagious virus. In such circumstances, access to other adults who might offer different conceptions of femaleness to the female child, as well as positive models of adult women, is likely to be blocked in complex ways. Alternative models for viewing roles of daughter and mother may be unavailable, so that images of women and the resulting 'mental representations of relationships', whether mother – daughter or husband – wife, may become highly constricted.

Maeve however had an aunt who did acknowledge to her when she was in her teens that she thought her father was too much of a disciplinarian, and this alternative perspective was described by Maeve as a starting factor in her ability to develop an oppositional voice. She left home as soon as she was able to get a job, and then married a man whose ability to manage events at first offered what she saw as safety, although she subsequently experienced his way of managing as also extremely controlling. He was never violent but would not let her make any decisions without his authority – she found she was treated like an incompetent person throughout a shared business life in which she in fact developed a particular skill in financial management. At the time she came to see me (she was then divorced) another painful factor was that her eldest son had treated her in the same manner as her former husband – and even worse her young daughter, who had been encouraged by her mother never to let herself be put down by her father, now sometimes treated her mother with the same voice of scorn used by her ex-husband.

What kinds of things could be helpful in enabling Maeve to recognise, name and amplify those aspects of herself in current relationships in which she was seen as competent rather than incompetent? I chose the workplace and her children as two areas in which she had clearly experienced herself as competent in the accounts she gave of her life. In relation to the workplace, I encouraged her to keep a diary of the very small precipitating events in her everyday life that had led her to believe she was incompetent, or more specifically, which had led to earlier male voices in her head telling her she was incompetent, for example the man she had employed to do the plumbing in the property business she ran, or the man with whom she had negotiated the rights for a particular contract. Each of these voices, because they were aggressive, reminded her of her father's and her husband's voices, and therefore became voices that disqualified her. I then encouraged her to substitute voices of men or women whom she knew had a high opinion of her, and we made a list of these so that their specific characteristics and opinion of her could be brought into her mind when she needed them. We planned who else's voice she could call on the next time she had to make a decision – whose voice was going to be annexed to provide an alternative to the 'over-dominant discourse' of her father and subsequently her husband. The question of when anyone is ready to allow an alternative voice to override or at least be 'in debate with' a powerful internal voice is key to its potential success, and is likely to depend on a trusting relationship with the therapist having been established.

In relation to the children, more direct interactive work was negotiated, and Maeve came with her son and daughter on a number of occasions to share with them some of the struggles she was having in changing her image of herself. These interviews were very powerful for her in that her adolescent children were able to describe vividly to her the strengths they had experienced in the way she had brought them up, while also voicing their concern about her self-destructive behaviour. One of the most important aspects of these interviews for Maeve was the way in which her daughter made it clear that she had not been harmed by her mother's collapses in the course of her recovery work; and showed her strength by telling Maeve about the plans for her own life. The two of them negotiated some different arrangements in relation to time spent together at home, in which Maeve's daughter took on board the fact that now her mother was stronger she was once more in charge of the house; although in turn Maeve had to begin the long process of recognising that her daughter had matured significantly by looking after her while she was ill. Her son was told by her that while she was really pleased that he had matured to the point where he could take all the decisions that his father used to take on her behalf, she – as his mother – didn't need that any more as she was enjoying taking them for herself. In the tearful exchanges during these sessions a legacy of disempowerment began to shift for Maeve, as she realised that she had in fact done a good job with her children, in spite of her own childhood experiences.

Talking with children about sexual abuse

Many young women and older girls perceive society as sending messages at many levels that encourage violence against them, and then denying their reports of violence when they assert that it has taken place. It is very important that professionals do not fall into the same trap. Girls who report rape, harassment or assault are likely to be telling the truth, and deserve the respect of being heard. There is a large literature on sexual abuse work with children, so only a few points relating to talking with children will be addressed here. It is also important to bear in mind that many adolescent boys have had sexually abusive experiences of different kinds, and these may form part of their underlying distress when presenting for overtly different reasons.

It is important to remember that children as well as adults may choose to dissociate from abusive experience and may not wish to report it directly. With encouragement some children want to talk, beginning with attention to specific details of where the event took place, for example the playground, the choir stall or vestry, the children's home or their father's flat. Having defined the context, and placed themselves within it in the security of knowing they are with another adult who will make the telling of the story safe, they may take time to decide how much they feel able to describe of the actual sexual events. Other children may create imaginative reenactments, creating a distinction between themselves and what was done to their bodies. For example when Anna first told her story at six years old, certain features were often repeated. She had learnt how to dissociate herself from painful or frightening experiences by turning herself into an automaton, saying that the person who was telling the story was inside a machine that could speak and all she had to do was press the button and get it to play. To demonstrate this she turned the wastepaper basket (metal) upside down, climbed onto it, pressed an imaginary button and began to speak in a high robotic voice, describing what had happened to her.

John, aged nine, could not talk about his abuse at all, but at his first interview he was encouraged to draw the man who had attacked him while he was playing just around the corner from his house and made him perform fellatio. Drawing the man on the blackboard with the help of the therapist, and getting him to colour in the jogging suit and then less neutral details such as his hands and face (although not his penis) allowed him to reveal his story to his mother and father bit by bit. Melina, aged fourteen, wanted to report on sexual abuse by her brother over a period of years. When telling her story to her mother, what helped her to find the words was being encouraged to describe for the first time all the details of the experience: where it had happened, the time of day, the exact clothes she was wearing. Therapists need to remember that there may not be a language in some families for 'hidden' parts of the body, and putting the story into words may involve the creation of a vocabulary. Melina's mother herself had no words for any of the 'women's parts' and told Melina that her own mother had slapped her when she tried to ask what her period was when she first 'came on', assuming it was the result of 'doing something naughty with boys'.

Children may present aspects of unpleasant experiences in a repeated or 'silly' form, but this should not prevent the therapist from recognising its seriousness to the children. For example a little girl describing 'sticky stuff in her hair' started dancing round the room shouting 'sticky stuff, sticky stuff', to her mother's embarrassment. Another child, showing her father attempting to enter her from behind, demonstrated this with two tiny dolls and then climbed onto a chair, dropped the dolls from a great height and shouted 'That will show you'. Boys may bring plastic monsters, with which they act out scenes of battle. It is always useful to have access to drawing things as well as non-specific representational material such as plasticine, which can be moulded. I also have a variety of small bendy dolls made of wire, which come in families of different colours and generational arrangements, as well as farm animals, wild animals, and prehistoric that can represent events less explicitly.

When working with all clients where sexual abuse has formed part of their experience, the therapist has to be particularly careful not to reimpose seductive or coercive frameworks on the meaning that develops in the sessions together (Jones, 1991). While some of the guidelines pertaining to work with clients who have been sexually abused, whether adults or children, apply equally to clients with other life dilemmas, they are of heightened importance in contexts where both the body and the mind have been involved against the wish of the person concerned and at a developmental stage where they were powerless to take effective action to prevent it. Key points include:

1. Do not push the client to go faster than she or he wishes to go.
2. Do not direct him or her into new courses of action until he or she expresses a wish to develop these in new ways.
3. Pick up any hints that you are being perceived as abusive and discuss it openly. Don't deny it, explore it.
4. Do not encourage the client to go further into an experience if she or he expresses a desire not to. It may be very frightening to be led into an area of terror that she or he does not feel ready to manage.
5. Do not tell the client that you can't manage what you are hearing or that you are frightened in a way that stops him or her proceeding with his or her own discovery/journey; seek consultation or supervision to strengthen your own position.
6. Do not only dwell on atrocities – remember the client's functioning self and the life that has to be managed when she or he leaves the room.
7. Remember and share areas of common gendered experience, where these can appropriately normalise aspects of oppressive behaviour in ways that illuminate the client's story.

Specific mistakes when working with any client who has been used sadistically include the following:

1. Trying to reinterpret the events in a less unfavourable way than they are described.
2. Becoming too interested in the 'truth' of what happened – this may become a preoccupation for client and therapist, partly as a result of the shock of what is described, and partly as a response to the self-image conjured up in oneself of a 'detective' or fighter for justice.
3. Attempting to be personally unresponsive or distant in manner (in a caricature of what is often associated with psychoanalytic therapies). This can easily be interpreted as rejection or abuse by a client if it replicates his or her earlier experience of having the pain within him or herself, and being coldly watched by observing adults (Cooklin and Gorell Barnes, 1994).

10

DOING THE WORK AND MAKING A DIFFERENCE

In writing an end note to this text the second edition of 'Family Therapy in Changing Times' I am bearing in mind my colleague Barry Mason's injunction to 'get a few key points across' (Gorell Barnes, in Mason and Sawyer, 2002).

Study your own coherence

The coherence of my approach over time interests me, as does the ongoing subjective truth of things I have written in the past. These include contemporary descriptions for which one may later be called to account. Meeting a young woman seeking her mother thirty-three years after I had placed her for adoption I was deeply grateful to my own recording as something that brought the event back to life for both of us and allowed me to enter her passionate quest now at a level both of us could engage in. So the first point is to try and be true to the complexities of the situation, the way the family perceive and narrate it and the way you work with it in your descriptions and in your recording.

A theory you can live and work by

The second key point is to try and build a theory of understanding about the interaction of family and individual that is useful to you and that you can live and work by. This will probably develop all your working life. In 1979 the Journal of Family Therapy published 'Psychodynamic and structural approaches to work with families', a paper reflecting my preoccupation at that time with the move from a psycho-dynamic model to one that, while 'systemic', focusing on pattern, and the relationship between the whole and the parts, still incorporated psychological, emotional, developmental principles. Attachment theory's own growth subsequently allowed the development of a more systemic model of the capacity of the individual to hold representations of sets of relationship in their mind. These were seen to act as working models guiding subsequent emotional relationship choices. This theorising based on extensive researched models of behaviour provided a way of including the idea of pattern, mutual influence in family life and the mutual influence of external systems influencing subsequent family life over time through internal representation of these. Attachment theory allows for individual instinctual drives and human need for shelter, security, and commitment to be placed within sets of relationship principles acknowledging the power of mutual influence in shaping the different ways these instinctual needs can be met. These ideas about core aspects of human need can be placed in balance with theorising socially constructed aspects of self. Acknowledging the power of attachment, while not specifying or privileging the essential nature of any particular family structure, also provides a framework for understanding the fragmentation of self that many people endure through losses of intimate relationship and transitions in life.

Recent work on disorganised attachment also offers a way of understanding the internal complexity of mind created by those abusive situations where the abuser is also the person on whom the child is dependant. This has particular resonance in relation to parental mental illness, to emotional and physical violence and to sexual abuse within the family.

Attention to text

Detailed attention to the text, whether this is spoken narrative (storytelling) written accounts, or couple and family process interaction is a key pathway to understanding the way that families and individuals reflect upon the way they live their own lives and the meaning they ascribe to discrete aspects of their own living. Careful listening and clarification of what is not clear will lead to a more reflective process that allows difference into the mind of the teller.

The development of 'reflective self function,' as it has been named from the perspective of attachment theory researchers (Main, 1985; Fonagy, 1992) can be seen as an essential aspect of all therapeutic intervention. It enables the individual who is telling the story to move themselves to a more differentiated position in relation to the dilemmas they are describing and this in itself allows a space for the emergence of new ideas, perspectives and action points. Such shifts also help the individual move from a sense of helplessness and entrapment into a space where they can think. The development of reflective self function is therefore an important step into the development of the capacity to heal as well as a better functioning mind. Since the process enabling this development is often painful, any means useful to clients of different ages should be utilised. As indicated, I use scraps of writing or poetry, drawings accompanied by comments, letters written by family members to myself, or to each other, or to imagined or to real others in the family. On occasion, audio-tapes are made and listened to. E-mails are often suggested now by clients but suffer the disadvantage in situations of high emotion of being able to be sent instantly after which they cannot be retrieved. This sometimes negates the value of the space created by writing which allows the writer the capacity to think about what has been written before it is placed before another.

In multi-person narratives or discourses with two or more people in the room, the therapist attends carefully not only to what people say but how they say it and asks themselves the question 'How does what any one person says *change* in relation to the presence of another?'. In relation to the presence of which others do thoughts, once clearly expressed, become confused or diminished? Gender and generation are usually components of such changes in voice. What is left out when certain others are present; what becomes dominant; what becomes diminished or disappears entirely? In extending these question to the outside world it is useful to ask where in everyday life voices disappear? How can an important or valuable voice be maintained in a context where it might otherwise not be heard?

The wider world and family life

This links to another key issue for therapists to attend to – the wider world and family life.Therapists have to be attentive to the larger discourses that permeate the life of the family and the minds of the individuals in families as well as to the structural effects of economics of poverty, class, nationalism, racism, and fundamentalism. Family therapy within the UK developed within the context of a welfare-state philosophy that connected the well-being of individuals to the wider functioning of a healthy society. This sense of 'work of each for weal of all', which followed the coming together of a nation in the aftermath of the Second World War, has been gradually eroded and fragmented by service structure changes, by more reliance from government on voluntary initiatives, and a permanent sense of overload experienced in the face of diminishing central government financial resources into social service, alongside increasing expectation and demand from clients and communities. Whereas systemic therapists may see a notional connection between the 'parts and the whole' as having possible resources for the future, linking families' well-being to community in their own minds, families often struggle with the experience of fragmentation searching for some sense of social and cultural coherence they have left behind and do not find here. Instead they often experience withholding, limitation and constraint. Reciprocally social services themselves no longer know how the shape of the field they are planning for will change. This requires us to attend more clearly to extended family ties, to links with friends and kin worldwide, to highlight the realities of loss in relation to community that has been left behind, and seek for links to smaller community developments which have reality in neighbourhoods in this country – a new outreach between systemic therapist eco-structures, and community development projects.

The realities of the intersection of worlds of work, economic survival, and family also need therapeutic attention. How does work diminish the capacity for attachment a couple may have for one another; how do demands of the work organisation compete with family organisation, the needs of children as well as the promotion of intimate development that care of children can promote in both men and women. Work overtly supports the construction of 'home' but it also provides a series of alternative links, loyalties and role requirements which may compete with desirable constructions of intimacy within the family. In a world where both partners are likely to work, and all single mothers are being conjured to do so by government, what may be in danger of being lost if an expedient executive work-centred self becomes dominant in all adults in the family? How do work pressures affect any couple's capacity to develop an intimacy demanding its own time and logic?

Many families are also affected by the requirements for world travel that current globalisation involves. In order to be mobile, sometimes on two or three continents, men and to a lesser extent women in business, have to be able to disconnect themselves from ties which would hamper their commitment. Throughout my professional life I have worked with fathers around the tension of commitment to their children and to their work; and increasingly mothers in executive positions have brought this struggle as well. Couples enter therapy when they are in conflict with definitions of themselves that they experience as discontinuous. The reality that is constructed within work settings, especially on continents where labour is cheap and service is plentiful may include expectations of partnership that are rejected by a marital partner. Indian, Chinese, and African couples have brought dilemmas around these issues as well as Western-born couples. Bringing these larger external economic and power issues into the conversation between a couple does not 'dissolve the problem' but does allow new meanings and new thought to enter previously over-rigid discourses defining 'gender realities' and presumptions about gendered relationships with children.

Attention to the fragility of relationships

The greater proportion of my work over the last twenty years has been with non-biologically connected families; with couples struggling to create diverse post-separation or post-divorce family forms; with couples fighting through the courts about residence and contact, with step-families again of various constructions; with gay and lesbian parenting; with adoptive families. The fragility of many emotional bonds between adults in distinction from the strength of many bonds between parents and children in second families requires attention and respect. Issues of constructing new contracts often enter the arena and something between mediation, therapy and post-modernist planning takes place as couples negotiate arrangements for staying in touch or staying together to maintain a family life with their children. I use research to inform my answers to questions that none of us yet know the answer to about how 'this and that' arrangement may affect children in their growing. I try and look more deeply into the meanings of resilience as researchers have struggled with these, drawing primarily on one put forward by Garmezy 'the maintenance of competent functioning despite interfering emotionality' as well as ideas from a variety of researchers about the promotion of resilience. I work reflexively, using my own life experiences and my research projects to inform my clinical work and to offer other perspectives on debates that affect all of us who live in non-nuclear families. I acknowledge and highlight conflicts of interest in warring parties but try and work to an approach which encourages the recognition and incorporation of change in each parent, on behalf of the resilience of the next generation.

Keeping an eye on oneself

Conversations that need maintaining in the changing arenas of life include those inner discourses of prejudice, attribution and blame arising from the belief systems of important others in our childhood. These often carry biases that as adults we are not fully aware of. In my experience such family voices are often found to be active and ongoing in our lives as young professionals and may well still be trying to influence the way we see or respond to the world. Here we may find the foundations of classism, sexism and racism, instilled through childhood stories, and half-heard conversations as well as fully fledged speeches around the kitchen table or Sunday lunch. Old baggage needs continuous re-examining and unless we can find ways of doing this ourselves, which we experience as having a useful effect, it seems inappropriate to invite our clients to join in similar experiments (Gorell Barnes, 2002a). In order to maintain openness and the capacity for enjoying and validating difference in our own minds, we have to practice curiosity, not only use it as a clinical concept. Find people who are different to yourself to have conversations with and keep doing it. Supervision alone is not enough.

The family as template for intimate emotions

The power of families to entangle and ensnare should always be balanced in our minds with their intention to love and do their best for their children. Abuse and violation coexist with love in the same household although not always within the same combinations of relationship within the family. Distinctions of loving, of the quality of loving and of positive intentions coexisting with bad acts does not exonerate bad actions themselves. Parents in conflict with one another or in conflict with the law over the care of their children often find these distinctions of intention and action useful, in trying to puzzle out why they continue to do things which they profess they do not want to do.

Many children who have grown up in conditions where love and abuse were side by side are helped by recognising where the strengths within their families lay and the legacies that they themselves can draw upon. Over thirty years, some of my clients have kept in touch in different ways, chance meetings in the street, Christmas cards, special events cards like weddings or births, as well as returns for further consultations. This has furthered my impulse towards the co-construction of therapeutic conversations: conversations in which both are participant although one is responsible for the observance of boundary more than the others. My background in sociology and social work, my ongoing interest in research within the ever changing structures of family living has been more securely guided by my early training in the maintenance of a safe therapeutic arena, whether someone's kitchen or a clinic space and has helped me to feel more free in exploration with clients on the ways in which social context and self mutually interact through a number of lenses including ethnicity, gender, class, sexual choice. I have also used ideas of resilience actively in looking for family and individual strengths trying to assist in the process of people moving towards what they hope for. In the words of one member of a family working with me, change occurs through 'using your recognition of strength, talent, and resilience as well as of the society that limits opportunities to hold onto who I am and how I would express myself if I could'.

What do we mean by resilience

As family therapists, we know that 'family' itself is a construction under continuous review and therefore the ways in which conception, childbirth and child-rearing will take place in the future will be more various than the constructs organising resilience research in many spheres have allowed to date. In looking for idiosyncratic 'local knowledge' and the wisdom of cultures, neighbourhoods and traditions in order to develop multiple versions of potentially resilient environments for children, and intersecting these with what we can learn from research, we may steer our practice a little more effectively on behalf of families and individuals in these ever-changing times.

REFERENCES

Adams, J. (1996) 'Lone Fatherhood', *Practice*, vol. 8, no. 1, pp. 15–26.

Andersen, T. (1992a) 'Relationship, language and pre-understanding in the reflecting process', *Australian and New Zealand Journal of Family Therapy*, vol. 11, no. 2, pp. 87–91.

Andersen, T. (1992b) 'Reflections on reflecting with families', in S. McNamee and K. Gergen (eds), *Therapy as Social Construction* (Newbury Park, CA: Sage) pp. 54–68.

Anderson, H. and Goolishian, H. (1988) 'Human systems as linguistic systems: preliminary and evolving ideas about the implications for systemic theory', *Family Process*, vol. 27, no. 4, pp. 371–93.

Archer, C. (2000) 'From the other side of the mirror: a worm's eye view of family therapy, *Context*, 52: 'The Magazine for Family Therapy and Systemic Practice', pp. 14–16.

Armesto, J. C. and Weisman, A. (2001) 'Attributions and emotional reactions to the identity disclosure ("coming out") of a homosexual child, *Family Process*, 40, pp. 145–62.

Arnold E. (2003) 'Broken attachments or women from the West Indies separated from mothers in early childhood', PhD University of London c/o author/Glenn House, Belmont Road, Leatherhead Surrey KT 22 7EN.

Arnold, E. and Adams, T. (eds) (2000) 'Attachment, loss and reunion: the unspoken price of immigration', *Separation and Reunion Forum* (NAFSIYAT, 278 Seven Sisters Road, London N4 2HI).

Asen, E. (1986) *Psychiatry for Beginners* (London: Unwin).

Asen, E. (2001) 'Intensive interventions with multi-problem families', in W. Yule (ed.) *Parenting: Applications in Clinical Practice*', p. 34, Association of Child Psychology and Psychiatry (occasional papers) no. 18, pp. 25–39.

Avigad, J. and Pooley, J. (2002) 'Strangers in foreign lands', in B. Mason and A. Sawyerr *Exploring the Unsaid: Creativity, Risks & Dilemmas in Working Cross Culturally* (London: Karnac).

Backett, K. (1987) 'The negotiation of fatherhood', in C. Lewis and M. O'Brien (eds), *Re-assessing Fatherhood* (London: Sage).

Bakhtin, M. (1984) *Problems of Dostoevsky's Poetics* (Manchester: Manchester University Press).

Bateson, G. (1973a) 'The effects of human purpose on conscious adaptation', *Steps to an Ecology of Mind* (St Albans: Paladin) p. 420.

Bateson, G. (1973b) 'Style, grace and information in primitive art', *Steps to an Ecology of Mind* (St Albans: Paladin) p. 115.

Bateson, G., Jackson, D. D., Haley, J. and Weakland, J. H. (1956) 'Towards a theory of schizophrenia', *Behavioural Science*, vol. 1, pp. 251–65.

Beardslee, W. R., Salt, P., Versage, E. M., and Gladstone, T. R. G. (1998) 'Children of affectively ill parents: a review of the last 10 years. *Journal of the American Academy of Child and Adolescent Psychiatry*, vol. 37, pp. 1134–41.

Bentovim, A. (1992) *Trauma Organised Systems: Physical and Sexual Abuse in Families* (London: Karnac).

Bishop, P., Clisverd, A., Cooklin, A. and Hunt, U. (2002) 'Mental health matters: a multiframework for mental health intervention', *Journal of Family Therapy*, 24, pp. 31–46.

Black D. and Urbanowitz, M. (1987) 'Family intervention with bereaved children', *Journal of Child Psychology and Psychiatry*, 28, pp. 467–76.

Boss, P., Caron, W. and Horbal, J. (1988) 'Alzheimer's disease and ambiguous loss', in C. Chilman, F. Cox and E. Nunnally (eds), *Families in Trouble* (Newbury Park, CA: Sage).

Bowlby, J. (1969) 'Attachment and Loss' *Vol. 1 Attachment 2nd edn* (1982). (London: Hogarth Press).

Bowlby, J. (1973) 'Attachment and Loss' *Vol. 2 Separation* (London: Hogarth, New York: Basic Books).

Bowlby, J. (1979) 'On knowing what you are not supposed to know and feeling what you are not supposed to feel' Canadian Journal of Psychiatry, 24, pp. 403–408.

Bowlby, J. (1980) 'Attachment and Loss' *Vol. 3. Loss, Sadness, and Depression* (New York: Basic Books).

Bowlby, J. (1988) *A Secure Base: Clinical Applications of Attachment Theory*. (London: Routledge).

Boyd Franklin, N. (2002) 'Creating risks and dilemmas', in B. Mason, & A. Sawyerr (eds) *Exploring the Unsaid: Working Cross-Culturally* (foreword pp. xiii–xxii) (London: Karnac).

Bratley, M. (1995) 'Parents' views of a contact centre', M.Sc. Dissertation. (London: Tavistock Clinic).

Brown, G. (1991) 'Life events and clinical depression', *Practical Reviews in Psychiatry*, series 3, no. 2 (Education in Practice Medical Tribune UK Ltd), pp. 4–6.

Brown, G., Harris, T. and Bifulco, A. (1986) 'Long term effects of early loss of a parent', in M. Rutter, C. Izard and P. Read (eds), *Depression in Young People: Developmental and Clinical perspectives* (New York: Guilford Press) pp. 251–96.

Browne, K. and Herbert, M. (1997) *Parenting, Family and Violence* (Chichester: Witey).

Buchanan, J. (2000) 'An adoptee's thoughts on adoption', *Context*, 52: *The Magazine for Family Therapy and Systemic Practice*, pp. 12–13.

Burck, C. and Daniel, G. (1995) *Gender and Family Therapy* (London: Karnac).

Burck, C. and Speed, B. (eds) (1994) *Gender, Power and Relationships* (London: Routledge).

Burghes, L. (1994) 'Lone parenthood and family disruption', Occasional Paper 18, Family Policy Studies Centre.

Burman, E. (1994) *De-constructing Developmental Psychology* (London: Routledge).

Burns, E., and Kemps, C. (2002) 'Risky business: the rewards and demands of cross cultural working with colleagues', in B. Mason, and A. Sawyerr (eds) *Exploring the Unsaid: Creativity, Risks and Dilemmas in Working Cross Culturally* (London: Karnac).

Byng-Hall, J. (1982) 'Family legends: their significance for the family therapist', in A. Bentovim, G. Gorell Barnes and A. Cooklin (eds), *Family Therapy: Complementary Frameworks of Theory and Practice* (London: Academic Press) pp. 213–28.

Byng-Hall, J. (1986) 'Family scripts: a concept which can bridge child psychotherapy and family therapy thinking', *Journal of Child Psychotherapy*, vol. 12, no. 1, pp. 3–13.

Byng-Hall, J. (1991) 'The application of attachment theory to understanding and treatment in family therapy', in C. M. Parkes, J. Stevenson-Hinde and P. Marris (eds), *Attachment Across the Life Cycle* (London: Routledge).

Byng-Hall, J. (2001) 'Attachment as a base for family and couple therapy', *Child Psychology and Psychiatry Review*, vol. 6, no. 1, pp. 31–5.

Campbell, D., Draper, R. and Crutchley, E. (1991) 'The Milan systemic approach to family therapy', in A. S. Gurman and D. P. Kniskern (eds), *Handbook of Family Therapy*, vol. 2. (New York: Brunner/Mazel).

Carter, E. and McGoldrick, M. (1980) *The Family Life Cycle: A Framework for Family Therapy* (New York: Gardner Press).

Cecchin, G. (1987) 'Hypothesising, circularity and neutrality revisited: an invitation to curiosity', *Family Process*, vol. 26, pp. 405–513.

Cecchin, G. (2001) 'Systemic practice', in D. Denborough (ed.) *Family Therapy Exploring the Fields Past, Present, and Possible Futures* (Adelaide: Dulwich Centre Publications), pp. 31–7.

Cederblad, M., Itöök, B., Irhammer, M., and Mercke, A. M. (1999) 'Mental health in international adoptees as teenagers and young adults: an international study, *Journal of Child Psychology and Psychiatry*, vol. 40, no. 8, pp. 1239–48.

Cederborg, A. C. (1994) 'Co-narration and voice in family therapy: voicing, devoicing and orchestration, *Family Therapy as Collaborative Work*, Linköping Studies in Arts and Science 106, Linköping University (Linköping, Sweden: Department of Child Studies).

Clulow, C. (2001) (ed.) *Adult Attachment and Couple Psychotherapy* (E. Sussex: Brunner: Routledge).

Cockett, M. and Tripp, J. (1994) *The Exeter Study* (Joseph Rowntree Foundation).

Cody, H. and Hind, G. W. (1999) 'Neuropsychological advances in child & adolescent mental health: the decade of the brain', *Child Psychiatry Review*, vol. 4, no. 3, pp. 103–8.

Colapinto, J. (1991) 'Structural family therapy', in A. S. Gurman and D. P. Kniskern (eds), *Handbook of Family Therapy*, vol. 2 (New York: Brunner Mazel).

Collins, B. (1994) 'Black patients in secure facilities and the implications for their families', in G. Gorell Barnes (ed.), *Ethnicity, Culture, Race and Family Therapy, Context*; 20 'The Magazine for Family Therapy and Systemic Practice'.

Cooklin, A. and Gorell Barnes, G. (1994) 'The shattered picture of the family: re-learning the therapist's views on human relations, the family, the therapists and therapy', in V. Sinason (ed.), *Treating Survivors of Satanist Abuse* (London: Routledge).

Cooklin, A. and Gorell Barnes, G. (2003) 'Family therapy when a parent suffers from psychiatric disorder', in M. Goepfert, J. Webster, and M. Seeman (eds) *Parental Psychiatric Disorder* (Cambridge: CUP, forthcoming).

Cooklin, A., Bishop, P., Bruggen, J. and Sturgeon, D. (1997) 'From patients to service systems: family intervention training as a strategy of change in mental health care delivery' (unpublished manuscript; see also Bishop *et al.*, 2002).

Cottrell, D. (1989) 'Family therapy influences on general adult psychiatry', *British Journal of Psychiatry*, vol. 154, pp. 473–7.

Cummings, E. M., and Davies, P. T. (2002) 'Effects of marital conflict on children: recent advances and emerging themes in process orientated research', *Journal of Child Psychology and Psychiatry*, vol. 43, no. 1, pp. 31–63.

CVS Consultants, (1999) 'A shattered world: meeting the needs of refugees and newly arrived communities' (27–29 Vauxhall Grove, London, SW8 1SY).

D'Ardenne, P. and Mahtani, A. (1999) *Transcultural Counselling in Action*, 2nd edn (London: Sage).

de Singley, F. (1993) *The Social Construction of a New Parental Identity in Fathers of Tomorrow* (Denmark: Ministry of Social Affairs, Conference Report, quoted in B. Simpson *et al.*, 1995), pp. 42–76.

Denborough, D. (ed.) (2001) *Family Therapy: Past, Present and Possible Future* (Adelaide, Australia: Dulwich Centre Publications).

Dowling, E. and Gorell Barnes, G. (1999) *Working with Children and Parents through Separation and Divorce* (Basingstoke: MacMillan).

Dowling, E. and Osborne, E. (1994) *The Family and the School: A Joint Systems Approach to Problems with Children*, 2nd edition (London: Routledge).

Downey, G. and Coyne, J. C. (1990) 'Children of depressed parents: an integrative review', *Psychological Bulletin*, vol. 108, no. 1, pp. 50–76.

Dunn J. (1988) 'Connections between relationships: implications of research on mothers and siblings; in R. A. Hinde and J. Stevenson-Hinde (eds) Relationships within Families: Mutual influences (Oxford: Oxford Science Publications).

Dunn, J. (2001) 'Children's development and adjustment in different family settings', in W. Yule (ed.) *Child Mental Health in Europe*, Occasional Papers, no. 17 (ACCP, St Saviours House, 39/41 Union Street, London SE1 1SD).

Dunn, J. (2002) 'The adjustment of children in step-families: lessons from community studies, *Child and Adolescent Mental Health*, vol. 17 no. 4, pp. 154–61.

Dunn, J., Davies, L. C. and O'Connor, T. (2000) 'Parents and partners life course and family experiences: links with parent–child relationships in different family settings', *Journal of Child Psychology and Psychiatry*, vol. 41, no. 8, pp. 955–68.

Dyregov, A. (2001) 'Telling the truth or hiding the facts: an evaluation of current strategies in assisting children following adverse events', in W. Yule (ed.) *Child Mental Health in Europe*, Occasional Papers no. 17 (ACCP, St Saviours House, 39/41 Union Street, London SE1 1SD).

Elizur,Y. and Ziv, M. (2001) 'Family support and acceptance: gay male identity formation and psychological adjustment, *Family Process*, vol. 40, no. 2, pp. 125–44.

Elliott, J. and Richards, M. P. M. (1992) 'Children and divorce: educational performance and behaviour before and after parental separation', in *International Journal of Law and The Family*, vol. 5, pp. 258–76.

Emde, R. N. (1988) 'The effect of relationships on relationships: developmental approach to clinical intervention', in R. A. Hinde and J. Stevenson-Hinde (eds), *Relationships within Families: Mutual Influences* (Cambridge: Oxford Scientific Publications).

Emery, R. and Forehand, R. (1994) 'Parental divorce and children's well being: a focus on resilience', in R. Haggerty, L. Sherrod, Garmezy, N. and M. Rutter (eds), *Stress, Risk and Resilience in Children and Adolescents; Processes, Mechanisms and Interventions* (Cambridge: Cambridge University Press), pp. 64–9.

Epston, D. and White, M. (1992) 'Experience, contradiction, narrative and imagination', *Selected Papers 1989–1991* (Adelaide: Dulwich Centre Publications).

Fernando, S. (1991) *Mental Health, Race and Culture* (Basingstoke and London: Macmillan, in association with Mind Publications).

Fernando, S. (1995) *Mental Health in a Multi Ethnic Society: A Multi Disciplinary Handbook* (London: Routledge).

Fitzgerald, J. (1992) 'Stepchildren in the child care system', in E. De'Ath (ed.), *Step-Families, What Do We Know and What Do We Need to Know* (London: Significant Publications).

Fonagy, P., Steele, M., Steele, H., Higgitt, A. and Target, M. (1993) 'The theory and practice of resilience', *Journal of Child Psychology and Psychiatry*, vol. 35, no. 2, pp. 231–57.

Forster, M. (1990) *Have the Men Had Enough?* (Harmondsworth: Penguin).

Forster, M. (1995) *Shadow Baby* (London: Viking).

Frommer, M. S. (1996) 'The right fit: a gay men's quest for Fatherhood', *In the Family*, vol. 2, no. 1, pp. 12–15.

Garmezy, N. (1991) 'Resilience in children's adaptation to negative life events and stressed environments', *Pediatric Aurals*, vol. 20, pp. 459–86.

Gelles, R. (1987) *Family Violence*, 2nd edn (London: Sage).

Glendinning, C. and Millar, J. (1987) *Women and Poverty in Britain* (Sussex, Wheat Sheaf).

Golding, J. (1996) 'Children of the nineties: a resource for assessing the magnitude of long-term effects of pre-natal and peri-natal events, *Contemporary Reviews in Obstetrics and Gynaecology*, vol. 8, pp. 89–92.

Goldner, V., Penn, P., Sheinberg, M. and Walker, G. (1990) 'Love and violence: gender paradoxes in volatile attachments', *Family Process*, vol. 29, pp. 343–64.

Golombok, S., Perry, B., Burston, A., Murray, C., Mooney Somers, J., Stevens, M. and Golding, J. (2002) 'Children with lesbian parents: a community study', *Developmental Psychology* (in press).

Goodman, R. (1994) 'Brain disorders', in M. Rutter, E. Taylor and L. Hersov (eds), *Child and Adolescent Psychiatry: Modern Approaches*, 3rd edn (Oxford: Blackwell).

Gorell Barnes, G. (1981a) 'Pattern and intervention: research findings and the development of family therapy theory', in A. Bentovim, G. Gorell Barnes and A. Cooklin (eds), *Family Therapy: Complementary Frameworks of Theory and Practice* (London: Academic Press).

Gorell Barnes, G. (1981b) 'A difference that makes a difference. Brief interventions in family pattern', *Journal of Family Therapy*, vol. 5, pp. 37–52.

Gorell Barnes, G. (1985) 'Systems theories and family theories', in M. Rutter and L. Hersov (eds), *Child Psychiatry, Modern Approaches* (Oxford: Blackwell).

Gorell Barnes, G. (1990) 'Making family therapy work: the application of research to practice', *Journal of Family Therapy*, vol. 12, pp. 17–29.

Gorell Barnes, G. (1991a) 'Ambiguities in post divorce relationships', *Journal of Social Work Practice*, vol. 5, pp. 143–50.

Gorell Barnes, G. (1991b) 'Consulting to a disaster unit: exploring contradictions in the system', *Context – a News Magazine of Family Therapy*, no. 9, pp. 14–19.

Gorell Barnes, G. (1994a) Commentary on 'Power, gender and marital intimacy', *Journal of Family Therapy*, vol. 16, no. 1, pp. 139–43.

Gorell Barnes, G. (1994b) 'The inter-subjective mind', in M. Yelloly (ed.), *Learning and Teaching in Social Work: Towards Reflective Practice* (London: Jessica Kingsley).

Gorell Barnes, G. (1994c) 'Family therapy in the 1990s', in M. Rutter, L. Hersov and E. Taylor (eds), *Child and Adolescent Psychiatry: Modern Approaches*, 3rd edn (Oxford: Blackwell).

Gorell Barnes, G. (ed.) (1994d) 'Ethnicity, culture, race and family therapy', *Context 20*, autumn: 'The Magazine for Family Therapy and Systemic Practice' (Canterbury: AFT Publishing).

Gorell Barnes, G. (1996a) 'Personal strengths and vulnerability in family and social contexts', in G. Edwards, and C. Dare (eds) *Psychotherapy, Psychological Treatments and the Addictions* (Cambridge: CUP) pp. 44–57.

Gorell Barnes, G. (1996b) 'Gender issues', in R. Davies, G. Upton and V. Varma (eds) *The Voice of the Child* (London: Farmer Press).

Gorell Barnes, G. (1998) 'Time past and time present: linearities, circularities and life', in *Journal of Family Therapy*, vol. 20, no. 2, pp. 177–86.

Gorell Barnes, G., (1999) 'Operationalising the uncertain: some clinical reflections (a response to Sir Michael Rutter)', *Journal of Family Therapy*, vol. 21, no. 2, pp. 154–59.

Gorell Barnes, G. (2002a) 'Getting it right and getting it wrong: developing an internal discourse about ethnicity and difference', in B. Mason and A. Sawyer (eds) *Exploring the Unsaid: Creativity, Risks and Dilemmas in Working Cross Culturally* (London: Karnac).

Gorell Barnes, G. (2002b) 'Fathers and Their Children Following Divorce: A Clinical Study (in progress).

Gorell Barnes, G. and Dowling, E. (1997) 'Rewriting the story: mothers, fathers and children's narratives following divorce', in R. Papadopoulos and J. Byng Hall (eds), *Multiple Stories: Narratives in Systemic Family Psychotherapy* (London: Duckworth).

Gorell Barnes, G. and Henesy, S. (1994) 'Re-claiming a female mind from the experience of sexual abuse', in C. Burck and B. Speed (eds), *Gender, Power and Relationships* (London: Routledge).

Gorell Barnes, G., Down, G. and McCann, D. (2000) *Systemic Supervision: A Portable Guide for Supervision Training* (London: Jessica Kingsley).

Gorell Barnes, G., Thompson, P., Daniel, G. and Burchardt, N. (1998) *Growing Up in Step-Families* (Oxford: Clarendon Press).

Gorney, C. (2000) 'Life's longing: a story of adoption, *Context*, 52: 'The Magazine for Family Therapy and Systemic Practice', pp. 7–9.

Green, R. J. (1996) 'Why ask, why tell? Teaching and learning about lesbians and gays in family therapy', *Family Process*, vol. 35, pp. 389–400.

Green, J. and Goldwyn, R. (2003) 'Attachment disorganisation and psychopathology: new findings in attachment research and their potential implications for developmental psycho pathology in childhood.' Journal of Child Psychology & Psychiatry, vol. 43, no. 7, pp. 835–47.

Harding, S. (ed.) (1987) *Feminism and Methodology: Social Science Issues* (Milton Keynes: Open University Press).

Hardy, K. and Laszloffy, T. (1994) 'Deconstructing race in family therapy', *Journal of Feminist Family Therapy*, vol. 3, no. 4, pp. 5–33.

Harris, K. and Maxwell, C. (2001) 'Meeting refugee mental health needs: the role of the psychologist', in G. Gorell Barnes and R. Papadopoulos (eds) *'Refugees' Context 54: 'The Magazine for Family Therapy and Systemic Practice'*, pp. 9–12.

Harris, T. and Bifulco, A. (1991) 'Loss of a parent in childhood, attachment style and depression in adulthood', in C. Murray, J. Parkes, J. Stevenson-Hinde and P. Marris (eds) *Attachment Across the Life-Cycle* (London: Tavistock).

Hart, B. (1993) 'Gender role self perceptions and attitudes of single fathers: implications for the feminist dialogues in systemic theory', M.Sc. dissertation (London: Tavistock Clinic).

Haskey, J. (1993) 'Divorces in England and Wales', *Population Trends*, vol. 74 (London: OPCS/HMSO) table 23.

Haskey, J. (1994) 'Step-families and stepchildren in Great Britain', *Population Trends*, vol. 76 (London: OPCS/HMSO) pp. 17–27.

Haskey, J. (1998) 'One parent families and their dependent children in Great Britain', *Population Trends*, vol. 91, pp. 5–14.

Hawley, D. R. and Dehaan, I. (1996) 'Towards a definition of family resilience: integrating a life span and family perspectives', *Family Process*, vol. 35, pp. 231–57.

Haworth, G. (2001) 'Romanian adoptions in a worldwide context: 'The Magazine for Family Therapy and Systemic Practice', in W. Yule (ed.) *Parenting: Applications in a Clinical Practice*, Association of Child Psychology & Psychiatry (occasional papers) no. 18, pp. 25–39.

Hetherington, E. M. and Kelly, J. (2002) *For Better or for Worse: Divorce Reconsidered* (New York: W. W. Morton).

R. A. Hinde and J. Stevenson-Hinde (eds) (1998) *Relationships within Families: Mutual Influences* (Oxford: Oxford Science Publications).

Hoffman, L. (1990) 'Constructing realities: an art of lenses', *Family Process*, vol. 29, no. 1, pp. 1–12.

James, A. and Sturgeon Adams, L. (1999) *Helping Families after Divorce: Assistance by Order?* (Bristol: Policy Press).

James, K. (2001) 'Feminist reflections on family therapy and working on the issue of men's violence', in D. Denborough (ed.) *Family Therapy Exploring the Fields Past, Present, and Possible Futures'* (Adelaide: Dulwich Centre Publications).

Jamison, K. R. (1995) *An Unquiet Mind: A Memoir of Moods and Madness* (London: Picador).

Jenkins, J., Smith, M. and Graham, P. (1988) 'Coping with parental quarrels', *Journal of American Academy of Child and Adolescent Psychiatry*, vol. 28, pp. 182–9.

Jenkins, J. M. and Buccioni, J. M. (2001) 'Children's understanding of marital quarrels, and the marital relationship', *Journal of Child Psychology and Psychiatry*, vol. 41, no. 2, pp. 161–8.

Jones, A. R. (1986) 'Writing the body: toward an understanding of ecriture feminine', in E. Showalter (ed.), *The New Feminist Criticism* (London: Virago).

Jones, E. (1991) *Working with Adult Survivors of Childhood Abuse* (London: Karnac).

Jones, E. (1993) *Family Systemic Therapy: Developments in the Milan Systemic Therapies* (Chichester: Wiley).

Jones, E. and Asen, E. (2000) *Systemic Couple Therapy and Depression* (London: Karnac).

Keith, D. and Whitaker, C. (1988) 'The presence of the past: continuity and change in the symbolic structure of families', in C. Falicov (ed.), *Family Transitions: Continuity and Change over the Life Cycle* (New York: Guilford) pp. 431–7.

Kiernan, K. E. (1992) 'The impact of family disruption in childhood on transitions made in young adult life', *Population Studies*, vol. 46, pp. 213–34

Kiernan, K. E. and Hobcraft, J. (1997) 'Parental divorce during childhood: age at first intercourse, partnership, and parenthood', *Population Studies*, vol. 51, pp. 41–55.

Kolvin, I., Miller, F. J. W., Fleeting, M. and Kolvin, P. A. (1988a) 'Social and parenting factors affecting criminal offence rates: in findings from the Newcastle Thousand Families Study, 1947–80', *British Journal of Psychiatry*, vol. 152, pp. 80–90.

Kolvin, I., Miller, F. J. W., Scott, C., Gatzuilz, S. R. M. and Fleeting, M. D. (1988b) *Adversity and Destiny: Explorations in the Transmission of Deprivation: Newcastle Thousand Families Study* (Aldershot: Gower).

Kraemer, S. (1993) *Fathers' Roles: Research Findings and Policy Implications* (London: Tavistock).

Kruk, E. (1992) 'Psychological and structural factors contributing to the disengagement of non custodial fathers after divorce', *Family and Conciliation Courts Review*, vol. 30, no. 1, pp. 81–101.

Kurdek, L. A. and Schmidt, J. P (1987) 'Relationship Quality of Partners in heterosexual married, heterosexual co-habiting and gay and lesbian relationships', Journal of Personality & Social Psychology, vol. 14, pp. 57–68.

Laing R. D. and Esterson, A. (1964) 'Sanity, madness and the family', *Families of Schizophrenics*, vol. II (London: Tavistock).

Laird, J. (2001) 'Women's stories', in D. Denborough (ed.) *Family Therapy Exploring the Fields Past, Present, and Possible Futures*' (Adelaide: Dulwich Centre Publications).

Laird, J. and Green, R. J. (1996) *Lesbians and Gays in Couples and Families: A Handbook for Therapists* (San Francisco, CA: Jossey Bass).

Lam, D. H. (1991) 'Psychosocial family intervention in schizophrenia: a review of empirical studies', *Psychological Medicine*, vol. 21, pp. 423–41.

LaSala, M. (2000) 'Lesbians, gay men and their parents: family therapy for the coming out crisis', *Family Process*, vol. 39, no. 1, pp. 67–82.

Lau, A. (1988) 'Family therapy and ethnic minorities', in E. Street and W. Dryden (eds), *Family Therapy in Britain* (Milton Keynes and Philadelphia: Open University Press).

Lau, A. (1994) 'Gender, culture and family life', in G. Gorell Barnes (ed.), *Ethnicity, Culture, Race and Family Therapy, Context,* 20: 'The Magazine for Family Therapy and Systemic Practice' (Canterbury: AFT Publishing).

Lau, A. (2000) *South Asian Children and Adolescents in Britain* (London: Whurr).

Laszloffy, T. A. and Hardy, K. (2000) 'Uncommon strategies for a common problem: addressing racism in family therapy', *Family Process,* vol. 39, no. 1, pp. 35–51.

Leff, J., Thornicroft, G., Coxhead, N. and Crawford, C. (1994) 'The TAPS Project 22: a five-year follow-up of long-stay psychiatric patients discharged to the community', *British Journal of Psychiatry,* supplement, Nov. pp. 13–17.

Leff, J., Wig, N. N., Ghosh, A., Bedi, H., Menon, D. K., Kuipers, L., Korten, A., Ernberg, G., Day, R., Sartorius, N. and Jablensky, A. (1987) 'Expressed emotion and schizophrenia in North India, III: influence of relatives' expressed emotion on the course of schizophrenia in Chandigarh', *British Journal of Psychiatry,* vol. 151, pp. 166–73.

Littlewood, R. and Lipsedge, M. (1988) 'Psychiatric illness among British afro-Caribbeans', *British Medical Journal,* vol. 296, pp. 950–7.

Long, J. (1996) 'Working with lesbians, gays and bisexuals: addressing heterosexism in supervision', *Family Process,* vol. 35, pp. 377–88.

Ma, J. L. C. (2000) 'Treatment expectations and treatment experience of Chinese families towards family therapy: appraisal of a common belief', *Journal of Family Therapy,* vol. 22, no. 5, pp. 296–307.

Maccoby, E. E. (1980) *Social Development, Psychological Growth and the Parent–Child Relationship* (New York: Harcourt Brace Jovanovich).

Maccoby, E. E. (1986) 'Social groupings in childhood: their relationship to pro-social and anti-social behaviour in boys and girls', in D. Olweus, J. Block and M. Radke-Yarrow (eds), *Development of Pro-Social and Anti-social Behaviour in Boys and Girls: A Research, Theories and Issues* (New York: Academic Press), pp. 263–4.

MacKinnon, L. and Miller, D. (1987) 'The new epistemology and the Milan approach: feminist and sociopolitical considerations', *Journal of Marital and Family Therapy,* vol. 13, pp. 139–55.

MacLean, M. and Eekelaar, J. (1997) *The Parental Obligation: A Study of Parenting Across Households* (Oxford: Hart Publishing).

Main, M., Kaman, N. and Cassidy, J. (1985) 'Security in infancy, childhood and adulthood: a move to the level of representation', in I. Bretherton and E. Waters (eds), *Growing Points in Attachment Theory and Research,* Monographs of the Society for Research in Child Development, vol. 50, nos 1–2, serial no. 209, pp. 66–104.

Malley, M., and Tasker, F. (1999) 'Lesbians, gay men, and family therapy: a contradiction in terms?', *Journal of Family Therapy,* vol. 21, no. 1, pp. 3–29.

Masten, A. S. and Garmezy, N. (1994) 'Chronic adversities', in M. Rutter, E. Taylor and L. Hersov (eds), *Child and Adolescent Psychiatry: Modern Approaches,* 3rd edn (Oxford: Blackwell).

McWhirter, D. P. and Mattison, M. (1934) *The Male Couple: How Relationships, Develop* (Englewood Cliffs, NJ: Prentice-Hall).

Miller, A. and Thomas, L. (1994) 'Introducing ideas about racism and culture into family therapy training', in G. Gorell Barnes (ed.), *Ethnicity, Culture, Race and Family Therapy, Context*, 20, 'The Magazine for Family Therapy and Systemic Practice'.

Minuchin, P. (1988) 'Relationships within the family: a systems perspective on development', in R. A. Hinde and J. Stevenson-Hinde (eds), *Relationships within Families: Mutual Influences* (Oxford: Oxford Science Publications).

Minuchin, S. (2001) Advanced Structural Family Training Course, University of Hong Kong, in Association with 6th Mental Health Institute of University of Beijing (personal record).

Minuchin, S. and Fishman, C. (1981) *Family Therapy Techniques* (Cambridge: Cambridge University Press).

Minuchin, S. and Minuchin, P. (1974) *Families and Family Therapy* (London: Tavistock).

Moffitt, T. E. (2002) 'Teen-aged mothers in contemporary Britain', *Journal of Child Psychology and Psychiatry*, vol. 43, no. 6, pp. 727–42.

Moltz, D. (1993) 'Bipolar disorder and the family: an integrative model', *Family Process*, vol. 32, no. 4, pp. 409–25.

Murray, L. and Cooper, P. (1997) *Post Partum Depression and Child Development* (New York: Guilford Press).

Nath, R., and Craig, J. (1999) 'Practising family therapy in India: how many people are there in a marital sub-system?', *Journal of Family Therapy*, vol. 21, no. 4, pp. 390–406.

Nwoye, A. (2000) 'Building on the indigenous; theory and method of marriage therapy in contemporary Eastern and Western Africa', *Journal of Family Therapy*, vol. 22, no. 4, pp. 347–59.

Ochiltree, G. (1990) *Children in Step-Families* (Sydney: Prentice-Hall).

Papadopoulos, R. (2001) 'Refugees, Therapists and Trauma', in G. Gorell Barnes and R. Papadopoulos (eds) *Refugees: Context* 54: 'The Magazine for Family Therapy and Systemic Practice'.

Papadopoulos, R. and Byng-Hall, J. (1997) *Multiple Voices: Narratives in Systemic Family Psychotherapy* (London: Duckworth).

Papadopoulos, R. (2002) (ed.) *Therapeutic Care for Refugees: no place like home* London: Karnac.

Papp, P. (2001) 'The process of changing family therapy', in D. Denborough (ed.) *Family Therapy Exploring the Fields Past, Present, and Possible Futures'* (Adelaide: Dulwich Centre Publications) pp. 81–8.

Parkes, C. M., Stevenson-Hinde, J. and Marris, P. (1991) *Attachment Across The Life Cycle* (London: Routledge).

Patel, N. and Fatimilehin, I. (1999) 'Racism and mental health', in C. Newnes, G. Holmes and C. Dunn (eds) *This is Madness: A Critical Look at Psychiatry and the Future of Mental Health Services* (Ross-on-Wye: PCCS).

Patel, N., Bennett, E., Dennis, M., Dosan, J. H., Mahtani, A., Miller, A. and Nadirshaw, Z. (2000) *Clinical Psychology, Race and Culture* (Leicester: BPS).

Patterson, C. J. (1994) 'Children of the lesbian baby boom: behavioural adjustment, self concepts and sex role identity', in B. Greene and G. M. Herek (eds), *Lesbian and Gay Psychology: Theory, Research and Clinical Applications* (Thousand Oaks, CA: Sage Publications), pp. 156–75.

Penn, P. (1985) 'Feed forward: future questions, future maps', *Family Process*, vol. 24, pp. 299–310.

Penn, P. and Frankfurt, M. (1994) 'Creating a participant text: writing, multiple voices, narrative multiplicity', *Family Process*, vol. 33, no. 3, pp. 217–31.

Peplau, L. A. and Cochran, S. D. (1990) 'A relational perspective on homosexuality' in D. P. McWhister, S. A. Sanders & J. M. Reinish (eds) Homosexuality: hetero-sexuality: Concepts of sexual orientation (New York: Oxford University Press)

Perelberg, R. J. and Miller, A. C. (1990) *Gender and Power in Families* (London and New York: Routledge, Tavistock).

Phoenix, A. (1999) 'Multiple racisms: racism peer commentary', *The Psychologist*, vol. 12, no. 3, pp. 134–5.

Place, M., Reynolds, J., Cousins, A. and O'Neill, S. (2002) 'Developing a resilience package for vulnerable children', *Child and Adolescent Mental Health*, vol. 7, no. 4, pp. 162–7.

Prynn, B. E. (2000) 'Family and social factors: the fit between adoptive children and their families', PhD thesis, University of East London, *Psychological Bulletin*, vol. 108, no. 1, pp. 50–76.

Quinton, D. and Rutter, M. (1984) 'Parents with children in care: 1. current circumstances and parents; 2. intergenerational continuities', *Journal of Child Psychology and Psychiatry*, vol. 25, pp. 211–31.

Rampage, C. (1994) 'Power, gender and marital intimacy', *Journal of Family Therapy*, vol. 16, no. 1, pp. 139–43.

Rampage, C. (2002) 'Marriage in the 20th century: a feminist perspective', *Family Process*, vol. 41, no. 2, pp. 261–8.

Reimers, S. (1999) 'Good morning Sir: "Axe handle", Talking at cross purposes in family therapy', *Journal of Family Therapy*, vol. 21, no. 4, pp. 360–76.

Reimers, S. (2000) 'Triple mindedness', *Journal of Family Therapy*, vol. 22, no. 1, pp. 24–8.

Reimers, S. (2001) 'Understanding alliances: how can research inform user friendly practise?', *Journal of Family Therapy*, vol. 23, no. 1, pp. 46–62.

Reiss, D. (1989) 'The represented and practising family: contrasting visions of family continuity', in A. Sameroff and R. Emde (eds), *Relationship Disturbances* (New York: Basic Books), pp. 191–4.

Reynolds, D. (2000) 'The ties that bind: a personal view', *Context 52*, 'The Magazine for Family Therapy and Systemic Practice', pp. 10–11.

Reynolds, S. J., and Mansfield, P. (1999) 'The effects of changing attitudes to marriage on its stability', in *The Lord Chancellor's Research programme: Research Series 2* (Crown Copyright UK).

Rutter, M. (1966) *Children of Sick Parents: An Environmental and Psychiatric Study*, Maudesley Monograph 16 (London: Oxford University Press).

Rutter, M. (1987) 'Psychosocial resilience and protective mechanisms', *American Journal of Orthopsychiatry*, vol. 57, pp. 316–31.

Rutter, M. (1990) 'Psychosocial resilience and protective mechanisms', in J. Rolf, A. S. Masten, D. Cicchetti, K. H. Nuechterlein and S. Weintraub (eds), *Risk and Protective Factors in the Development of Psychopathology* (Cambridge: Cambridge University Press), pp. 181–214.

Rutter, M. (1998) 'Developmental catch-up and deficit following adoption after severe global early privation' (The English & Romanian Adoptees Study Team), *Journal of Child Psychology and Psychiatry*, vol. 39, pp. 465–76.

Rutter, M. (1999) 'Resilience concepts and findings: implications for family therapy. *Journal of Family Therapy*, vol. 21, no. 2, pp. 119–45 (see also responses by Gorell Barnes and Smith).

Rutter, M., and Quinton, D. (1984) 'Parental psychiatric disorder: effects on children', *Psychological Medicine*, vol. 14, pp. 853–80.

Sapphire (1996) *Push: The Life of Precious Jones* (London: Secker & Warburg).

Scheflen, A. (1981) *Levels of Schizophrenia* (New York: Brunner Mazel).

Schlosser, A. and De'Ath, E. (1995) *Looked After Children and their Families. Fact File 2* (Step-family Association London UK).

Schuff, G. H. and Asen, E. (1996) 'The disturbed parent and the disturbed family', in M. Goepfert, J. Webster and Seeman, M. V. (eds) *Parental Psychiatric Disorder* (Cambridge: Cambridge University Press).

Scott, G. (2001) 'Parent training; where are we now', in W. Yule (ed.), *Parenting: Applications in Clinical Practice*, Association of Child Psychology and Psychiatry (occasional papers) no. 18, pp. 25–39.

Siegel, S. and Walker, G. (1996) 'Connections: conversations between a gay therapist and a straight therapist', in J. Laird and R. J. Green (eds), *Lesbians and Gays in Couples and Families: A Handbook for Therapists* (San Francisco, CA: Jossey Bass), pp. 22–68.

Simpson, B., McArthy, P. and Walker, J. (1995) *Being There: Fathers After Divorce* (Relate Centre for Family Studies, University of Newcastle).

Slater, S. (1995) *The Lesbian Family Life Cycle* (New York: Free Press).

Sluzki, C. E. (1979) 'Migration and family conflict', *Family Process*, vol. 18, no. 4, 379–90.

Smith, A. (1997) *Navigating the Deep River* (Cleveland, Ohio: United Church Press).

Smith, G. (1999) 'Therapists reflections: a response to Sir Michael Rutter on resilience', *Journal of Family Therapy*, vol. 21, no. 2, 154–9.

Solomon, J. and George, C. (1999) 'The development of attachment in separated and divorced families: effects of overnight visitation, parent and couple variables', *Attachment and Human Development*, vol. 1, no.1, pp. 2–33.

Speed, B. (1991) Reality exists OK? An argument against constructivism and social constructionism', *Journal of Family Therapy*, vol. 13, pp. 395–411.

Sroufe, L. A. and Fleeson, J. (1988) 'The coherence of family relationships', in R. A. Hinde and J. Stevenson-Hinde (eds), *Relationships Within Families: Mutual Influence* (Oxford: Oxford Science Publications).

Stern, D. (1977) *The First Relationship: Infant and Mother* (London: Fontana Open Books).

Stern, D. (1985) *The Interpersonal World of the Infant. A View from Psychoanalysis and Developmental Psychology* (New York: Basic Books).

Sveaas, M., and Reichelt, S. (2000) 'Refugee families in therapy: from referrals to therapeutic conversations', *Journal of Family Therapy*, vol. 23, no. 2, pp. 119–134.

Tamura, T. and Lau, A. (1992) 'Connectedness v. separateness. Applicability of family therapy and Japanese families', *Family Process*, vol. 31, no. 4, pp. 319–40.

Tasker, F. L. and Golombok, S. (1997) *Growing Up in a Lesbian Family* (New York: Guilford Press).

Tasker, F. L. and McCann, D. (1999) 'Affirming patterns of adolescent sexual identity: the challenge', *Journal of Family Therapy*, vol. 21, no. 1, pp. 30–54.

Thomas, L. (1995) 'Psychotherapy in the context of race and culture: an intercultural therapeutic approach', in S. Fernando (ed.), *Mental Health in a Multi-ethnic Society: A Multi-disciplinary Handbook* (London: Routledge).

Tizard, B. and Phoenix, A. (1994) *Black, White and Mixed Race* (London: Routledge).

Thompson, M. C., Rea, M. M., Goldstein, M. J., McKlowitz, D. J. and Weisman, A. G. (2000) 'Difficulty in implementing a family intervention for bi-polar disorder', *Family Process*, vol. 39, no. 1, pp. 105–20.

Tomm, K. (1984) 'One perspective on the Milan systemic approach', *Journal of Marital and Family Therapy*, vol. 10, pp. 113–25, 253–71.

Tomm, K. (1987) 'Interventive interviewing: Parts I and II', *Family Process*, vol. 26, pp. 3–13, 167–83.

Tomm, K. (1988) 'Interventive interviewing: Part III. Intending to ask lineal, circular, strategic or reflexive questions', *Family Process*, vol. 27, pp. 1–15.

Vetere, A. and Cooper, J. (2001) 'Losing it and owning it: addressing responsibility for family violence therapeutically', in W. Yule (ed.) *Occasional Paper 18: Association for Child Psychology and Psychiatry* (St Saviour's House, 39/41 Union Street, London SE1 1SD).

Wadsby, M. (1993) 'Children of divorce and their parents', Linköping University Medical Dissertations, no. 405 (Linköping, Sweden: Department of Child and Adolescent Psychiatry, Faculty of Health Sciences, Linköping University).

Walsh, F. (1996) The concept of family resilience: crisis and change', *Family Process*, vol. 35, no. 3, pp. 261–81.

Walsh, F. and McGoldrick, M. (1988) 'Loss and the family life cycle', in C. Falicov (ed.), *Family Transitions: Continuity and Change over the Life Cycle* (New York: Guilford Press) pp. 311–36.

Walters, M. (1990) 'A feminist perspective in family therapy', in R. J. Perelberg and A. C. Miller (eds), *Gender and Power in Families* (London and New York: Routledge, Tavistock).

White, M. (1986) 'Negative explanation, restraint and double description. A template for family therapy', *Family Process*, vol. 25, no. 2, pp. 169–84.

White, M. (1987) 'Family therapy and schizophrenia: addressing the "in the corner" lifestyle', *Dulwich Centre Newsletter*, Spring, pp. 47–57.

White, M. and Epston, D. (1990) *Narrative Means to Therapeutic Ends* (New York: W. W. Norton).

Wilson, J. (1999) *The Illustrated Mum* (London: Corgi).

Winnicott, D. W. (1971) *Playing and Reality* (London: Tavistock).

Wolin, S. J. and Wolin, S. (1993) *The Resilient Self: How Survivors of Troubled Families Rise Above Adversity* (New York: Villard).

Woodcock, J. (1994) 'Family therapy with refugees and political exiles', in G. Gorell Barnes (ed.), *Ethnicity, Culture, Race and Family Therapy, Context*, 20: 'The Magazine for Family Therapy and Systemic Practice' (Canterbury: AFT Publications).

Woodcock, J. (2001a) 'Threads from the labyrinth: therapy with survivors of war and political oppression', *Journal of Family Therapy*, vol. 23, no. 2, pp. 136–54.

Woodcock, J. (2001b) 'A dozen differences to consider when working with refugee families', in G. Gorell Barnes and R. Papadopoulos (eds), *Refugees, Context*, 54: 'The Magazine for Family Therapy and Systemic Practice', pp. 24–5.

Xiong, W., M. R. Phillips, X. Hu, R. Wang, Q. Dai, J. Kleinman and A. Kleinman (1994) 'Family-based intervention for schizophrenic patients in China: a randomised controlled trial', *British Journal of Psychiatry*, vol. 165, pp. 239–47.

INDEX